Museum Basics
Second Edition

W9-CBG-429

Museums throughout the world have common needs and face common challenges. Keeping up to date with new ideas and changing practice is considerably demanding for small museums where time for reading and training is often restricted. *Museum Basics* has therefore been written for the many museums worldwide that operate with limited resources and few staff.

Drawing from a wide range of practical experience, the authors provide a basic guide to all aspects of museum work, from museum organisation, through collections management and conservation, to audience development and education. Organised on a modular basis with over 100 Units, *Museum Basics* can be used as a reference to support day-to-day museum management and as the key textbook in pre-service and in-service training programmes. It is designed to be supplemented by case studies, project work and group discussion.

This second edition has been fully updated and extended to take account of the many changes that have occurred in the world of museums in the last decade. It includes a glossary, sources of information and support as well as a select bibliography.

Timothy Ambrose is an international consultant working in the field of cultural heritage. He is a Fellow of the Society of Antiquaries of London and a Fellow of the Museums Association. He has particular interests in the role of museums in destination development and has published widely.

Crispin Paine is a museums and heritage consultant, writer and lecturer. He is a Visiting Fellow at University College Chichester, a Fellow of the Museums Association and a Fellow of the Royal Geographical Society. He has particular interests in local community museums, and in the material culture of religion.

Museum Basics

Second Edition

Timothy Ambrose and Crispin Paine

Routledge
Taylor & Francis Group

LONDON AND NEW YORK

First published 2006
by Routledge
2 Park Square, Milton Park, Abingdon, Oxon OX14 4RN

Simultaneously published in the USA and Canada
by Routledge
270 Madison Ave, New York, NY 10016

Routledge is an imprint of the Taylor & Francis Group an informa business

© 2006 Timothy Ambrose and Crispin Paine

Typeset in Garamond 3 and Frutiger by
Florence Production Ltd, Stoodleigh, Devon
Printed and bound in Great Britain by
TJ International Ltd, Padstow, Cornwall

British Library Cataloguing in Publication Data
A catalogue record for this book is available from the British Library

Library of Congress Cataloging in Publication Data
Ambrose, Tim.
    Museum basics / Timothy Ambrose and Crispin Paine – 2nd ed.
        p. cm.
    Includes bibliographical references and index.
    1. Museums – Handbooks, manuals, etc. 2. Museum techniques – Handbooks,
    manuals, etc. I. Paine, Crispin. II. Title.
    AM5.A43 2006
    069–dc22   2005024697

ISBN13: 978–0–415–36633–5 (hbk)
ISBN13: 978–0–415–36634–2 (pbk)

Contents

Section 3 The development and care of the museum's collections   133

Section 4 **The museum and its buildings   205**

Section 5 **The museum and its management   235**

Section 6 **Supporting resources** 305

Foreword

On behalf of the International Council of Museums (ICOM), I welcome this second edition of *Museum Basics*. Since this book was first published, the museum world and the environment in which it operates have experienced substantial changes. We commend the authors and publisher for having recognised the need to update this significant contribution to the museum profession.

Originally developed during Alpha Oumar Konaré's presidency at ICOM, in co-ordination with the ICOM International Committee for the Training of Personnel (ICTOP) and supported by UNESCO, this book on good museum practices has since proven itself worldwide and has met the needs of many museum workers as a sound foundation for their activities.

We are certain that this new edition will particularly help museums with limited staff and budgets to tackle the challenges they face today: among others, financial pressures, resource optimisation, exploiting new technologies, managing cultural tourism and expanded ethical obligations on the profession.

Encouraging the creation of tools such as *Museum Basics* has been and will remain an ICOM priority in providing service to the museum community, through the sharing and dissemination of specialised knowledge.

Alissandra Cummins, President, International Council of Museums

Acknowledgements

This second edition of *Museum Basics* is a product of the international museums community. Both the first and second editions have benefited from advice and encouragement from museum workers in all parts of the world. Their recognition of the value and importance of *Museum Basics* as an everyday handbook for museums with few professional staff and limited financial resources has continued to be a continuous source of encouragement throughout its development.

This second edition has built closely on the work of the first edition and the various translations that followed its publication. The following individuals helped us to test sections of the first edition 'in the field', and advised us on its international applications. We have continued to apply their original advice to the second edition.

Mr Martin Akanbiemu, Nigeria
Mr Luhfti Assiarto, Indonesia
Sra Lucia Astudillo de Parra, Ecuador
Dr Ahdoulaye Camara, Senegal
Profesora Serafina Traub Borges do Amaral, Brazil
Dr Gary Edson, USA
Dr Saraj Chose, India
Sra Cecilia Bákula, Peru
Dr Ahi A. Derefaka, Nigeria
Professor Joe D. K. Nkrumah, Ghana
Dr Petr Suler, Czech Republic
Mr F. Karanja, Kenya
Dr Carol Stapp, USA
Mr Yui-tan Chang, Taiwan
Ms Alissandra Cummins, Barbados
M. Claude Daniel Ardouin, Senegal
Profesora Miriam Arroyo de Kerriou, Mexico
Mr Kit Neuman, USA
Ms Umebe N. Onyejekwu, Nigeria
Ms Verna Wheeler, USA
Sra Alejandra Pena, Paraguay
Mr Kenneth Perry, USA

Sr Sergio Duran-Pitarque, Peru
Dr Piet Pouw, The Netherlands
Ms Nicky Ladkin, USA
Dr Eilean Hooper-Greenhill, UK
Mr Andrew Hall, USA
Dr Susanne Peters, France
Dr Karyl Robb, USA

In addition, we would like to thank Professor Eilean Hooper-Greenhill of the University of Leicester, Alex Dawson of mda, Jonathan Gibbon of Spiral Productions, Jon Hall of Heritage Resource Agency, Lucy Trench of the Victoria & Albert Museum and Sean Young of Locum Consulting for their help and support and for permission to use examples of their work in the text.

We are most grateful to Alissandra Cummins, President of ICOM, for writing the Foreword and for ICOM's continued support of the publication.

Our thanks are also due to Andrew Wheatcroft of the University of Stirling for his continued support and to Catherine Bousfield, Matthew Gibbons and Amy Laurens at Routledge, and Sue Leaper at Florence Production for their help and encouragement throughout the production process.

While we must take final responsibility for this second edition of *Museum Basics*, we cannot of course take the final credit. We have continued to lean on the work, published and unpublished, of colleagues throughout the international museums community. While it is not possible to acknowledge them all individually, it is nonetheless a very real pleasure to record the value of their work in providing the foundations of this publication. We hope that the second edition of *Museum Basics* will continue to be of benefit to our international colleagues and help museums realise their full potential worldwide.

Timothy Ambrose and Crispin Paine
Lewes, East Sussex and Liss, Hampshire
June 2005

Section 1
Introductory

About this book

The main purpose of *Museum Basics* is to provide a basic outline of good practice for museums with few professional staff and limited financial resources worldwide. Many museums internationally have inadequate staffing and resources to meet their responsibilities fully. They have common needs and face common challenges. Despite this, they individually and collectively care for a unique resource – their collections – which represent a significant part of the world's heritage. This book has been written to help museums care for and provide access to those collections and meet the management challenges they face.

The original edition of *Museum Basics* was written in consultation with a wide variety of museum workers in many different countries. Their ideas and comments on themes and topics, text and layout, helped shape and substantiate the first edition and increased its relevance to museums in countries that have different traditions of museum development. This second edition has built on their earlier inputs and has similarly benefited from comments and advice from professional colleagues.

The second edition of *Museum Basics* takes into account the fundamental changes that have occurred within the professional environment of museums over the past ten years. These include:

- the significant increase in the number of museums worldwide;
- the wider context within which museums work, including globalisation;
- new information and communication technologies and the growth of the Internet;
- macro-political changes;
- the increasing use of private finance in museum development;
- international tourism; and
- the recognition of the widespread need for appropriate pre-service training and ongoing professional development.

The opportunity has been taken to enhance the usefulness of the book by revising and restructuring the text and including more process diagrams and illustrations, increasing the number of study examples, adding a range of new Units and updating the information on support resources, including web-based information.

This edition has retained the organisation of the book into six sections. Each section moves from a general introduction to more specific issues. The Units within the different sections can be read individually or in groups as a basic introduction to the subject being studied. Individual Units may be used as study texts within training programmes and have been written with the curriculum devised by ICTOP firmly in mind. For each Unit, signposts to related Units are provided. Similar ideas and suggestions recur in different Units. This is a deliberate approach designed to encourage readers to think about their application to different aspects of museum work.

Museum Basics is also supported by suggestions for further, in-depth reading in the different topic areas. These are restricted to key textbooks likely to remain reasonably available to readers.

The book also includes a glossary of terms used in the text. Understandably there are variations in the use of terms in museum work internationally. While every effort has been made to make the text as applicable as possible internationally, readers should refer to the glossary where there is any doubt about the meaning or use of a word or phrase. We have included special *key word sections* throughout the text to explain particular terms in detail.

The coverage of the book is purposefully wide-ranging. It is based on ideas that are already being used every day in museums with few staff and limited budgets. It places a particular emphasis on:

- managing collections effectively – the unique resource of museums;
- achieving an appropriate balance between caring for and managing collections and making them as widely accessible as possible to public audiences;
- effective market research, marketing and audience development, an approach to museum work that may be unfamiliar in some countries;
- caring for visitors and users and meeting their needs;
- managing staff and volunteers; and
- managing resources.

These are all aspects of museum work that have received particular attention in recent years, especially but not exclusively in the context of the massive growth in international tourism. Their emphasis is also a reflection of the significant increase in the numbers of new museums being established and redeveloped worldwide.

Keeping up to date with new ideas, changing practice and agreed standards, and learning from other museums about success and failure is a considerable challenge for museum staff. This is true especially in small museums where access to information, time for reading, and opportunities for training are often restricted. *Museum Basics* will therefore be regularly revised to help museum staff keep up to date with the changing contexts in which they are working.

No book about museums and their work can pretend to be comprehensive. While *Museum Basics* has been designed to address the main, day-to-day concerns of museum managers, and has been written with the museum with limited resources in mind, there will be other themes or topics that readers will want to explore. The authors and publishers are concerned that later editions accurately reflect needs in the field. We therefore continue to welcome suggestions for future editions that readers and reviewers may wish to make. Please write to the authors, care of Routledge, 2 Park Square, Milton Park, Abingdon, Oxfordshire OX14 4RN, United Kingdom.

One of the best characteristics of the international museums community is the willingness to share ideas and network information on good practice. This second edition of *Museum Basics* has built on this commonwealth of expertise and experience and we trust that future editions will continue to do so.

Key words

Museum manager – the term museum manager is used to describe any member of staff with responsibility for managing resources – people, finance, collections, buildings or equipment. The term has been used throughout *Museum Basics* to demonstrate that many people manage resources and contribute to a museum's efficiency and effectiveness.

Museum director – the term museum director is used to describe the senior member of staff who has overall responsibility for the museum's day-to-day operation and who reports to the museum's governing body.

Unit
2

About museums

Related Units – Units 3–7

Each year, in countries throughout the world, millions upon millions of people visit museums. As a result of growing interest in their collections and their work, the number of museums of all kinds increases year by year. Their popularity is assured. It is not the purpose of *Museum Basics* to discuss the advantages and disadvantages of the phenomenal upsurge of museum developments worldwide in the last fifty years or so. However, it is this growth of interest in museums and allied cultural institutions that represents the broad context within which *Museum Basics* will be used. It is appropriate therefore that we comment briefly on museums in their wider setting at the beginning of the new century.

In professional circles, the arguments rage as to whether there are too many museums chasing limited resources, whether quantity and growth damage quality and sustainability, and whether new forms of partnership and co-operation are required to cater for a cost-effective scale of provision. The pattern of historical development and current provision of course vary from country to country.

In Europe, for example, it is estimated that for each museum that existed in 1950 there are four today. In other parts of the world, museum development is only just beginning. While the form of museum provision differs from one country to another, so too do standards – standards of collections management, standards of user service and standards of museum management and administration. Improving standards of provision in a balanced way is a critical professional concern.

Whatever the case for growth or containment, museums in every country need to operate within a national policy for museums that has been and continues to be informed by appropriate comparisons with other countries. The development and distribution of museums, the resources that they need, and the range and quality of services to the public that they should provide all need to be discussed on an informed basis with reference to international standards. Professional and political resolution of these issues needs to be found through the process of policy development.

In the context of a country's museums service, adequate financial resources are needed to enable museums to attain appropriate standards and undertake the full spectrum of their responsibilities. These include appropriate training and professional development programmes for staff and governing bodies at all levels, proper standards of collections care and management, high-quality facilities and services for users, effective planning regimes and a commitment to sustaining existing audiences and developing new audiences through well-considered marketing and learning initiatives. All of these are essential if the museums service is to flourish to the benefit of the country and its people and their visitors.

The status and standing of a country today is in large part measured by the attention it pays to its cultural policies and programmes and its investment in its cultural facilities. International tourism, and the widespread economic gains it can bring if managed sensitively and sustainably, now represents a major reason for investment in museums and their work throughout the world. Museums as key cultural attractors have an important contribution to make to the development of tourist destinations, whether those destinations are countries, regions, cities and towns or areas of countryside.

The increasing importance of resurgent national, regional and local identity, where museums through their displays and exhibitions can serve to reflect change and continuity in traditional cultural values, is of major significance in museum development in many countries. Taken as a whole, their collections represent a unique resource reflecting change and continuity in a country's historical development, its achievements and progress and the challenges it has met internally and externally through time.

As keepers of the collective memory, museums can play a valuable role in providing an understanding of identity and in fostering a sense of belonging to a place or community for their users. In the face of immense and often painful political and cultural change in many countries, their museums can provide a valuable sense of connection between the past and the present and serve as a springboard for the future.

As a cultural phenomenon, museums have a long history. Perceptions of their role and value have changed through time as the political and cultural values around them have themselves altered and developed. Today, museums can play a strong role in the social, cultural and economic life and well-being of a country in urban and rural settings. Both individually and collectively, museums can provide many benefits (see Unit 4). Identifying and articulating those benefits within a clear policy framework helps to build the case-for-support for museums at all levels.

Types of museums

Related Unit – Unit 2

Museums are the treasure-houses of the human race. They store the memories of the world's peoples, their cultures, their dreams and their hopes.

Before modern museums developed, different societies found different ways of preserving objects and collections they held important. In ancient India, chitrashalas – painting galleries – were a means of education as well as a source of enjoyment, the paintings and sculpture providing lessons in history, religion and art. In Asia, precious items were often deposited for safekeeping in temples, while in Europe, churches sometimes preserved not only treasures, but curiosities too.

In many societies, custodians were appointed for objects important to the group. For example, in the Cross River region of West Africa, certain masks were assigned an elder or other respected person to take responsibility for them. The fifteenth-century Scottish crosier shrine (bishop's staff) of St Fillan was taken to Canada by its hereditary keeper in 1818; today it is back in Scotland, in the Royal Museum of Scotland. In Imperial China, collections of precious paintings were as important to members of the ruling class as they are in the West today.

Museums in the modern sense developed in Europe in the seventeenth century. The first use of the term 'museum' in English was in 1682; it described the collection of strange, rare and exotic things that the gentleman Elias Ashmole gave to the University of Oxford. From the private collections of courtiers and gentlemen, museums became the public educational institutions we know today.

Yet today museums vary enormously. They range in size and activity from great international museums such as Washington's Smithsonian Institution to the smallest one-room village museum. They vary enormously, too, in their purpose. Some are intended purely to amuse and entertain holidaymakers; others preserve the data on which scientific and historical research is based. They vary in their collections: from insects to historic industrial machinery, from ancient statues to pathological specimens, from modern paintings to revolutionary flags. They vary in who runs them. They vary in the public they seek to serve.

Museums vary most controversially in the function they perform. Often the function that its managers ascribe to a museum is quite different to the function its critics accuse it of carrying out. Many national museums, for example, claim to exist to promote national unity by fostering national culture. Their critics, though, claim that their hidden function is to encourage the public to accept the status quo, and thus to keep the present governing class in power. There has been much discussion in recent years of the need to analyse the underlying function, implicit and explicit, of public institutions such as museums.

The one thing that every museum has in common with every other museum is collections. Compare the definitions of 'museum' given in Box 3.2: do you know any museums that fit into none of these definitions? If you do, why do you think they are called 'museums'?

Box 3.1 Some types of museums

Classified by collections:

- general museums
- archaeology museums
- art museums
- history museums
- ethnography museums
- natural history museums
- science museums
- geology museums
- industrial museums
- military museums

Classified by who runs them:

- government museums
- municipal museums
- university museums
- independent (charitable trust) museums
- army museums
- commercial company museums
- private museums

Classified by the area they serve:

- national museums
- regional museums
- city museums
- local museums

Classified by the audience they serve:

- general public museums
- educational museums
- specialist museums

Classified by the way they exhibit their collections:

- traditional museums
- historic house museums
- open-air museums
- interactive museums

What other types of museum can you think of?

Box 3.2 Definitions of museums

The International Council of Museums definition:

A museum is a non-profit making, permanent institution in the service of society and of its development, and open to the public, which acquires, conserves, researches, communicates and exhibits, for purposes of study, education and enjoyment, material evidence of people and their environment.

The Museums Association (United Kingdom) definition:

A museum is an institution which collects, documents, preserves, exhibits and interprets material evidence and associated information for the public benefit.

'Institution' implies a formalised establishment that has a long-term purpose. 'Collects' embraces all means of acquisition. 'Documents' emphasises the need to maintain records. 'Preserves' includes all aspects of conservation and security. 'Exhibits' confirms the expectation of visitors that they will be able to see at least a representative selection of the objects in the collections. 'Interprets' is taken to cover such diverse fields as display, education, research and publication. 'Material' indicates something that is tangible, while 'Evidence' guarantees its authenticity as the 'real thing'. 'Associated information' represents the knowledge which prevents a museum object being merely a curio, and also includes all records relating to its past history, acquisition and subsequent usage. 'For the public benefit' is deliberately open ended and is intended to reflect the current thinking, both within our profession and outside it, that museums are the servants of society.

The American Association of Museums definition:

A non-profit permanent, established institution, not existing primarily for the purpose of conducting temporary exhibitions, exempt from federal and state income taxes, open to the public and administered in the public interest, for the purpose of conserving and preserving, studying, interpreting, assembling, and exhibiting to the public for its instruction and enjoyment objects and specimens of educational and cultural value, including artistic, scientific (whether animate or inanimate), historical and technological material. Museums thus defined shall include botanical gardens, zoological parks, aquaria, planetaria, historical societies, and historic houses and sites which meet the requirements set forth in the preceding sentence.

Key word

Heritage centre – a term widely used to describe a facility interpreting the natural and/or cultural heritage of a place or an area. In many cases, heritage centres are collections-based and are thus functionally museums, even though 'heritage centre' may be thought to sound more attractive to visitors.

Unit

4

The case for museums

Related Units – Units 2–3, 5–7

The functions of museums have been described in Unit 3. In this Unit, we explore the wider role of museums in society and the benefits that they can give to the communities and locations within which they are located. In developing the case-for-support for museums, identifying, explaining and, where possible, quantifying the benefits that the creation of a new museum or the development of an existing museum will provide is a powerful way of demonstrating its value to investors.

SOCIAL AND CULTURAL BENEFITS

Museums can provide a significant range of social and cultural benefits for the locations or destinations in which they are set. Many of these are described in greater detail in later Units. Examples include:

- contributing to the preservation and conservation of the community's cultural and natural heritage;
- serving as a cultural focus and a place of shared 'memory' for the community;
- engaging with educational organisations and offering students of all ages opportunities to learn through contact with original material;
- providing accessible cultural facilities, e.g. exhibition spaces, meeting rooms, lecture theatres;
- representing the history and culture of minority groups;
- organising accessible cultural events and activities;
- acting as a centre of objective professional expertise;
- providing opportunities for community involvement through volunteer programmes, Friends' groups or training programmes;
- working in partnership with other cultural bodies, e.g. libraries, archives, theatres, arts centres to develop joint programmes and projects.

In a very real sense, museums are able to inspire people and enhance the quality of their lives. They can play an important role in developing a sense of identity and community cohesion for the area in which they are located. Of particular importance are the opportunities that museums have to engage with those who are socially disadvantaged, through special programmes built around their collections.

Museums too are important centres for learning, whatever size or type. They provide often unique resources for formal education and for informal learning at all levels. As learning centres, they provide opportunities to work with a wide range of natural and cultural heritage material to which few other learning institutions are likely to have access. And many museums provide access to local resources along with the information and knowledge that help to enhance their significance for the user.

But to be successful in providing such social and cultural benefits, museums need to be effectively managed and well resourced.

ECONOMIC AND REGENERATION BENEFITS

Museums can play an important role in regeneration programmes in urban and rural areas. Such programmes may be concerned with physical regeneration, economic regeneration or social regeneration; often all three aspects are combined in regeneration programmes. The role of museums in economic regeneration is perhaps less well understood in many countries than their cultural or social regeneration role.

Museums may serve as an important tourist or cultural element in an overall redevelopment or regeneration programme for a location. In urban areas, for example, where the traditional industrial or manufacturing base may have been destroyed, the development of service industries or tourism may represent an alternative economic strategy for the community. In a location where the tourism economy is important, a museum can play a significant role as an attractor for a tourist destination. In rural areas, for example, where economic development may need to take place because of changes to the traditional agricultural economy, a museum can have a useful role to play in serving as a focus for explaining economic and associated cultural change to the local community and visitors.

Museums can make an important contribution to the cultural infrastructure of a location or area, often alongside other cultural facilities such as theatres, libraries, archives or concert halls. A critical mass of high-quality cultural facilities and services can often be a powerful mechanism for attracting a business or organisation to invest in and locate to an area. Such facilities make the area more attractive for its workforce and their families who will live there for the future. Museums can thus help to regenerate or develop local economies in times of economic change through supporting job creation and continued employment.

Where tourism is an important part of the local economy, a museum can act as a magnet or attractor for encouraging tourist visitors to visit the wider destination. Visitors to a museum will also spend money within the local economy, for example in shops, restaurants, hotels, garages and markets. Through ongoing market research, it is possible to quantify the amount of money that visitors spend in the economy in these ways and the number of jobs supported or created through such spending. In this way, the museum can quantify the economic benefits that it brings to the local economy.

The jobs in many museums also have an economic value in their own right within the local economy. Permanent staff will make different forms of direct and indirect contribution to the economy, for example through the taxes they pay and the money they spend locally. Through the nature of their work, museums can also attract part-time or temporary staff, perhaps as part of government training schemes or research projects. Training or research programmes provide valuable support to the museum itself, but will also generate additional economic benefits beyond its walls through the spending power of those participating in such programmes.

Museums may also attract financial investment or grants from external agencies, such as government or international agencies, for their programmes and projects. This is of particular value for museums in areas where local financial resources may be constrained. It is possible to support the museum's arguments for such external investment by reference to the museum's broader economic potential within the community.

Altogether it is worth considering, and quantifying where possible, the range of economic and regeneration benefits that your museum does or might bring to the local community (see Unit 83). List all the economic benefits that the museum provides, such as providing permanent or temporary jobs, attracting visitors to the area, attracting grants or providing skills development and training; then calculate how much they add to the economy. Quantifying the museum's 'economic value' in these terms can help to support other arguments to the museum's governing body for increased resources as well as attract external support for the museum's work.

POLITICAL AND CORPORATE BENEFITS

Museums can provide important 'political' benefits. The organisation running a museum, whether it is a public body such as local government or an independent organisation such as a foundation or trust, should take every opportunity to demonstrate the museum's contribution to the life of the community and seek to foster a sense of local pride in its work. Demonstrating how the museum benefits the community helps to promote 'political' support for the museum particularly within local and central government authorities or agencies, who are after all accountable to the communities they serve. This is an important element in the argument for financial investment. Demonstrating how the museum can use and has used that investment successfully to help deliver local or central government policies of relevance to its community helps sustain such support.

Museums that are part of larger organisations such as local authorities can play a valuable corporate role in public relations and publicity for their administrations. Where they are part of larger departments responsible, for example, for cultural or educational services, or tourist or community services, they are at the front end of delivering services and represent an important 'public face' for their administrations. The quality of their facilities and services is therefore indicative of the quality and values of the larger organisation to which they are responsible.

In dealing with businesses or companies in the private sector, for example as part of a sponsorship programme, museums also have to show how they deliver benefit to their sponsoring body. Sponsorship is a two-way process with both parties looking to benefit from the other on the basis of contributions of equal value. A museum can bring a range of benefits to a corporate sponsor while a corporate sponsor can bring a range of benefits to a museum. Museums need to consider carefully what benefits they can provide, for example through publicity and brand promotion, as the basis for their case-for-support for sponsorship (see Unit 87).

THE CASE FOR INVESTMENT

All of these benefits – social and cultural, economic, political and corporate – can be used by museum directors and managers to underpin arguments for investment. Investing in museums provides an array of benefits in return and it is essential that museums marshal all of the arguments they can to show the benefits accruing from support and investment. Where such benefits are provided – and are seen to be provided – the reputation and standing of the museum is thereby enhanced. It is a matter of judgement as to which benefits can be identified and used to help the museum director to make the case for resources. The balance will vary from one museum to another depending on local circumstances. Identifying what benefits your museum provides in all of these areas is a useful exercise.

The role of a museum is thus much more than a simple functional description. The successful museum director will ensure that all the benefits that their museum provides to the local community and beyond are defined and used to advantage.

STUDY EXAMPLE 4.1

A museum seeking investment from a local planning authority first acquired a copy of the authority's policy statements on future development in the area. The museum carefully analysed the policy statements and planning objectives of the authority in these documents. It was then able to draw up a case-for-support for investment based closely on the planning authority's own policies and planning requirements. The museum identified all of the benefits and support it could bring to help the authority meet its objectives and was successful in obtaining financial support.

For example, one of the planning authority's aims was to encourage people to stagger their journey home, in order to lessen overcrowding on buses and trains. The museum proposed to open in the evenings, with special activities organised jointly with local cafés. In another example, the local authority aimed to encourage development in a rural area. The museum proposed using its large collection of textiles and costume to open a branch museum there.

Analysing what benefits a museum can bring through its services to those who are able to support it is a powerful way of arguing for resources. At the same time, it reinforces the role and status of the museum in the eyes of its supporters and users.

Museums and sustainability

Unit 5

Related Units – Units 4, 6

SUSTAINABILITY AND THE WIDER WORLD

Given their concern with the different relationships between the natural and the human world through time and space, museums have an important to role to play in explaining and promoting sustainability.

Sustainability is a key organising principle underpinning the goals, policies and processes of society. It promotes a way of life that seeks to secure and conserve the natural capital upon which society depends. All societies are ultimately dependent for their economic and social well-being on the resources and systems that sustain life on Earth. These systems have limits, and as the results of global warming are beginning to demonstrate, we go beyond them at our peril. Economic activity of all types must therefore be constrained within those limits. Sustainability recognises the importance of efficient and ethical resource management in all forms, especially those resources derived from the natural world.

Museums, as public institutions concerned with change and continuity in the cultural and natural world, are well placed to promote the importance of sustainability and the need to pass on to future generations a healthy and diverse environment, and natural capital undamaged by economic development. They can play an important leadership role in promoting the principles of sustainability as well as demonstrating good practice in sustainability through their day-to-day work.

SUSTAINABILITY IN MUSEUM MANAGEMENT

Sustainability is also a useful management concept at the micro level. A sustainable approach to museum work can help to ensure that an appropriate balance across all of the museum's systems and functions is maintained. A policy for sustainability for example will recognise the interdependency of different museum activities, and help to demonstrate how resources can most efficiently and effectively be managed in meeting the museum's mission and strategic objectives.

Passing on the museum and its collections 'in a healthy state' to future generations is a fundamental management responsibility. Sustainable management approaches help to provide for the long-term care and safe-keeping of collections for future generations.

At the same time museums can play an important role in encouraging environmental sustainability. They can demonstrate effective approaches through the care that they take of their own environment in and around the museum, develop exhibitions and study programmes exploring the principles and practice of environmental sustainability, and promote environmental sustainability through education and learning services.

A conscious, proactive programme dedicated to sustainability should be at the heart of each museum's work.

STUDY EXAMPLE 5.1

As part of the development of its collections storage facilities, an independent museum undertook a detailed assessment of the different options available to it. Different criteria were used to assess the options, a number of which were directly concerned with sustainability issues. They included assessment of the energy efficiency of the new storage facilities and the costs of use, confirmation that the different types of wood to be used in the construction and fit-out could be sourced from sustainably managed woodlands, and appraisal of the different modes of transport needed for moving collections and staff to and from the stores.

The museum was able to take full account of the sustainability of the new collections stores in the options analysis and to demonstrate that its preferred option for development met with its sustainability policy.

Museums and ethics

Unit
6

Related Units – Units 42–3, 51, 80

As museums have developed over the centuries, so those working in them have sought to establish codes of rules and professional behaviour to regulate their work. Some of this is enshrined in law, although legislation affecting museums varies significantly from country to country. To help provide an international standard on which different countries and museum organisations can draw in developing their own codes of ethics, the International Council of Museums (ICOM) has established its *Code of Ethics for Museums*. The *Code* has been designed to provide a means of professional self-regulation and is regularly reviewed in the light of changing circumstances. ICOM's *Code* is based around a set of minimum standards of professional conduct and performance and serves as a benchmark against which those working in and for museums can assess their performance.

The *Code* is presented as a series of principles supported by guidelines of desirable professional practice. These principles are supported and accepted by the international museum community and have informed the different Units in this book. The *Code* is essential reading for all those engaged in museum governance and day-to-day activities, and should be used to inform both the museum's policies and working practices. In many countries, museum associations have also established their own codes of ethics that reflect ICOM's *Code* but are tailored to the particular circumstances under which their museums operate. These too should be essential reading and underpin policy and practice.

The key principles on which ICOM's *Code of Ethics for Museums* is founded are the following:

Museums preserve, interpret and promote the natural and cultural inheritance of humanity. Museums are responsible for the tangible and intangible natural and cultural heritage. Governing bodies and those concerned with the strategic direction and oversight of museums have a primary responsibility to promote and protect this heritage as well as the human, physical and financial resources made available for that purpose. (Guidelines cover institutional standing, physical resources, financial resources and personnel.)

Museums that maintain collections hold them in trust for the benefit of society and its development. Museums have the duty to acquire, preserve and promote their collections as a contribution to safeguarding the natural, cultural and scientific heritage. Their collections are a significant public inheritance, have a special position in law and are protected by international legislation. Inherent in this public trust is the notion of stewardship that includes rightful ownership, permanence, documentation, accessibility and responsible disposal. (Guidelines cover acquiring collections, removing collections and the care of collections.)

Museums hold primary evidence for establishing and furthering knowledge. Museums have particular responsibilities to all for the care, accessibility and interpretation of primary evidence collected and held in their collections. (Guidelines cover primary evidence, museum collecting and research.)

Museums provide opportunities for the appreciation, understanding and promotion of the natural and cultural heritage. Museums have an important duty to develop their educational role and attract wider audiences from the community, locality or group they serve. Interaction with the constituent community and promotion of their heritage is an integral part of the educational role of the museum. (Guidelines cover display and exhibition and other resources.)

Museum resources provide opportunities for other public services and benefits. Museums use a wide variety of specialisms, skills and physical resources that have a far wider application than in the museum. This may lead to shared resources or the provision of services as an extension of the museum's activities. They should be organised in such a way that they do not compromise the museum's stated mission. (Guidelines cover identification services.)

Museums work in close collaboration with the communities from which their collections originate as well as those they serve. Museum collections reflect the cultural and natural heritage of the communities from which they have been derived. As such, they have a character beyond that of ordinary property, which may include strong affinities with national, regional, local, ethnic, religious or political identity. It is important therefore that museum policy is responsive to this possibility. (Guidelines cover origin of collections and respect for communities served.)

Museums operate in a legal manner. Museums must conform fully to international, national, regional or local legislation and treaty obligations. In addition, the governing body should comply with any legally binding trusts or conditions relating to any aspect of the museum, its collections and operations. (Guidelines cover legal frameworks.)

Museums operate in a professional manner. Members of the museum profession should observe accepted standards and laws and uphold the dignity and honour of their profession. They should safeguard the public against illegal or unethical professional conduct. Every opportunity should be used to inform and educate the public about the aims, purpose and aspirations of the profession to develop a better understanding of the contributions of museums to society. (Guidelines cover professional conduct and conflict of interest.)

Section 2
The museum and its users

Museums are for people

Unit 7

Related Units – Units 2, 4, 8–12

MUSEUMS AND REPRESENTATION

Year by year attitudes to museums and the demands that people make of them continue to change worldwide. Increased international travel and first-hand experience of museums in other countries, greater exposure to museums and their collections through broadcasting, and personal access to museums and museum services through the Internet are all important change factors. They make people more directly aware of the standards museums are achieving in their work and encourage people to interrogate the role of museums in society.

Internationally, there is for example a growing critical awareness of the 'political' nature of museums and their historic role in maintaining the cultural values of elite or privileged groups in society. As political structures change, the powerful role of cultural facilities, such as museums, run or supported by the state, comes under intense public scrutiny. Questions about whose culture is being portrayed or transmitted in museums and who is portraying or transmitting it for whom are to be heard in countries throughout the world. This debate, with the recognition of the powerful position that museums and similar facilities have in explaining and transmitting cultural values, is an exciting and challenging one. Museums need to explain the rationale for their mission and their core values to their users, and engage their users in helping them shape mission and values.

Museum users are increasingly expecting a greater degree of representation in the work of museums. For example, in multicultural societies, minority ethnic groups or groups who may have traditionally been under-represented in museums, such as women or children, are becoming more interested in having their culture appropriately represented through displays and exhibitions, collections and databases. This is especially true where museums have implicitly or explicitly denied opportunities for balanced representation in the past.

ENCOURAGING INVOLVEMENT AND ENGAGEMENT

Museum users now expect more involvement and a more active, participatory experience in their contact with museums. Involvement may take many forms, for example serving as a volunteer, taking part in management committees or working parties, or helping in fundraising activities. Closer engagement with the museum might simply mean being able to handle collections and take part in special events and activities programmes. The spectrum is a wide one and building closer relationships with people provides multiple long-term benefits.

For example, the changing style of museums and the changes affecting presentation methods through the application of new information and communication technologies are generating greater interest in 'hands-on' experiences for users. It is not enough for museums to present collections and information to visitors in a passive way. Museums have to engage interest through active involvement with their users and build on this to achieve their objectives. Museum managers should encourage users to explore and discover the museum's collections and services for themselves. This is in contrast to the traditional approach still prevalent in many museums where expertise resides in the museum alone and users are perceived as passive recipients of what the museum determines should be on offer.

This rising public demand for involvement and participation in the 'process' of museum work and engagement with what museums have to offer the user means that museums have to understand the social and economic context within which they are working to a far greater degree than in the past. Everything that a museum does is ultimately for the public benefit. Understanding the public's interests and concerns, likes and dislikes, needs and wants, is of critical importance in providing successful services and developing successful museums. Museums are for people, and the successful museum recognises the opportunities that participation and involvement can bring to its work and the need to engage people ever more closely with the services it provides.

These changes in attitude and interest place a heavy responsibility on the shoulders of those managing museums, especially where public money is involved. Managing museums efficiently and effectively for the public benefit requires a detailed understanding of, and sympathy with, the various different interest groups within the museum's public. Developing such an insight requires detailed research on a continuous basis. It is only when the museum's public is thoroughly understood that the museum can effectively respond to the public's needs and requirements through its services.

Throughout *Museum Basics* there is a strong emphasis on the relationship of the museum with the people whom it serves. The concept of a 'market' where the museum, along with other educational and entertainment facilities, 'sells' or 'advertises' its 'wares' is developed in succeeding Units. The idea of a museum operating in a 'market' may be unfamiliar to some readers, but it is of immense value in helping to analyse the relationships between people and museums, and in exploring how museums can respond to people's needs and interests.

The term 'market' also signifies competition. Museums in all parts of the world are in competition, not simply with one another, but with all the other calls on people's leisure time. Operating within a market means being 'competitive', providing products and services that the public want and are prepared to pay for either directly or through their taxes. Successful museums are oriented towards the market and are outward-looking. They recognise that their future depends on people sympathetic to their objectives and on people who are prepared to be involved in what they have to offer. As we have noted, this involvement may go far beyond a casual visit to the museum, and may extend into fundraising programmes, voluntary work, patronage, membership of the Friends' group, donations, fieldwork and oral history, and collecting programmes to name but a few. Building public interest and support is essential for a museum's long-term success.

In the twenty-first century, the greatest challenge facing museums is to recognise that museums are for people, and that future success depends on meeting their identified needs.

Unit 8

Access and accessibility

Related Units – Units 9–13

There are many ways in which museums prevent people from visiting them. This Unit looks at some of the barriers museums unconsciously erect against visitors, and at ways we can knock them down again.

▋ 'IT'S NOT FOR PEOPLE LIKE US.'

One of the main reasons that people do not visit museums is that they think they will not feel comfortable there. Sometimes, indeed, the idea of visiting a museum may not even have occurred to them. In almost every country, museum-going tends to be an activity of the better-educated and better-off.

Too often, museums seem to make special efforts to make ordinary working people feel uncomfortable. Many earlier museums were designed to look like palaces, and though they may have been meant to be 'palaces of the people', in fact they are easily associated in people's minds with the elite. Many of the most famous museums, too, attract a very large number of foreign tourists. As a result, local people feel that they are 'not for us'. Like the big tourist hotels, they may make people feel like strangers in their own country.

What can we do to counter this alienation, to make ordinary local people feel that their museums belong to them? The first step is to recognise and understand the problem. A market survey (see Unit 9) will reveal what people think about the museum, but many lessons can be learned simply by visiting the museum and trying to see it with the eyes of a modest person who has never been to a museum before. Or perhaps you might invite representatives of different ages or ethnic groups to visit the museum with you and discuss their visit in detail with them.

Can the outside of the museum be made to seem more friendly, perhaps by flags and banners, by 'welcome' signs, or by pictures showing what is to be found inside?

Can special marketing campaigns be aimed at sections of the community who do not visit? If you can discover what it is that discourages them, perhaps appropriately designed leaflets, posters, radio and TV can be used to reassure them.

Could special openings and events be arranged for special groups? Rather than trying to attract individuals or families, it may be easier to arrange special visits for existing groups, for example, women's groups, religious groups or shared-interest groups. Not only will the group members feel more secure and comfortable among people of their own kind, whom they already know, but the museum may be able to arrange special talks or other activities suited to their interests (see Unit 17).

The museum reception and security staff must be trained to be equally welcoming to all sorts and conditions of people. In some countries museum security staff are traditionally drawn from one particular minority group: this may be off-putting to visitors from other groups.

What about the café? Is the food it sells acceptable and familiar to local people? Are toilets available? If the local custom is to sit on the floor rather than on chairs, is that comfortably possible? In general, is there anything else that can be done to make the ordinary person feel at home in your museum?

'IT'S NEVER OPEN.'

Too often museums seem to have opening hours to suit the convenience of museum staff rather than that of visitors. It is of the greatest importance to find out when your potential visitors could come to the museum. If the local custom is for such visits to be made in family groups, led perhaps by father or grandfather, then it is clearly essential for the museum to be open when he is not working: that may be in the evenings or at weekends, or at certain seasons of the year.

'IT'S TOO TIRING.'

It's easy to get tired in museums; old people and children may tire particularly quickly. Not only should the displays be designed to counter the 'museum effect' through changes of atmosphere and pace (see Unit 29), but plenty of seating should be provided throughout the museum, with refreshments − if only water − readily available.

'BUT I CAN'T TAKE THE CHILDREN.'

Is the museum designed with children in mind? Are there places where they can run around and let off steam? Is there a special children's section? Is there a crèche where small children can be safely left while their parents explore the displays? Are there special guidebooks and worksheets designed for children? Is there some-where where babies' nappies (diapers) can be changed? Are the stairs safe for small children? Are pushchairs and baby buggies welcome?

Few museums will have all these things, but the more the museum is welcoming to children, the more their families will come too. This is important because the majority of visits to museums take place in family or social groups.

▌'HOW CAN I GET THERE?'

Where is the museum located? Many museums are in the richer parts of town, well away from the areas where most people live. Many others are designed to be convenient for car-drivers. Yet even in the richest industrialised societies of the West, perhaps 50 per cent of the population may not have daily access to a car. We should remember this and try to find ways of helping people get to the museum.

It may be possible to persuade the local bus company to run buses to the museum. It may be possible for the museum to run its own bus or transport service from the town centre, perhaps offering a cheap ticket combined with other facilities.

▌'I CAN'T AFFORD IT.'

How much are visitors paying to come to the museum? They will have to pay for the transport to get there, the admission charge, refreshments and perhaps some small souvenirs for the children, and transport home again. For a family party this may add up to quite a large sum. What is the average weekly income of the sort of family we want to attract to the museum? Can they afford it? Does the museum provide free admission on certain days for the local community? Are there special admission rates for families and regular visitors?

▌'I CAN'T MANAGE THE STAIRS.'

Many of the museum's potential visitors will have impaired mobility. Some will be in wheelchairs, but more will simply walk slowly and painfully, will use a stick or simply find stairs difficult (see Unit 12).

Every museum should ensure that it is as accessible as it possibly can be to visitors who find it difficult or impossible to walk. All doors and displays must be wide enough for wheelchairs, stairs and steps should be as few as possible and always matched by lifts, escalators or ramps (see Unit 8).

▌'MY EYES AREN'T GOOD ENOUGH THESE DAYS.'

Many of the museum's potential visitors will have impaired eyesight. No curator who has watched the concentration and joy on a blind child's face as he or she feels museum objects will need persuading of the value of arranging handling sessions and 'to-be-touched' displays.

Many more visitors simply have poor eyesight, and for them it is important to remember:

- to keep light levels as high as is compatible with conservation (see Unit 56);
- to provide good lighting on stairs;

- to provide handrails wherever possible;
- to provide large lettering on labels (see Unit 31);
- to train staff to understand and watch out for visitors' difficulties, and to offer discreet and tactful help when necessary.

Unit

9

Understanding your market

Related Units – Units 8, 10–12

A museum's *market* can be thought of as the overall social and economic context within which the museum operates. All museums operate within a market and all provide a supply of services that meet a market demand. The market will vary from place to place, region to region, country to country. The numbers of museums and the numbers of users will vary. Researching your market in terms of supply and demand and understanding its composition will help you to determine whether your museum is offering the right type or mix of services to your users, at the right location, at the right time(s), at the right level and at the right price. Understanding the nature and composition of your market is of paramount importance for success.

Market analysis and *market research* are necessary whether you are starting up and developing a new museum, or managing an existing one. Market analysis helps to provide quantitative information about the marketplace you are working within; market research helps to provide qualitative information. Market research should be a continuous exercise helping you to develop or change your services to your users in the light of their needs and responses to the museum. It will help you to address new *market segments* and develop new audiences. Market research is not the preserve of specialist companies, although these can often be very helpful. It is essentially common sense, and you can – as many museums do – work out your own market research plan. It is about finding out a range of relevant information from users and non-users that will help your museum meet its aims and objectives. Market analysis and research will also help in drawing up a forward plan for the museum (see Unit 81) and in developing a marketing plan (see Unit 10).

RESEARCHING YOUR USERS AND COMPETITORS

People use museums to meet all kinds of needs. Some are straightforward, such as seeking information, somewhere to meet their friends, somewhere to take visitors or children when they are on holiday; some are more complex, such as to discover the history and heritage of a place, to find a sense of personal identity, to spend time by oneself. Research will help you to understand the motivations of your users more accurately and develop services to meet their needs and interests. Critically, it will also help to explain why people do *not* visit your museum.

You can find out a great deal about the museum market using external information, both quantitative and qualitative, derived from published and unpublished sources. You can also use internal information derived from your own observation, surveys and records, or specially commissioned research. By the time you have completed your fact-finding, you should have answers to the following questions:

- Why will people visit my museum?
- What motivates them?
- Who will visit my museum?
- What are their characteristics?
- When will they come to the museum?
- Will they return and how often?
- How much time will they spend in the museum?
- Who are my museum's competitors?
- What are their strengths and weaknesses?
- What can my museum learn from them?
- What will my museum's *market share* be?
- Is my museum's market getting larger or smaller year by year?

This information will help you to build up a picture of the market for your museum and help to determine the nature and scale of the demand for your museum and its services.

CARRYING OUT MARKET ANALYSIS

To find out more about the size and composition of your target markets and to allow you to answer some of these questions, you need to gather quantitative information from published and unpublished sources. Published and Internet-based information might include:

- central and local government statistics related to family/household expenditure on services/goods, lifestyle groups and trends in the marketplace;
- research publications and journals providing relevant case study material on museums;
- specialised publications on marketing, giving information about the interests and attitudes of different groups;
- local trade organisations and business people holding information on local markets;
- consultancy reports on museum developments that include market research.

Compare your market share, anticipated or actual, with other museums. Are there trends in the market place apparent over three, or five, or ten years?

Are visitor numbers or numbers of museums on the increase or decrease? Why is there this pattern? Is the museum business in your country successful or unsuccessful at the moment? How will it fare in the future? Discuss these figures with colleagues and advisers to get a better understanding of where your museum fits into the overall market both in terms of supply and demand.

This *'desk research'* can bring together valuable information and is an important method of building a picture about your market and its different market segments. Not all of these sources may be available to you, but make use of what you can acquire and develop information over a period of time. Of particular importance is to identify changing trends over time.

MARKET RESEARCH SURVEYS

To complement this external *quantitative* information, an important and useful method of gathering information is the market research survey. Market research surveys can help to provide a range of *qualitative* information about users and non-users.

On the one hand, market research surveys can be very specialised and detailed. Specialist companies experienced in gathering market information and carrying out analysis of the results may carry them out for your museum. On the other hand, they can be relatively simple and carried out internally by the museum itself. They do nevertheless need to be well designed and to provide information that will complement quantitative information and allow you to build up a more detailed picture of your market and its composition.

Regular use of survey questionnaires can also help to identify changing trends in your museum audience, and help to explain why people do not come to the museum!

A simple visitor survey questionnaire might, for example, gather the following information about a sample of your visitors:

- age range – up to 12, 12–18, 18–25, 26–35, 36–45, 46–55, 56–65, 66–75, 75 and over;
- gender – male/female;
- group numbers – adults/children;
- occupation/occupation of head of household;
- type of transport to museum – foot, bicycle, bus/coach, train, car, other;
- distance travelled from home or holiday residence;
- location of home or holiday residence;
- reason(s) for visit;
- length of visit;
- frequency of visits;
- enjoyment of visit;
- suggestions for improvements.

The minimum size of sample should be somewhere between 200–300 visitors. There are different approaches to sampling, with the goal of achieving a representative sample of the population. However, the museum should seek to reach a balanced and representative sample of the population being studied. A random sampling approach may need to be balanced by a degree of selection.

Market research surveys of people who do *not* use the museum can also help to pinpoint the reasons why people do not visit your museum. Some of these factors will be beyond your control or influence. But finding out about why people do not visit your museum provides the first steps for developing or improving services for the future to attract new audiences. The museum may also wish to hold discussions with groups or representatives of different communities to discover people's attitudes to the museum and its services.

Remember: market research should be a continuous process as it will help to inform your forward planning and your marketing approaches! At a simple level, observation of visitor behaviour, talking to visitors, noting visitor characteristics, can all be carried out on a day-to-day basis, and recorded. More complex research programmes may be undertaken, perhaps seasonally or annually. Much will depend on the museum's resources.

RESEARCHING YOUR COMPETITORS

Research and observation in other museums and similar facilities can also provide very valuable data as well as ideas for your own developments. Try to find out who visits other museums and analyse the services that are provided for them. Look at the pricing policies and opening times of other museums. Examine how their brand identity is presented in the marketplace through advertising, web sites or print matter. Ask what makes for success and why these museums are successful or unsuccessful. Test for yourself the range and quality of services on offer.

Look at other organisations too. Analyse what is happening in other service environments. Assess shops, restaurants, hotels, offices – what quality of design and standard of environment and service are people expecting from these facilities? Won't they expect your museum to offer a similar level and quality in services and surroundings?

People face increasingly complex choices over what they might do with their leisure time. If the quality of your museum is below acceptable standards, they will go elsewhere for their leisure and entertainment.

FACTORS INFLUENCING MUSEUM VISITING

These are some of the factors that you might find helpful in thinking about what motivates your visitors and non-visitors and affects their decision-making:

- location of museum;
- cost of transport to the museum;
- distance to be travelled to the museum;
- availability of transport;

- type of transport;
- time spent travelling;
- prior knowledge of museum;
- marketing and advertising;
- signage;
- appeal of subject;
- pricing policy;
- range of facilities and services available;
- accessibility – physical and intellectual;
- opportunities for participation in museum work;
- quality and depth of the museum's web site;
- previous experience of the museum;
- peer group recommendations;
- weather conditions;
- season of the year;
- available time;
- level and range of interest in the museum's collections;
- family/partner/social group agreement.

PEOPLE IN HOUSEHOLDS

It is useful to know what sort of individuals and social groups visit museums. Household types for research purposes include:

- living alone;
- married couple or partners, no children;
- married couple or partners, with dependent children;
- married couple or partners, with non-dependent children;
- single parent with dependent children;
- multiple occupation;
- extended family.

GATHERING INFORMATION

Sources of information for market research include the following:

- publications;
- unpublished reports;
- visitor counts;
- observations of visitor behaviour in the museum;
- market research surveys;
- self-completion questionnaires;
- administered questionnaires;
- interviews with visitors and non-visitors;

- talking to visitors;
- analysis of group bookings;
- analysis of comments in visitor books.

ASSESSING YOUR MUSEUM IN THE MARKETPLACE

The task of your museum is to respond to the actual or latent market demand that you have been able to identify through your market analysis and research. At this stage, it is as well to stand back and consider the museum's current or planned state. Examine the range and quality of services and experiences on offer to your users. Ask what benefits the museum is providing its users in the light of what you know of their needs and expectations through your market research.

Ask yourself the following questions:

- What 'business' is my museum in: the history business, the education business, the leisure business, the conservation business?
- What overall *'product'* or 'service' is the museum providing?
- What is the quality of the museum's public facilities and services? What does it not have to offer the public?
- Does the museum 'stand out' in the marketplace? Does it have a recognisable *brand identity*?
- Are there strong events and activities programmes to encourage regular and repeat visitation?
- Is the museum accessible in physical, cultural or intellectual terms?
- Is the museum reaching out beyond its walls through outreach services, educational services or web site provision?
- Is the museum affordable to people in terms of its pricing?
- Do people know about the museum and its work? How do they know about it?
- Do enough people know about the museum?
- Do they speak well of it? Are they satisfied?

It is unlikely that you will have the money or resources to provide for *all* of the needs of *all* of your possible users. You will have to decide what developments are required and what balance of services it would be best to provide with the resources that you have to attract your target users. Market analysis and research will give you the basis on which to make these decisions.

Remember that many people will use your museum, but not necessarily visit it. They may require information by telephone or by letter, or request products from the museum shop to be sent by post. They may make use of information resources on the museum's web site. They may meet their friends outside the museum because it is a well-known landmark, or simply accept it as part of their cultural 'landscape'. It may serve symbolically to give them a sense of cultural status. There are many ways in which people use museums.

MEETING MARKET DEMANDS

Market analysis and research will help to identify those people who need the services and benefits that your museum is offering. In reality, there is not one uniform market of users, but a collection of many smaller groupings or *segments*. Each of these represents a potential target for the museum. There are many ways of dividing or segmenting your market. They include the following characteristics:

- *Age* – people of different ages have different needs and the museum will need to cater for a range of age groups. How will your museum cater for different age groups successfully?
- *Gender* – many people visit museums in family or social groups. Is your museum able to cater equally for men and women?
- *Income* – different income groups have different spending power. Will your museum target specific income groups or aim to appeal to all?
- *Education* – the level of education of your users may well determine the approach you take to exhibitions and displays, events and activities. How will your museum cater for different levels of educational attainment? Will your users have literacy and numeracy difficulties? How can these be overcome?
- *Location* – museum users can be divided up by where they live, where they work and the places/facilities that they visit. Do you know where your users are coming from, and how they travel to your museum?
- *Leisure participation* – visiting museums is only one type of leisure or cultural activity. Do you know what else your visitors like to do in their leisure time? Does this suggest possibilities for the delivery of services?
- *Lifestyles and values* – different households and families have different lifestyles and values. Which lifestyles will your museum cater for? Will you have long opening hours, for example, to allow visitors to come after their work? How will you address different religious values?
- *Patterns of use* – visitors to museums may visit once, several times or regularly. Very many people visit museums in family or social groups. Does your museum attract people on a regular or irregular basis and why?

However you segment your market and whatever combination of characteristics you use, you need to ask the following questions:

- Can each market segment that you select as a target be quantified through market research? Can you estimate the number of potential users in each segment? How often will these users visit the museum and at what times of the year? For example, census records may tell you how many families with young children there are in your area; your market research can tell you what proportion of that potential market segment is coming to your museum.
- Is the size of the market segment significant? Are there enough users in each segment to justify providing services for them? Can the museum attract more users from this segment through new developments or changes in marketing strategies?

- If income is a consideration for your museum, is the market segment a profitable one? Will users from this segment cover the costs of the service on offer? What level of income will they generate?
- Can you reach and communicate with the market segment effectively? Is it possible to inform the market segment of your services? How will you do this and what are the cost implications? You may have to make special efforts for those who cannot read or write and for those who speak minority languages.

All of this market analysis and research should be designed to make you examine the quality, range and delivery of your museum's services and improve them where required. The successful museum provides services to meet the needs of its users. The successful museum understands who its users are and what they need. It has researched its market.

Key words

Market – the overall social and economic context within which a museum operates. The term implies an exchange between the museum in terms of its services and products and the 'marketplace', which consists of people using or purchasing the museum's services and products.

The notion of competition within the 'marketplace' also encompasses other services and products that are competing with museums for people's time and money.

Market segmentation – a method of dividing the market up into groupings with specific characteristics in order to target services at them.

Market penetration – the degree to which a museum is successful in attracting users from the market as a whole and from particular market segments, and encouraging take-up of services.

STUDY EXAMPLE 9.1

An industrial museum wanted to find out more about its visitors and their levels of satisfaction with the museum. Everyone visiting the museum was offered a free cup of tea in the museum café if they completed a simple survey questionnaire first. By the end of the year, the museum had collected over 10,000 questionnaires at a cost of just £500.

From the detailed analysis of the questionnaires, the museum gained new insights into where its visitors came from. However, comments from the questionnaires also led to three key improvements – in the organisation of the museum shop, the siting of the museum's donation boxes and a different seating and serving arrangement in the café. These improvements in turn provided a net increase in income of 400 per cent and improved customer satisfaction.

This was a simple example of good qualitative market research providing a range of benefits both to the museum and its users.

STUDY EXAMPLE 9.2

A museums service in a medium-sized industrial city wanted to discover why people living on its peripheral housing estates did not visit the service's four museums in the city centre. A small team of researchers interviewed a range of people in their homes, chosen to be representative of the various types and lifestyles of people living on the estates. Each interviewee was given a voucher to purchase food in local shops in payment and spent between one and two hours discussing their cultural interests and attitudes to museums with the interviewers. The interviews were transcribed and a report on the findings presented to the museums. In the light of the comments from the residents, the museums were able to develop new services and marketing plans to encourage visitation from these areas of the city.

Market research had helped the museums service identify and reach new audiences.

Unit
10

Marketing your museum

Related Units – Units 9, 11–12

Market analysis and research (see Unit 9) will have shown who your users are or might be, why they visit the museum and use its services, and what their needs are. It should also have given you insights into why people do not visit the museum or use its services. Successful marketing of the museum depends on a combination of factors, sometimes known as *the marketing mix*, and conveniently described as product, price, place and promotion.

Within the marketing mix, the museum has to strike a balance between these four factors. It has to develop products or services to meet the needs and interests of identified market segments. It has to ensure that the way in which that product is priced or made available will generate demand. Where possible, for example with a new museum building, it has to ensure that its physical position or outlets are effectively sited. Finally, it has to promote and publicise its presence and its services in the marketplace using a variety of techniques.

The museum also has to develop good working relationships and good public relations with its users and patrons in order to maintain and develop interest in the museum's services and to fulfil its mission.

PRODUCT

What is the *museum product*? Understanding the museum product and developing it in line with your users' needs is the task of museum management and a key component in the marketing mix. It is an amalgam of services, people, buildings, facilities, atmosphere, customer care, accessibility, corporate presentation, collections, events and activities and many other quantifiable and non-quantifiable factors. It is what differentiates your museum from any other museum, or market competitor. It is essentially what makes the museum's identity and personality, and has a key part to play in the development of the museum's brand – the perception of the museum in people's minds.

PRICE

Managing any museum carries with it costs – costs associated with staffing, displays, exhibitions, conservation, documentation, security, promotion and all the other responsibilities of a museum. How those costs are met will vary from museum to museum. Some museums will have their costs met wholly or in part by public authorities; others will have only minimal public funding and rely heavily on admission charges and other forms of income generation such as retail and catering for their income. How the museum will meet its costs is a task of management, but the prices charged for admission and/or services are a key component in the marketing mix. The successful museum ensures that its pricing policy does not exclude potential users, and allows it to meet the full range of its responsibilities.

PLACE

What is the best location for a museum? A museum's location may be a strength or it may be a weakness. Museums are established in many different types of location in town and country, in specially built or reused buildings, in rich or poor communities. Their location is one of the key factors in their accessibility, and a determining factor behind who visits them and how successful they are in meeting their mission.

Museums can play an important part in social and economic regeneration, providing cultural 'anchors' in developing tourist destinations (see Unit 4). The interrelationships between the museum and other cultural facilities, as well as other services and infrastructure related to the location as a whole, may be an important factor in considering where to develop a new museum. A museum that is playing a full part in social and economic regeneration in a particular location may well have access to capital and revenue funding and other support not available in other locations. Identifying the best location for a new museum needs careful consideration; factors such as physical accessibility, synergy with other cultural and allied facilities, potential for investment and contribution to regeneration programmes need to be borne in mind in examining options for a museum's location (see Unit 71).

PROMOTION

How can museums effectively promote themselves in the marketplace? One of the most important points to bear in mind in setting up a marketing or promotional strategy for your museum is how you can test its impact. If there is only a limited amount of money available for promotion through posters, advertising, mail-outs, leaflets and the broadcasting media, you will need to know whether your marketing budget is being spent to the best effect. Evaluating the success of a marketing strategy is at least as important as devising and implementing one.

In marketing your museum ensure that all of the benefits to the user are stated clearly, and wherever possible seek creative advice. Much money may be wasted on poorly conceived marketing materials, which are poorly distributed and poorly received by potential users. Promoting the museum may cost nothing other than enthusiasm, hard work and the creative use of existing information providers such as the press and radio. Bear in mind that good word-of-mouth publicity from satisfied users is ultimately the most powerful means of developing support for the museum.

Developing a good working relationship with your users is important in marketing the museum. But developing and maintaining a good working relationship with the museum's patrons and stakeholders is also important. Managing effectively the relationships between the museum, the museum's users and the museum's patrons is a central task of the museum management.

The museum's patrons and stakeholders might include central and local government agencies, corporate sponsors, charitable trusts, individual donors, international funding bodies and local businesses. The museum's success will depend in large part on how well your achievements and successes, as well as needs, are understood by these supporters or potential supporters. Significant amounts of time need to be spent on keeping them informed of, and inspired by, your work in order to maximise their assistance.

Promoting success and encouraging your users to demonstrate their satisfaction with the museum to patrons will help secure the investment needed by the museum to carry out its work successfully. If insufficient attention is paid to one of these areas of responsibility, and too much emphasis is placed on one area to the exclusion of another, the museum will suffer. It follows that effective *public relations* for all your constituencies of interest are of importance. Good relations with your public form an essential complement to marketing.

There are various means of promoting the museum in the marketplace. The communications and promotional strategy that you employ, whether it is through the broadcasting media, print and/or audio-visual materials and web site, will help to attract audiences to your museum and keep your museum in public focus.

What methods are available to market the museum? The following checklists give an indication of the wide range of methods available to you. In practice, some will be unsuitable or inappropriate depending on circumstances, but all are worth serious consideration.

SOME ADVERTISING AND PUBLICITY MEDIA

Newspapers

- daily
- weekly
- weekend
- colour magazines
- domestic
- foreign
- international
- news stories
- features
- photographs/captions
- editorials
- letters
- advertising
- advertising features
- competitions/prizes

Magazines

- weekly
- monthly
- quarterly
- annual
- occasional
- domestic
- foreign
- international
- general readership
- special readership groups
- trade/commercial
- news stories
- features
- photographs/captions
- editorials
- letters
- advertising
- advertising features
- competitions/prizes

Television

- features
- news stories
- interviews
- documentaries
- talk-shows
- quizzes
- advertising
- associated publications
- associated web sites

Radio

- features
- news stories
- interviews
- documentaries
- talk-shows
- quizzes
- advertising
- associated publications
- associated web sites

Printed material

- posters
- leaflets
- direct mail/mail-shots
- brochures
- personalised letters
- information flyers
- banners/flags
- advertising flyers
- financial appeal literature

Displays

- tourist information centres
- shops
- travel centres
- other cultural facilities
- fairs

- promotional events
- government offices

Web sites

- information pages
- e-exhibitions
- interactive pages
- hyperlinks to other linked sites
- associated publications

MARKETING YOUR MUSEUM

Marketing and promoting your museum and its services to the public requires careful consideration. Your market analysis and research will have identified a variety of audiences for the museum, and you will have developed services to meet the needs of your target market segments. How do you reach them, and reach them efficiently, ensuring value for money? Paid advertising, whatever media you use, means that the museum is in charge of what it wants to say and how it wants to say it. Free editorial copy in a newspaper or news coverage on the radio or television can be helpful, but it is also selective and others are in control of editing and presentation.

Targeting your marketing effectively at your market segments is the key to obtaining value for money; some media are better than others in this respect. Do not be afraid to take professional advice and do not be afraid to experiment. Whatever form or mix of marketing is used, the museum should ensure that the choice of medium is appropriate and marketing materials are of good quality and well presented, whatever the target audience at which it is aimed. Your marketing materials should be designed to create an identity or personality for your museum in the public mind, and this identity should consistently reinforce the museum's brand. If you are using a variety of advertising media to promote your museum in the marketplace, consistency of brand identity is of particular importance.

Remember that there is enormous competition with other organisations seeking to gain attention and communicate with the marketplace; your marketing strategy needs to attract attention, identify the key benefits on offer and be memorable. Successful museums target their marketing on the basis of good market analysis and research. They use creative ideas. They maintain consistency of brand identity. They build up constituencies of long-term support by providing the benefits to the user that they have promised.

Developing new audiences

Related Units – Units 7–10, 12

> *Everyone has the right freely to participate in the cultural life of the community, to enjoy the arts and to share in scientific advancement and its benefits.*
>
> (Article 27 of the Universal Declaration of Human Rights)

No museums should ever be content with their present visitors, even if millions come through the door every year. Who are our visitors? Who uses our services? Are we really attracting all those people we want to attract?

The term 'audience' has been borrowed from the arts and sport to mean those groups of people who visit the museum, or who use its other services.

Museums too often reflect the divisions that exist in their societies. For example, museums often find themselves reflecting the interests and traditions of the wealthier local residents, or of the larger and longer-established community, or of older people, or of men. Poorer people, immigrants, the young or women can find themselves excluded. In some countries, too, museums are visited mostly by foreign tourists, even those museums designed to appeal to local people.

Every museum should carry out regular visitor surveys to find out who their visitors are (see Unit 9). Larger museums will commission full professional surveys, but even the smallest museums can ask every visitor three or four simple questions, perhaps on the way in or out:

- Where do you come from?
- What work do you do?
- Why did you come?
- What one thing could increase your enjoyment of the museum?

If the answers are noted down, together with the time or day, day of the week, time of the year, the weather, and the group the visitor came in, it will be possible to work out detailed information on who visits the museum, when and (to some extent) why. We can then decide whether we are attracting the type of visitors we most want to attract.

Perhaps some groups are obviously missing from our visitor profile. For example, perhaps we are attracting only wealthy, professional people, yet we (and our stakeholders) believe the museum should serve *all* the people. What can we do to attract those we are missing? Possible steps are of three kinds:

- Change what the museum offers, to make it more attractive.
- Do more to promote the museum.
- Improve access to the museum.

Much can probably be done to make exhibits more attractive and interesting to new audiences, and temporary exhibitions can be used to target distinct groups of people (see Units 29 and 34). The museum's publicity can be reviewed to make sure that the right message is getting to the new audiences (see Units 9 and 10). And the location, appearance and ease of access of the museum can all be considered, and any possible improvements planned (see Unit 8).

It can be useful to set out plans to develop new audiences in a formal Audience Development Plan. The key section will be one that describes exactly who is going to do what, what it will cost and how its success can be measured (see Study example 11.1).

Museums cannot solve all the problems of the world! We need to be a bit modest, and remember that museums cannot usually work miracles. But museums do have a responsibility to ensure that we are serving as wide a spectrum of audiences as we possibly can. We can at least play our part in promoting social equality and mutual understanding; we can do our best to help.

STUDY EXAMPLE 11.1

A museum found that its current audience was almost exclusively composed of well-educated local people and foreign tourists. It drew up an Audience Development Plan with the objective of widening its audience; this is part of that Plan's key section.

Exhibit improvements: proposal	Who?	By when?	Cost?	Measure
Rewrite labels in more accessible form	Curator with local teacher	End August	To be determined	Survey of visitors
Include interactives	Curator with local teacher	End August	To be determined	Survey of visitors
Review publicity	Curator with local teacher	End August	Staff time	Survey of visitors
Secure regular slots on local radio	Director	December	Staff time	Length of slot/ listener numbers
Exhibition openings by local sportspeople	Director	Ongoing	Staff time	Increase in visitor numbers/new audience segments
Make museum look more attractive: flags, etc.	Director with designer	End May	To be determined	Increase in casual visitors
Improve external signposting	Director with designer	End July	To be determined	Survey of visitors

A local museum carried out a simple survey of visitors and non-visitors, and was shocked to realise that almost all its visitors came from just one of the 'tribes' who lived locally. For many local residents, the museum was simply alien territory in which they would not feel comfortable. What could be done? The museum could not easily be moved to a more neutral location, and even if it could, it might risk losing its existing audience. Instead, the museum organised an event each year that involved groups from the different local communities putting on a festival. The main event was held at the central sports stadium, which was seen as neutral ground where everyone felt comfortable, but an accompanying exhibition was held at the museum, and was heavily publicised. Although the museum staff had to give a great deal of their time to organising the festival, this audience development policy succeeded; after three years not only were there many more visitors, but another visitor survey showed that they were much more representative of the local population.

Unit 12

Special audiences: museums and people with disabilities

Related Units – Units 8–11

Disability does not discriminate. People of all ages and in all walks of life can suffer from various forms of physical or mental disability on a permanent or temporary basis. A substantial proportion of people in any community will suffer from some form of disability. We are all likely to suffer from some form of disability as old age approaches. People may have difficulty in walking, people may be blind or partially sighted, people may be deaf or hard of hearing, or people may have a mental handicap or suffer from fear of heights, open spaces or closed spaces.

In making your museum accessible and hospitable to all, you will need to take account of the needs of people with disabilities and develop policies and programmes of practical action to provide for disabled people. Legislation on disability varies from country to country, and the museum will have to take account of the legislative framework within which it is working and meet any necessary legal requirements.

In considering how to make the museum more accessible to people with disabilities, it is useful to undertake an Access Audit, an assessment of all the aspects of the museum that might provide barriers to access. This can then help the museum establish a plan of action and prioritise improvements for the future. Access Audits are best carried out in conjunction with people with different forms of disability so that the museum's response can be appropriately informed. This checklist provides an indication of the sort of questions museum managers should be asking of the external and internal features of museum buildings in considering access for people with disabilities:

OUTSIDE THE MUSEUM

Orientation for disabled visitors. Are there appropriate signs/landmarks for blind/ partially sighted visitors? Are marketing materials available in large text size?

Access routes/paths. Are access routes clearly marked and free of obstructions? Are kerbs and edges defined and surfaces slip-free? Are signs, gratings, litter bins a hazard? Do windows/doors open outwards or inwards?

Ramps and steps. Are entrances well signposted and accessible for people in wheelchairs? Are ramps for wheelchair users at the correct gradient? Are there handrails alongside ramps and steps? Is there adequate lighting?

Entrance doors and halls. Are doors wide enough for wheelchair users? Is the door too heavy to open? Are there steps associated with the door? Can people see through the doors? Are glazed doors clearly marked? Can automatic doors be used instead of swing doors? Do halls and lobbies allow for wheelchair manoeuvre?

INSIDE THE MUSEUM

Orientation. Is there sufficient, legible signing for partially sighted visitors? Are there aural or tactile landmarks to assist blind/partially sighted visitors? Do the surface colours of walls/floors aid or impede orientation?

Levels. Are there warnings about changes in floor levels? Are stairs well lit and signposted? Are information desks/hooks/washbasins/shop displays/telephones at a suitable level for wheelchair users?

Lifts. Are control buttons easily seen and located? Is there a handrail inside the lift? Are signs and directions clearly marked and lighted?

Seating. Is there sufficient seating available for visitors? Is it stable and at varied heights?

Materials and surface finishes. Are surface finishes chosen with a view to avoiding discomfort or injury? Are there sharp angles on walls or junctions? Is sound or light reflection an aid or a hindrance? Can colours be used to provide guidance? Are displays presented without distracting surfaces behind them so that objects stand out effectively?

Lighting. Are windows designed to minimise glare? Can they be opened and locked easily? Is display lighting effective for partially sighted visitors?

Heating. Are heating systems such as radiators dangerous to touch?

Disaster management. Will disabled people be able to get out of a museum building easily in the case of fire or other disaster? Are there procedures laid down for staff to follow? Do staff know what to do in case of emergencies?

Induction loops. Is the museum/gallery/lecture room/education centre fitted with an induction loop to help people who use hearing aids?

Signs. Are signs legible and consistent? Are they positioned well? Are Braille letters within hand reach and at an appropriate level and angle?

Touch exhibitions/displays/tours/workshops. Does the museum provide touch exhibits/handling opportunities for blind or partially sighted visitors?

Café/restaurant. Are serving arrangements accessible and appropriate for visitors in wheelchairs?

Toilets. Are there specially designed toilets for disabled visitors?

Guided tours. Does the museum organise guided tours and events specifically for people with disabilities?

These are only a few of the questions that museum managers should be addressing in the design of new museums, the adaptation and development of existing buildings and the provision of visitor facilities and services, whether these be displays/exhibitions, education services, guided tours, publications or demonstrations and workshops. Understanding the needs of people with disabilities in order to put improvement programmes into action or to ensure new facilities/activities meet their needs effectively requires proper communication and consultation with disabled people.

A museum manager should take every step to liaise with disabled individuals or liaison groups to identify needs. There is a wide range of organisations and publications available to provide general and specific advice on needs. The museum may wish to establish an advisory panel to help inform its policies in this area. At the same time, consideration should also be given to the museum's own policy of employing disabled people as staff or volunteers.

Working with disabled people can be a rewarding experience for museum staff. There is a need however for all staff to be trained in such work, and in assisting disabled visitors in appropriate and sensitive ways. It is worth remembering that many disabled people do not appear disabled. The museum should make every effort to publicise how it is able to assist disabled visitors. Disabled people need to know in advance whether it is worth their effort to visit a museum, and publicity material should provide information on access and accessibility. Every museum should aim to create a universally accessible environment, and equal opportunities for all to use the museum's services. In many cases, making the museum accessible for people with disabilities enhances the standard of facilities for all visitors.

STUDY EXAMPLE 12.1

Recognising that many blind and visually impaired people find visiting places outside their homes difficult, especially for the first time, a museum established a special gallery for visitors with visual impairment. The gallery had a series of changing tactile exhibitions with items selected for their tactile interest and the museum provided a number of workshops in which individuals and groups discussed touch items and handling collections.

The museum developed this service for its users by working with associations for the blind and visually impaired, and sending invitations on audio-tape to all registered blind people in their area. Museum staff were trained in receiving blind and visually impaired people into the museum, and in appropriate methods of guiding them.

Exhibition staff also visited a number of blind people in their homes in conjunction with helpers from the local associations for the blind and visually impaired to encourage them to use the new facility. The museum later established a special users' group that encouraged members to act as advocates for the museum's services for the blind and visually impaired and helped to develop a new and important audience for the museum.

By working in this way, museum staff gained new understanding of groups with special needs and a section of the community was better served.

Unit

The museum visit

Related Units – Units 14–21

A visit to a museum is a complete experience, to which every aspect contributes. Dirty toilets or offhand staff or poor publications will spoil the visit just as much as poor displays. The museum staff should consider how to monitor and improve every aspect of the visitor's experience.

Here is a checklist of the things that go to make up the visit experience. How well does your museum measure up?

Pre-visit publicity. How do visitors find out about the museum? How is interest aroused in what the museum has to offer? What expectation does the museum's publicity generate?

Transport. How do visitors get to the museum? How far away does signposting to the museum begin? Is there enough directional signage? Can access be made easier? Could public transport be improved, or could the museum provide transport of its own? Is the car park large enough and well designed (see Unit 8)?

Arrival at the museum. Is the walk from the bus stop or car park pleasant and easy, not only for fully fit people, but also for elderly people, small children or people in wheelchairs (see Units 8 and 12)? Is it well signposted? Can the way be made more pleasant or informative, and can tourists be protected from harassment by touts selling souvenirs, taxi drivers, etc.?

Appearance. Is the museum easy to recognise? It should be announced with a large well-designed sign. Does the museum look attractive? Even a poor building can be improved with well-designed signs and perhaps flags or banners. Is there a well-designed notice giving opening hours and the price of admission? Are the museum staff at the entrance to the museum smart, efficient and above all welcoming (see Units 10, 11, 75, 76)?

Buying a ticket. If there is a charge to visit the museum, is it obvious where to buy a ticket? Is the ticket-office itself well designed? Does the ticket-seller have plenty of change? The ticket itself should be attractive and well printed. Does the price of the ticket represent good value for money? Can one buy a season ticket, to allow repeat visits? The ticket-seller is probably, for the visitor, the most important person in the museum. The museum will be very largely judged on the friendliness and efficiency of the ticket-seller. He or she should be carefully trained to give every visitor a smile and a word of welcome, and to be able to answer the most common questions visitors ask – or to direct them to an information desk (see Unit 75).

Opening hours. Is the museum open at times convenient to most potential visitors? Too many museums are open at times to suit their staff, forgetting that many people work every day, and can visit museums only in the evening or on public holidays.

Cloakroom. Is there a cloakroom where visitors can safely leave bags, coats, umbrellas or parcels? If visitors leave bags and coats they will feel more comfortable and at home, and the museum's security will be improved.

Psychological orientation. As the visitor leaves the busy street, he or she needs to relax and adopt a calm, receptive mood before entering the displays. It is instructive to look at how temples are designed in many parts of the world: they very often have an entrance court, garden or hall where the worshipper can get into the right mood before entering the temple itself (see Unit 74). The design and 'mood' of the museum's entrance hall will greatly affect the mood in which the visitor enters the displays.

Physical orientation. Before entering the displays, the visitor needs to know what there is in the museum, and how to find it. It is also important to know roughly how long the visit will take. If possible, every visitor should be given, when buying the ticket, a leaflet with a plan of the museum and a brief description (with photographs) of the displays, listing the most important items. There should be a clear plan of the museum at the entrance, and in a larger museum there should be signposting throughout the museum (see Units 75, 76).

Intellectual orientation. Before entering the displays, the visitor also needs to know what he or she is going to see and what he or she might learn. The leaflet given to the visitor with their ticket is one way of telling the visitor this; another is by an Orientation Gallery. An Orientation Gallery tries to tell the visitor what he or she is going to see, and also to suggest how to see it – what aspects to look at and what questions to ask. For example, an exhibition of Coptic icons could be looked at from different points of view: how were they made? Who are the saints depicted? How were they used by worshippers? How did the artistic style change over the centuries? An Orientation Gallery could encourage the visitor to look at the exhibition from one or other points of view. By changing the orientation it is possible, to some extent, to change the visitor's experience of the exhibits (see Unit 76).

The museum staff. The museum staff are the most important element of all in the visit experience. According to how efficient, smart, helpful and friendly they seem, the museum will be judged (see Units 90, 93, 95, 97).

Sequence and flow. If the displays are designed to be seen in one particular order, it must be obvious to the visitor which way to go. The designer can use various techniques to encourage the visitor to follow the proper sequence: physical barriers, pools of light that attract, arrows, numbered panels. Generally, visitors should circulate in the direction in which they read (see Unit 74).

Pace. 'Pace' refers to the variety of stimuli the visitor receives and the changes in his or her environment as he or she walks around the museum. Visitors quickly get bored if all parts of the museum look and feel much the same. By changing the floor surface, light levels, colours, display style, and ceiling height the display designer can help keep the visitor alert and interested (see Unit 76).

Food and drink area. The quality of the museum's food and drink area, its appearance, comfort, service and food is of enormous importance to the visitor's experience of his or her visit (see Unit 20).

Toilets. The toilets are important, especially in a large museum. There must be enough to meet visitors' needs, conveniently located. They must be regularly checked and kept spotlessly clean.

Seating. There should be plenty of places throughout the museum where visitors can sit down; this is important to all visitors, not just those with mobility difficulties (see Unit 12).

Visitors with special needs. Not all museum visitors are fit adults. Consider how your own museum provides for:

- elderly and infirm visitors;
- visitors in wheelchairs;
- blind or visually impaired visitors;
- nursing mothers;
- small children;
- visitors with learning difficulties.

Everyone should be welcome in a museum, and everyone should be able to use and enjoy its facilities (see Units 12, 18, 21).

Photography. Some museums still forbid visitors from taking photographs. There seems no good reason for this. The ability to take a few photographs to remember the visit by often adds greatly to the visitor's enjoyment of the museum. The introductory leaflet should say that photography (without tripod or flash, which may annoy other visitors) is permitted for personal use only; photographs for publication or commercial use require a permit.

The museum shop. The museum shop, even if it is very small indeed, is an important part of the visit experience, and its quality will – like that of the food and drink area – reflect on the museum (see Unit 14).

Publications. All except the smallest museums need five different kinds of publication. But they do not have to be elaborately or expensively produced:

- A simple leaflet – free or very cheap – which describes briefly what is to be found in the different parts of the museum, and which contains a plan.
- A booklet, if possible in colour, which describes the contents of the museum in more detail. It should be as attractive as possible, with many photographs, so that visitors will buy it as a souvenir of their visit. It should be priced so that almost all visitors buy one.
- A guide booklet for children. This should be specially written for children, and will probably contain drawings to colour, puzzles to solve and quizzes to answer. It should be very cheap so that children can buy it.
- A full guidebook and catalogue that describes most of the objects or groups of objects in the museum.
- Scholarly publications: books, monographs and journals (see Unit 36).

Learning in museums

Related Units – Units 15–17

In recent years, the emphasis has moved from *education*, which implies museums teaching things to children, to *learning*, which implies individuals of all ages using the museum for their own benefit.

Moreover, museums have benefited greatly from research into how people learn. This research is still developing very fast, and much of what we think we know now may change; the insights of neuroscientists studying the human brain will greatly help educational psychologists studying how people learn in general, and how people learn in museums in particular. However, most recent research has been carried out in the West and we need to understand whether people in different cultures learn in the same way.

Learning is not just about facts – it also includes experiences and emotions. Learning is something we *do*, and we all do it in different ways. It is also important to remember that for many people learning is a social experience – something that is most enjoyably (and so most easily) done in company with others.

Museums are special places, where the learning that visitors do has special characteristics. Museum learning has been called 'free-choice learning', because people do it at their own speed, taking their own direction, and because they want to. Research has emphasised the active role the visitor plays. The old 'positivist' theory, that knowledge is 'out there' waiting to be acquired, has given way to a new 'constructivist' theory that knowledge is actively constructed by the visitor. However, there is still a great deal of debate, and in practice museums use both understandings to make their displays and programmes.

HOW PEOPLE LEARN

Specialists have developed a range of theories about how people (especially children) develop and how they learn. Some of these have been influential in museums, both in the design of exhibitions and in the construction of education programmes. A few of the best-known theories are summarised very briefly here.

The *behaviourist* approach believes that behaviour is largely learnt from practice and experience. It has been criticised as suggesting that human beings do not choose, but just respond to stimuli in the environment. In museums the approach has been applied by treating the exhibit as a stimulus, and by studying how effectively it holds visitors' attention.

The *cognitive-developmental* approach believes that the child understands the world only by acting on it; learning is an active exchange between the learner and the environment. In museums this approach has underlain many interactive exhibits, particularly in science museums.

'*Discovery learning*' suggests three modes in which children represent the world: the enactive (where representation occurs through actions), the iconic (where representation involves building up a mental picture of things one has experienced) and the symbolic (where representation takes place through symbols). Many science museums have tried to create exhibitions that encourage discovery learning.

The theory of *Multiple Intelligences* suggests that all human beings use nine or more different intelligences to learn:

1 Linguistic: talking, writing, reading.
2 Musical: melody, rhythm, playing music, singing.

Box 14.1 What is learning?

Compare these three definitions of learning. Which seems to describe best what you want to happen in your museum?

> We learn many different kinds of things. We accumulate facts and information and digest this knowledge into opinions. We continue throughout life to develop know-how: how to use new technology, how to tell a good story. We learn to make new discriminations and learn new preferences. We develop new dispositions, learn new roles and new aspects of character, and broaden our emotional range.
>
> (Claxton 1999: 7–8)

> Learning is an active process of collecting information, a process of utilizing this information to build complex, internal knowledge structures called schemata. Every individual's schemata are unique and appear to have a physical reality represented by many branching connections of neurons within the brain. Schemata are accessed both as places in which to store new information and as places from which to retrieve old information. By virtue of differences in both genes and experience, every individual uniquely acquires, processes, and stores information. . . . The process of learning can be conceptualised as involving seven major factors. These are the influences of: prior knowledge and experience; subsequent, reinforcing experiences; motivation and attitudes; culture and background; social mediation; design and presentation; [and] the physical setting. To fully understand the nature of the museum learning process requires an understanding of the role, independently and collectively, of these seven influences.
>
> (Falk and Dierking 2000)

> Learning is a process of active engagement with experience. It is what people do when they want to make sense of the world. It may involve increase in or deepening of skills, knowledge, understanding, values, feelings, attitudes and the capacity to reflect. Effective learning leads to change, development and the desire to learn more.
>
> (UK Museums, Libraries & Archives Council)

3 Logical-mathematical: numbers, systems, logical thought, problem-solving.
4 Visual/spatial: how things look, imagination, creating images, using space.
5 Tactile/physical: doing, building, touching, moving (sports, dancing . . .).
6 Interpersonal: communicating with others, rapport.
7 Intrapersonal: self-awareness, objectivity.
8 Intuitive: perceiving information not available to 'the senses'.
9 Creative: finding new solutions, new ideas.

This highly-influential approach has encouraged museums to use as many different techniques as possible, to appeal to as many of these intelligences as possible.

'*Social cognition*' believes that it is society that teaches children what and how to think. Children learn by solving problems with others, especially with adults, and schools (and museums) can be seen as a 'social setting specially designed to modify thinking'.

'*Constructivism*' proposes that learners construct knowledge for themselves, individually or with others creating meaning as they learn. It has been very influential in museums, which naturally provide opportunities for people to interact with their environment and construct their own world.

Play has been identified by many researchers as crucially important to children's development. Through play children learn to explore and discover, to stretch their imaginations, to define and solve problems, to role-play, and to create meanings around objects. Some museums have designed exhibitions that encourage play, and have used artistic activity to achieve the same ends in a rather more structured way.

One of the most promising areas of research is into the ways in which the museum experience can build on and modify prior knowledge – the understanding that visitors bring with them to the museum.

Unit
15

Museum education services: inside the museum

Related Units – 14, 16, 17

Museums have an important role in providing education services to users, whether these are children or adults. Some education services will provide a range of formal teaching opportunities in the museum; others will work closely with teachers to allow teachers to make better use of the educational resources available through displays and exhibitions, databases, handling collections and museum staff.

The look of wonder on a child's face can be the reward for a lifetime's work in museums. It is the aim of museum education to foster contact between people – whether children or adults – and objects: not to teach facts, but to sow a seed of interest, a spark of inspiration.

In an ideal world, every museum would have at least one education specialist who would be a trained teacher who also had an understanding of museums and museum collections, and a vocation to help people – especially children – use and learn from them.

For most museums the establishment of such a post should be high priority. A museum education specialist can be of enormous value to a museum. He or she may be the only member of staff with training in the psychology of learning, and may have considerable experience of analysing complex concepts and presenting them in a simple way to a non-specialist audience. The education specialist may be, indeed, the only professional communicator or interpreter in the museum.

It is clearly sensible, therefore, for the museum to make full use of his or her skills, and to involve him or her in all aspects of interpretation and the planning of new displays and exhibitions. Museum education is not just about teaching children, though children may be its principal audience.

Many small museums may not be able to employ an education specialist of their own. For them, there are other possibilities. One is that the local Schools Service may be able to co-opt a teacher to the museum, perhaps for two or three years, who could be trained to apply teaching skills to the museum context. Another is that suitable volunteers may be available in the community – perhaps retired teachers, or teachers not presently working – who may be willing to give some of their time to the museum. Another possibility is sponsorship: a large company might be willing to finance the appointment of an education specialist for a few years.

CONTACT WITH SCHOOLS

Whether or not the museum is able to provide an education specialist, it is an important part of the work of every museum to establish strong links with its local schools. Someone on the museum staff – perhaps the director – should have responsibility for maintaining contact with the teachers at local schools. He or she should make sure that the schools know what is going on at the museum and how they can make use of it, and that the museum staff know about developments in the schools.

Unfortunately few teachers learn, as part of their training, about how to use museums in their teaching. Teachers of art or history may be familiar with museums, but teachers of (for example) mathematics or craft and design or languages may need to have the possibilities museums offer presented to them.

Every museum should try to organise – perhaps once a year – a training day for teachers. Ideally, this would be arranged through the local Schools Service, and the teachers be given time off to attend. It should be held at the museum, and might be led by a museum education specialist brought in for the day. However, all the museum staff should be involved, because museum staff and teachers getting to know each other will be a major benefit of the day. The day must be carefully planned, especially if it involves some real teaching of real children!

EDUCATION MATERIALS

Museums should help teachers make use of museums by providing education materials. What these should be will depend very much on the character of the museum, and the needs of the local schools. The first step will be to ask local teachers what they need. They may find simplified catalogues of the collections most useful, or booklets describing projects based on the displays, or worksheets or web-based materials that can be downloaded for use in the classroom.

Many museums provide worksheets for visiting schoolchildren. Some teachers value these; others dislike them. The sign of a good worksheet is that it encourages the user to look at material on display. If the user can answer the questions without really looking, it has been badly constructed. Questions that ask children to count things, for example, are less useful than ones that ask how something was made or how it was used — i.e. that require deduction from observation.

Museums hoping to attract visits from more than one or two schools should publish a booklet describing the services they can provide to schools and provide the same information on their web site. It should include:

- a description of the displays;
- the name of the museum's education specialist;
- how to book a class visit;
- what services are available, e.g. talks, guided visits, events;
- the facilities available to visiting groups:
    - education room;
    - worksheets, audio-visual materials, models;
    - shop;
    - catering facilities;
    - toilets;
    - clipboards, pencils, etc.
- information about access: is it suitable for children with disabilities?

PLANNING A MUSEUM VISIT

Teacher and curator or museum education specialist should together plan every school visit to a museum. It is essential that teachers visit the museum before they bring any children, and essential that every visit be booked in advance.

The visit should be part of the work the children are doing at school, not just an 'end of term treat'. The preparation for the visit will therefore take place in the classroom. When the children get to the museum, they will already have a good idea of what they are going to see and what work they are going to do. It should lead on naturally from the schoolwork they have been doing in the classroom. The skilful teacher is one who can ensure that the children's work is guided and purposeful, but can use the special stimulus and inspiration that museums can provide.

THE MUSEUM EDUCATION ROOM

If possible, every museum should have an education room. It should be big enough to accommodate a normal-size school party, and at least should have seats. It might also contain:

- a clean water supply;
- a blackboard or whiteboard;
- a projector and/or slide projector and/or overhead projector;
- paints and paper.

Many museums will not be able to provide these things, or even a separate education room. They might, however, consider providing basic equipment such as clipboards and pencils.

THE SCHOOL VISIT

Schoolchildren arriving at the museum deserve a warm, relaxed and friendly welcome. They need:

- to be welcomed by a member of staff;
- to be shown where to put their belongings;
- to be given an opportunity to use the toilets;
- to have an introduction to what they will be seeing and doing;
- to be given any necessary materials.

The introductory talk should be very short. Museums still sometimes get asked by unimaginative teachers to provide 'a general tour'. Such requests should be discouraged, since the children will learn little. Instead, the museum staff should discuss with the teacher more effective ways of using the children's precious time in the museum.

Even if the museum's education specialist is leading the particular class visit, the children's teacher must be present throughout and fully involved in the programme. It is he or she who will be leading the follow-up work back at school.

FOLLOW-UP WORK

Just as the museum visit should continue naturally from the work the children were doing in the school classroom, so the museum visit should be followed by further work at school. Ideas for follow-up work include:

- Written work, perhaps an imaginative account of the lives of the people who made or used some of the objects seen, or of the 'lives' of the objects themselves.
- A display of classwork deriving from the visit or a classroom 'museum' or exhibition.
- Drama, dance and music. Could the class create a play based on their museum work, or learn songs and dance of the period or people being studied?
- Models, using measured drawings, or costume-figures or imaginative historical reconstructions.
- Crafts. Many craft activities, that relate to the museum's collections, can be carried out by children.
- Artwork might include making a frieze or collage, creating life-size models or printing fabric or paper using designs copied from museum objects.

Unit 16

Museum education services: outside the museum

Related Units – Units 14–15

The liveliest museums are not content to wait for people to come and visit them: they take their services out into the community. Similarly, museum education services are not limited to helping visiting schoolchildren – they include many different ways of taking the museum out into schools and into other parts of the community. Some of these ways are noted in this Unit.

SCHOOL LOAN SERVICES

The lending to schools of objects from the museum collections or from special loan collections is commonly called a 'School Loan Service'. The choice of material to be used in this way must take into consideration conservation and security requirements. The principle of a School Loan Service is that real museum objects are lent for short periods to schools, so that teachers can integrate learning from objects into their normal classwork.

School Loan Services vary greatly in size. The smallest simply mean that teachers are encouraged to borrow objects from the museum collections. The largest services have big collections, specially built up for the purpose and quite distinct from the main museum collections. The objects are provided in specially designed boxes, and are accompanied by notes for teachers. Objects can be ordered from a published catalogue, sent every term to every school in the area, and are delivered by the

Loan Service's own vehicle. Such large services employ many staff: education specialists, technicians, drivers and clerical staff.

The benefits a Loan Service can bring are very great. Objects that might otherwise simply remain in store are serving a real educational purpose in the hands of teachers and children, while using objects in school encourages teachers and children alike to visit the museum itself.

However, any museum considering setting up a School Loan Service should also weigh seriously the drawbacks:

- If objects are borrowed from the museum collections they may decay or be damaged more quickly.
- If a special loan collection is set up, might it be competing for objects with the museum itself?
- Administering even a simple service is very time-consuming while a large service can be very expensive.

MOBILE SERVICES

A few museums have set up 'mobile museums', large vans containing museum objects and displays, which can take a small taste of the main museum out to local schools, or – for example – to rural villages. They have been found particularly beneficial in large countries such as India and Canada, though on a smaller scale they have been successful in the UK in both cities and countryside. In Australia and Sweden, museum trains have been used to bring museum collections and displays to more remote communities. In Sweden indeed, the *Riksutställningar* (Swedish State Exhibitions) has pioneered new ways of reaching a wider public.

TALKS IN SCHOOLS

Children always appreciate someone other than their teacher talking to them, so even curators who feel shy of talking to children are often made to feel very welcome!

CHILDREN'S CLUBS AND HOLIDAY ACTIVITIES

Nothing gives such an impression of liveliness in a museum as a rich programme of holiday activities for children. Many children who have been involved in them have been inspired with an appreciation of their environment and a love of art that has benefited them throughout life.

Before rushing ahead and announcing such activities, the museum would be well advised to consider what resources they would require. Is the effort required cost-effective in terms of the number of children who will benefit? How can the children the museum most wants to reach be encouraged to come? Sometimes much of the museum's educational effort seems to go into amusing children who are already privileged.

However, if the educational benefit has been well thought through, and the marketing of the programme well targeted, museum activities for children can be hugely beneficial. Holiday activities are usually open to any child who wants to come, and they take place on various days during the school holidays. Children's clubs usually meet at weekends or after school and they are limited to members, though any child can join if there is a place.

A museum without an education specialist could very possibly attract one or more local teachers – or possibly retired teachers – to undertake holiday activities, while a children's club for older children could be run by a curator, and could do really useful work for the museum. The range of possible activities involving children and museums is limited only by the imagination of the organisers.

SPECIAL EVENTS

One of the most effective ways of providing a museum education service is by organising special events (see Unit 17). These can last half a day, a weekend or two weeks. They can take all sorts of forms. A common approach is to choose one theme – which might be an activity like 'cooking', or a class of object such as 'wheels' or a historical period. If intended for schools it should relate to the schoolwork the children who take part are doing, though if it takes place in the holidays a seasonal theme might be appropriate. A whole programme of events and activities is then planned around the theme, and school parties or individual children book places to take part.

Another approach is the Living History day, when children come to the museum and act out a story from history, often dressed in reproduction period clothes, and trying out some of the crafts and activities associated with the chosen time and country (see Unit 26). These days need very careful planning if they are to be successful.

Special events are perhaps particularly appropriate in a small museum because limited resources can be concentrated on a short period of time. Staff or volunteers can be hired specially, the event can be marketed effectively and disruption is limited to just a few days.

SETTING LEARNING OUTCOMES

One of the advantages a museum education service has over – say – a school is that it need not be so formal, and is not tied to a precise school curriculum. Even so, for any educational activity, the museum should consider carefully what learning outcomes it is trying to achieve, and how those outcomes tie in with the mission of the museum on the one hand, and the aims of the school or college on the other. It is also important to set out in advance how the educational activity will be evaluated, and assess how effectively the learning outcomes were achieved.

Box 16.1 Learning from objects

One of the aims of museum education must be to help people learn to look at objects, and, by asking questions, to learn directly from the objects themselves. Here is a sample worksheet, taken from Gail Durbin, Susan Morris and Sue Wilkinson, *A Teacher's Guide to Learning from Objects* (1990).

Initially you may want to give children a worksheet like this to help them analyse an object. Ultimately, they should be able to frame their own questions and set about answering them.

Looking at an object – the main things to think about	*Some further questions to ask*	*Things found out through looking*	*Things to be researched*
PHYSICAL FEATURES What does it look and feel like?	What colour is it? What does it smell like? What does it sound like? What is it made of? Is it a natural or manufactured substance? Is the object complete? Has it been altered, adapted, mended? Is it worn?		
CONSTRUCTION How was it made?	Is it handmade or machine-made? Was it made in a mould or in pieces? How has it been fixed together?		
FUNCTION What was it made for?	How has the object been used? Has the use changed?		
DESIGN Is it well designed?	Does it do the job it was intended to do well? Were the best materials used? Is it decorated? How is it decorated? Do you like the way it looks? Would other people like it?		
VALUE What is it worth?	To the people who made it? To the people who used it? To the people who keep it? To you? To a bank? To a museum?		

Box 16.2 Museum Education Policies

Many museums are finding it useful to write a formal Museum Education Policy; it helps them to define their priorities, and to present their ideas to others. The following example of a Museum Education Policy is adapted from Eilean Hooper-Greenhill, *Writing a Museum Education Policy* (1991).

The Education Policy

Aims

1 To enhance the education of children and adults through the imaginative use of the museum and its collections.

- Excitement and motivation are the foundations of successful learning; museum visits should be challenging, memorable experiences resulting in personal enrichment for all.
- The study of evidence in museums should promote enquiry and interest and be concerned mainly with the process of learning and the acquisition of skills. Knowledge, although important, should be part of a broader learning process that has interest and understanding as its principal objective.

2 To assist the museum to maximise the educational potential of its collection, buildings and other resources.

- The experience and expertise of the museum education service should be used to assist the museum to realise its commitment to education in accordance with the Collections Management Policy, and to promote the status of education within the museum generally.
- The educational effectiveness of the museum is affected by the public's perception of the museum as a whole, and is not restricted to the displays. All aspects of the museum's interface with the public should therefore be 'user friendly' and create a positive and harmonious atmosphere conducive to effective learning.

Audiences

To provide a service for the following groups, in order of priority:

- Teachers and pupils from schools and colleges funded by the local Schools Service.
- Educational institutions/organisations funded by the local Schools Service or by any other county council source, such as pre-school playgroups, social and welfare groups.
- Adult education groups.
- Museum staff.

Box 16.2 continued

Type of provision

1 To provide direct teaching to schools, colleges, educational institutions and organisations and to adult education groups.

- Teaching will generally take place in the museum's schoolroom and the relevant galleries, although extra-mural teaching may be undertaken at the discretion of the education specialist.
- Teaching styles will take cognisance of the principles of good practice.
- Wherever possible teaching styles will be used that focus students' attention on the artefacts. These might involve handling real artefacts, using replicas and creating situations that promote students' interest and inquisitiveness in the artefacts. This could be achieved through the use of project or topic work, active learning and drama, across the curriculum.
- Visits by schools and adult education groups should promote understanding of museums and their role in contemporary society.

2 To provide learning resources that support the educational use of the museum.

- Resources to include ideas for worksheets, teachers' notes and information on related sites/visits in the county.

3 To assist with enquiries of an educational nature.

- The museum is an invaluable database for local studies. As far as is practicable and in keeping with museum guidelines regarding conservation and security, access to the reference collections by interested parties should be facilitated.

Staffing

- Although it is anticipated that the education specialist will do most of the work outlined above, specialist advice and assistance from curatorial staff will be necessary on occasions, as well as additional assistance from volunteers and freelance workers.
- The production of teachers' packs may involve a working party comprising local teachers.

Resources/budget

- To increase and diversify the range of items available for handling and study purposes.
- To increase the involvement of curatorial staff and volunteers in the implementation of the education programme.
- To explore alternative methods for funding freelance workers such as writers and artists in residence.

continued

Box 16.2 continued

- To upgrade existing administrative provision with particular reference to the use of information technology.
- To allocate approximately 75 per cent of education staff time and funds to the provision of schools-based activities and resources.

Roles and functions within the museum

- To ensure that educational considerations are included in managerial decisions and the formulation of museum policies.
- To establish and maintain an entitlement to key resources such as funding and the allocation of space, in line with the museum's other core activities.
- To take an active role in the planning and evaluation of temporary exhibitions and permanent displays.
- To monitor goods on sale in the museum shop in terms of educational value, and advise on possible new lines.
- To encourage a balanced programme of publications of general as well as specialist interest.
- To improve the provision of facilities for visitors, particularly for disabled and handicapped people.
- To ensure that the layout of the museum is readily comprehensible through clear and accurate signposting.

Networks outside the museum

1 In order to keep abreast of developments in museums and education and to provide an effective and worthwhile service capable of responding to the needs of its clientele, close links should be maintained with the local Schools Service and museum professionals.

2 Contact should also be maintained with the following:

- Specialist teachers groups, e.g. local history teachers.
- Professional education centres.
- Field study and outdoor education centres.
- Professional groups.
- Local archaeological teams.
- Societies with local involvement.

Training

1 The museum education specialist should:

- Have professional educational and museum qualifications, or be prepared to undergo the necessary training.
- Be an effective classroom practitioner.

Box 16.2 continued

- Comply with the relevant Code of Conduct for museum professionals.
- Develop managerial skills through participation in management training courses in order to become more effective in senior management.

2 To provide in-service training for teachers and museum staff:

- In order to promote the educational role of the museum, teachers and museum staff should have some understanding of the principles of good practice under-lying both professions. In-service training should therefore facilitate opportunities for discussion and the interchange of ideas between both parties, and provide opportunities for working together.
- In-service training should assist teachers to use the museum's resources to respond to local and national initiatives, where appropriate. Museum staff and volunteers should be kept informed of recent educational developments, and of the implications for the museum.

Marketing

In order to keep people informed about the nature of the services provided, and to attract new audiences within the county, the education specialist will continue to use the following channels:

- participation in local Schools Service courses and meetings with advisory teachers and probationary teachers;
- meetings of local teachers;
- entry in local Schools Service handbook listing local educational resources;
- publicity for special events in Schools Circular and fly posting to schools.

Evaluation

- Wherever feasible evaluation should be carried out in order to ensure the continuing effectiveness and credibility of the museum's education service.

Events and activities: creating programmes

Related Units – 10–11, 14–16

Lively programmes of informal events and activities that support the museum's mission are a powerful means of building support for the museum. Events and activities programmes – physical and virtual – can significantly affect the ways in which the public perceives your museum and help develop market interest.

Programmes of events and activities can be developed to enhance the core services that the museum provides and to meet the needs of specific target groups or market segments (see Units 9–10). Arranging events and activities programmes within the museum itself on-site or on-line is one approach. Another approach is for the museum to organise activities in other locations, perhaps in partnership with other institutions or organisations, and thus to develop new audiences for the museum and its work.

In many cases, these events and activities can be income generating and might also attract financial support through grants and sponsorship and thus form an important strand of additional income for the museum. Decision on which events and activities to provide free and which events and activities to charge for is a policy decision for the museum to make.

IDEAS AND OPPORTUNITIES

The list here gives an indication of the range of opportunities for informal events and activities available to museums. The list does not include formal education programmes (see Units 15–16), but many of them have significant learning potential. Neither does it include events that are not directly related to the museum's mission, such as letting the museum's facilities for conferences or receptions to external bodies (see Unit 21).

Events and activities in the museum

- Temporary exhibitions of objects/specimens of the month/week/day exploring items from the collections, loans or new acquisitions.
- Film/video programmes.
- Touring exhibitions from the museum.
- Workshops for children/families on these/objects in the museum.
- Print/picture loans.
- Family workshops in art or science.
- Hospitality mornings/evenings organised by museum support groups.

- Museum stands/exhibitions/demonstrations at local fairs/shows.
- Lectures and illustrated talks programmes.
- Special interest/special needs group meetings.
- Recorded music clubs.
- Meetings.
- Guided walks programmes.
- Fieldwork programmes with volunteers.
- Training events for the public such as photographic recording, map reading, oral history recording or caring for collections.
- Training events for museum professionals.
- Arts festivals.
- Foreign visitor days.
- Oral history recording and workshops.
- Demonstrations of museum skills, e.g. conservation.
- Competitions and quizzes for children/families/special interest groups.
- Craft exhibitions.
- Publication launches.
- Exhibition previews.
- Dance performances.
- Hospital visiting programmes.
- Dramatic performances.
- Informal education programmes.
- Transport rallies.
- Historical re-enactments.
- Pageants.

Not all of these suggestions will be relevant to every museum. Some museums will include a number of these approaches in their core services, others will only be able to develop a few ideas because they have limited money or staff. Together, they provide a menu of opportunities from which museums can pick and choose to suit their own needs. There are of course many more ideas that can be added to this list.

By organising regular events and activities programmes of this type, active museums can develop general interest in their work, and build political as well as public support for their services. By experimenting with different approaches for different market segments, the museum can develop a body of valuable marketing experience.

Opportunities will always exist to develop events and activities programmes in collaboration with other museums or other organisations. Sharing experience, costs and resources can often help to make a programme possible where otherwise a museum might be unable to undertake the programme on its own. Raising financial support for joint programmes can also be easier, as the constituency of support for the programme can often be broadened and more people involved in the activities. Forging new working relationships with other bodies by undertaking events and activities programmes is another valuable benefit for the museum.

POLICIES

Organising events and activities programmes – on-site, off-site or on-line – is time-consuming. A careful balance has to be struck between allocating resources for events and activities and allocating resources to other areas of the museum's work.

In policy terms, the museum's management has also to decide where the emphasis of its work is going to be put within a spectrum of formal education through leisure learning to entertainment. Some museums will wish to focus resources on their formal education responsibilities, while others will wish to see these balanced by developing informal educational activities or leisure learning events and activities.

Using the museum's facilities for cultural purposes broadly related to the museum's mission and the collections, for example music recitals or dramatic performances, is different to using the museum for purposes that are unrelated to the mission or collections. Hiring the museum's facilities to outside bodies, for example for corporate entertainment, business conferences or weddings, may have income-generating benefits, but the museum will need to consider whether the impact on other aspects of its work is positive or negative (see Unit 21).

PLANNING PROGRAMMES

What steps does the museum need to take in developing events and activities programmes? We examine here the middle of the spectrum described earlier – informal education or leisure learning. Formal museum education provision is discussed in Units 15–16; facilities use and entertainment are discussed in Unit 21.

In planning events and activities, it is helpful to draw up a matrix with the types of event and activity along the vertical axis and their details along the horizontal axis. Types of event for the vertical axis are suggested previously, while details for the horizontal axis might include the following:

- Physical location of event in the museum.
- Spatial needs.
- Visitor capacity – per hour, per day, per week.
- Frequency of event – per day, per week, per month, per year.
- Target audience for event.
- Public or restricted access.
- Type of public engagement – general through to specialist user.
- Type and extent of mediation by staff required.
- Free/paid admission.
- Visitor dwell time (hrs).
- Service providers/partners for the event.
- Average persons attending.
- Number of persons per year attending.
- Cost of provision.
- Source(s) of income.
- Estimated income.

- Profit/loss.
- Possibilities of virtual access or on-line support.
- Type of evaluation proposed.

The matrix thus provides detailed guidance on individual events and activities and suggests what mix of events and activities might form the year's programme. The museum can then make a choice from the planning list and run the selected programme(s) over whatever timescale is chosen.

Suggestions and ideas for activities can be obtained from a wide variety of sources – museum staff, professional colleagues in other museums or educational centres running similar programmes, published case studies, visitors, schools, community groups, market research reports, etc. – the list is a long one. Activity leaders may be found within the museum's staff, or may be artists or craft workers, teachers, performers in dance, music, drama, mime, puppetry, community workers or volunteers with special skills.

The museum should establish an archive of ideas for events and activities that can be progressively developed as information becomes available. It should also develop a list of available and possible activity leaders for the future.

AUDIENCE GROUPS

People of all ages learn more effectively through participation (see Unit 15). While the museum may ultimately be able to offer events and activities or leisure learning programmes to all of its visitors, it may be better to target specific groups and develop experience progressively. Some of the groups at which events and activities programmes can be targeted include:

Families – families cut across age and special interest groups, and are represented in every socio-economic group. Museum visiting is for many people a social activity, and families form an important social grouping for the museum to target.

Pre-school children and their carers – pre-school children and their carers are also present across the socio-economic spectrum, and this group has special needs often disregarded by museums.

Children – children represent the museum-visiting audiences of the future. Children's events and activities programmes not only help the museum, but also will always be of interest to other members of the family.

Young people – young people respond readily to events and activities specifically related to their needs and interests. Programmes organised by young people tend to attract other young people.

Adults – adults are often interested in leisure learning activities that are related to their occupation or leisure activities. The museum may find it worthwhile to approach adults through organised groups such as clubs or societies or workplace groups.

People with disabilities – provided that physical access to the museum is appropriately designed, people with disabilities will respond to events and activities programmes as enthusiastically as any other group. Museums should be prepared to take suitable activities programmes to disabled groups or people in hospitals or other venues where visiting the museum is not possible.

Care must be taken to publicise your events and activities effectively to ensure take-up. Marketing materials need to be appropriately designed for the intended target groups.

The museum should as a matter of course evaluate the success of a particular activity in a written report or case study, and where possible or relevant record the activity with photographs or video. These reports will also help to ensure continuity of understanding and expertise within the museum. The body of information thus built up can be a powerful method of demonstrating success to others such as governing bodies, funding organisations, press and media contacts. Evaluation reports can serve as an important component in a case-for-support to funding bodies for future events.

TEMPORARY EXHIBITIONS

The value of *temporary* exhibitions for a museum is that they provide change and variety, and can focus on collections or topics not otherwise presented in the museum's displays. They may also allow the museum to extend coverage of a topic or subject that has only limited coverage in displays and provide opportunities to present material from reserve collections. Virtual temporary exhibitions may also be developed on the museum's web site and can be a powerful means of extending the museum's reach and building audience interest.

The value of a *touring* exhibition hired into the museum is that it provides a ready-made temporary exhibition and thus can save time on the part of curatorial and design staff. It may be designed to a higher standard than is possible in-house and help to influence standards for the future. It may be based on collections/information that the receiving museum may not otherwise be able to provide for its users. A touring exhibition may complement existing collections or provide new material to extend the museum's services. Bringing in touring exhibitions to the museum may however be expensive and every care should be taken to ensure an accurate understanding of the full cost and staffing implications.

If museums are to develop programmes of temporary exhibitions, there are a number of issues of policy and practice that should be borne in mind (see Units 32–4). The following checklist provides some points to note:

Policy

- What sort of temporary exhibition policy should be established?
- How do temporary exhibitions relate to the museum's mission and overall policy objectives?

- What balance of space should be given to temporary exhibitions and displays in the museum?
- How do temporary exhibitions relate to the museum's policies for communications and education?
- What type of temporary exhibitions will the museum make available? Will they include a percentage of touring exhibitions hired in? Will they include some exhibitions designed in-house to tour to other museums? Will they include temporary exhibitions on the museum's web site?
- Will external organisations such as community groups be allowed to develop temporary exhibitions within the museum?
- What controls over standards or quality will the museum wish to exercise?

Ideas and planning

- What themes or topics should be explored?
- How are these determined? Through market research?
- What curatorial objectives does the museum have in developing temporary exhibition programmes?
- What resources will need to be made available – staff time, money, space, equipment?
- What educational and events and activities will be developed in association with the exhibition?

Development

- Who will draw up the exhibition brief?
- Are collections available for the chosen theme of the exhibition? Is additional collecting/borrowing required?
- Will additional research be needed?
- What is the timetabling requirement?
- Who will design the exhibition?
- Who will prepare the storyline or select objects?
- What additional information/graphics are needed?
- Will a catalogue or other print matter need to be produced? What are the timetable implications for these?

Collections care and management

- What are the conservation constraints on the material to be exhibited?
- What remedial conservation is needed for the exhibits? What are the time implications of the conservation programme?
- What are the security constraints?
- What type of display equipment and materials should be used?

- What are the packing and transport requirements of a touring exhibition hired into the museum or an exhibition to be toured by the museum?

Administration

- What are the administrative requirements for exhibitions that the museum has developed for touring or that are hired in to the museum?
- What hire fees will the museum charge for its own touring exhibitions?
- Will there be an admission charge for special temporary exhibitions?
- What are the conditions imposed by the museum on exhibitions originated for touring – security, preventive conservation, promotion, acknowledgements to the museum?
- What are the delivery/collection arrangements for touring exhibitions?
- Whose responsibility is it to erect/dismantle/pack a temporary or touring exhibition?
- Are there possibilities for collaboration with partners in the production, administration and marketing of exhibitions?

These questions are not designed to be comprehensive, but they do give an indication of the sort of questions that the museum will need to be aware of in developing temporary exhibition programmes and associated events and activities programmes.

Key words

Outreach – the method by which a museum can take services out into the community which it serves through, for example, touring exhibitions, School Loan Services, events and activities programmes. It reflects the opportunities for museums to reach wider audiences outside the walls of the museum building(s).

Carer – children are looked after by many different people – parents, relatives, child-minders, friends. In many cases, children are looked after by 'carers' when their parents are at work. The term 'carer' is used here to encompass all these.

STUDY EXAMPLE 17.1

A museum organised six temporary exhibitions each year. For each of these exhibitions, it targeted a special user group and developed a programme of events and activities for the group. The programme was carried out in conjunction with a variety of different organisations and individuals. In particular, a balance between science and arts activities was sought. Each of the programmes was recorded with a mixture of colour-slide and audio-recording to produce tape-slide programmes, and videotape.

For each exhibition, the museum drew up a detailed report to a standard format analysing the resources that had been required, staff time, costs and practical successes and difficulties encountered. The reports and the visual records were developed over a five-year period to demonstrate to the museum's governing committee and funding bodies the work that the museum was carrying out to attract new audiences.

As a result, additional resources were made available to the museum to further the museum's marketing programme and to sustain the events and activities programme. Later the reports were published as a textbook helping other museums learn from this museum's experience.

Unit
18

Facilities for visitors

Related Units – Units 9, 13, 19–21

The range and quality of the facilities and services that you provide for visitors to your museum will in large part determine the success of the museum. Visitors should be made to feel welcome and comfortable, and encouraged throughout their visit to return again and again and to recommend the museum to others.

The museum director and the museum's staff should ensure that support facilities or services are of the highest quality and contribute to the success of a visit. Even the smallest museum with very limited resources can make visitors feel very welcome and provide basic visitor facilities. At the very least, museum staff can give guidance to visitors as to where car parks, bus stops, refreshments, or toilets are located, if the museum itself has none of its own.

The checklist and questions here give an indication of the basic facilities that museums should consider providing for their visitors.

Seating. Is there somewhere for your visitors to sit down? Are they able to sit down in the display/exhibition areas? Is there a special rest area? Is it furnished appropriately with comfortable chairs, tables for reading matter, etc.? How can it support the museum's educational objectives through information provision? Is it kept tidy and clean? Is it clearly marked a no-smoking area?

Coats/hats/umbrellas. Is there somewhere for visitors to leave their coats, hats or umbrellas? Is the area safe and secure? Can it be effectively staffed? Is it an appropriate size?

Toilets. Does the museum have toilets for visitors? Are they kept appropriately supplied, and clean and tidy on a regular basis? Are they equipped effectively for disabled visitors? Are they properly signposted?

Information points. Does the museum provide an information point or desk where visitors can obtain information about the museum, its collections and services? Are staff effectively trained to handle enquiries? Are they able to use languages familiar to the main groups of the museum's users (see Unit 8)?

Shops/sales areas. Is there a shop or sales area in the museum selling souvenirs, education material, publications, etc. (see Unit 19)? Is this well presented and maintained?

Food/drink. Does the museum provide refreshments for visitors? Is the area kept clean and tidy on a regular basis? Are visitors allowed to smoke in the area or not (see Unit 20)?

Special needs. Does the museum make sufficient provision for visitors with special needs, such as visitors with disabilities (see Unit 12), children, family groups with young babies, school groups, etc.?

Voluntary support. Can visitors who are interested in the work of the museum offer to support its work through volunteer help? Are they encouraged to do so in the museum?

Admission charges and times. Are the opening hours of the museum convenient for visitors? Are the admission charges sensitively set to different groups of visitors? Does the museum provide special discounts?

Web site. Is the museum's web site kept up to date? Does it provide sufficient information about the museum and its collections? Are there opportunities to develop it so that it provides interactive opportunities for visitors?

Other facilities. Depending on the size of your museum, you may wish to develop further facilities. In particular, there may be opportunities to create special study facilities available to particular groups. A number of museums make their in-house library collections available to the public, and others provide special study rooms for students incorporating a range of equipment such as study collections, micro-fiche readers, interactive video disc and web access. Special education centres with classrooms or lecture theatres may be used for a wide range of uses and audiences. Special provision in the museum may also need to be made for volunteers, Friends' groups, or corporate supporters.

External areas of the museum, such as gardens or parks, can also be used for a wide range of events and activities, and special facilities such as marquees or demonstration units can be erected on a temporary basis to cater for visitors.

All of these ideas and questions are not meant to be exhaustive. They are cited to act as triggers for museum managers to analyse the range of visitor facilities and services provided to visitors at present, and to question whether these might be extended or improved. In a number of cases, we explore different types of facilities in greater depth in other Units in this book.

Museum managers should put themselves in the place of their visitors, and ask themselves (as well as their visitors through ongoing market research) whether the museum visit *as a whole* can be made more enjoyable. Try visiting your own museum perhaps with some friends or members of your family to experience what the visitor experiences in the round. A first-class experience for the visitor will encourage repeat visits, and good word-of-mouth publicity encourages others to visit; a poor experience can damage the museum's reputation and standing.

Finding out about your visitors' needs is an important part of market research (see Unit 9). Caring for visitors, looking after their needs and wants through the provision of good-quality visitor facilities and services, is one of the principal responsibilities for all museums.

STUDY EXAMPLE 18.1

Over a period of two years, a museum carried out a detailed survey of its visitors to examine their needs. The survey showed visitors wanted better facilities, above all for disabled and infirm people. As a result, it was able to implement a phased development programme, which included the building of a new visitor reception centre providing a range of facilities designed to accommodate visitors of all types, including those with special needs. The new visitor reception centre was constructed because it would have been too expensive to adapt existing facilities effectively to serve disabled people.

Funding for the centre was derived in part from a number of organisations with special responsibility for disabled groups. The centre allowed the museum to market itself more widely and as a consequence, the museum saw its visitor numbers increase substantially.

It had put the care of its visitors first and reaped the benefits.

Unit
19

Providing services: shops and sales points

Related Units – 18, 86

Shops and sales areas play an important role in museums of all sizes (although in some countries there are still, surprisingly, legal restrictions on selling in museums). They provide opportunities for visitors to take home a souvenir of their visit, help to provide more information about the collections, serve as a point of personal contact with staff and, of course, generate income for the museum. They therefore have an important educational and public relations role to play as well as contributing to the museum's financial sustainability.

LOCATION AND LAYOUT

The location of the shop or sales point needs to be carefully considered. Most museums site their shops at the exit/entrance, for the simple reason that most visitors tend to buy goods at the end of their visit. For small museums, one advantage of siting the shop at the museum's entrance/exit is that it may be possible for reception staff to service both incoming and outgoing visitors. Wherever possible, museum shops should be accessible independently of a visit to the museum to increase sales, and customers should be encouraged to use the shop on a regular basis rather than only on a visit to the museum. Shops and sales points may also be located in other off-site locations on a temporary or permanent basis – much will depend on the scale of the museum's retail operation.

The design and layout of a shop or sales point need careful consideration. Is the approach to be self-service or over the counter? Self-service, where customers can pick up and handle goods in advance of purchase, normally generates more sales than traditional over-the-counter shopping particularly among foreign visitors. However, whatever method is chosen, the sales area needs to present its goods in a well-designed, attractive and organised way, clearly labelled and priced. Both layout and presentation need to encourage people to buy, but also need to ensure security against theft. High-value items will need special protection, perhaps behind glass or beyond reach.

STOCK

Decisions on what stock to obtain for sale should be taken in the context of a clearly defined purchasing policy. The museum director should determine how the shop will support the museum's mission, what the objectives of the shop are, and what range of stock can best serve those objectives. Museum shops should stock items that are well designed and of good quality. All items should provide value for money, and stock should relate in a general or a specific way to the museum's collections. Of course original historic artefacts or natural history specimens should never be sold!

Stock items can be bought in ready-made from wholesalers or specially produced by manufacturers or printers for the museum directly and can be customised with the name or logo of the museum. It is well worth having packaging, such as carrier bags, also printed with the museum's name or logo for publicity purposes. In public relations terms, items bought from a museum shop should continue to promote the museum long after the purchase.

In selecting items for sale in the shop, it is also important to identify and guard against possible competition from other sales outlets. A museum is well placed to develop items for sale based on its collections and its work that are not available elsewhere, thus giving it a competitive edge over other retail outlets.

INCOME AND EXPENDITURE

The museum's buying policy is important. The museum must ensure that it is not tying up hard-earned capital in buying in too much stock or in holding stock that is slow to sell and that can progressively go out of date or fashion. Having the right range of stock that your visitors want and from which you can maximise profits needs careful consideration. It is often a good idea to test the customer response to new stock lines before purchasing any significant quantities.

The museum shop must make a profit if it is to contribute effectively to the museum's income, and therefore the shop's pricing policy is important. It is worthwhile looking at the prices of goods in other shops with which to compare your museum's prices and to learn more about the levels of mark-up on items that have been bought in wholesale.

Museums may wish to license other organisations to produce sales items based on their collections. In this way, the museum itself may not have any production or purchase costs to meet, but can simply earn a percentage of the profits made by the licensee. The museum may itself take some of the licensed items for sale through its shop. This approach can mean that an item based on the museum's collections such as a print or a replica is sold far more widely, perhaps internationally, than would otherwise be the case through the museum's own on-site shop. Merchandising collections in this way can be a powerful way of generating income. Care needs to be taken in the contractual arrangements between the museum and licensee and professional legal advice should be sought. Reference should be made to ICOM's *Code of Ethics for Museums (paragraph 2.10)* on the issue of licensing (see Unit 6).

Shop stock should be considered as an important financial asset, and looked after appropriately. Storage conditions for items for sale should be clean, tidy and secure. The museum director should ensure appropriate records are maintained of transactions and that a regular stock audit is carried out. Cash receipts from the shop should be scrupulously recorded and banked on a regular basis.

Careful attention should be paid to each 'line' or category of item stocked to find out the pattern of sale. The person responsible for managing the shop and purchasing stock should provide regular reports on the shop's sales performance to the museum manager or director.

Many museums are now extending their web sites to support their in-house retail operation. Having an on-line shop has many advantages in that the museum can potentially reach many more customers. However, care needs to be taken in the development of on-line retailing and specialist advice should be sought on the practical and financial implications of setting up and maintaining such a service.

CUSTOMER CARE

Museum shops are an important point of direct personal contact with visitors. Friendly and courteous service is essential, and staff working in the shop whether on a full-time or temporary basis should be effectively trained in their duties. The museum may also wish to consider training shop staff in the languages of their main visitors. Customers should be made to feel welcome, encouraged to buy items and thanked for their patronage.

STUDY EXAMPLE 19.1

Bulk purchase of items for resale in a consortium of museum shops was developed by a museums' co-operative forum. Unit costs on a range of items were reduced, and the museum shops were able to stock a wider range of items than they would have been able to do individually. One museum took a lead role in co-ordinating the administration of the project for a small handling fee. The forum later entered into a range of merchandising projects, and established a joint trading company to run and develop a purchasing programme. Later still, the company began a mail order catalogue and distributed the museums' shop goods very widely.

By working together museums were able to extend the range of services available to users and to generate profits from co-operative activity.

STUDY EXAMPLE 19.2

A small museum began to sell local craftspeople's products, insisting on only the best quality. Visitors were surprised to find such unusual and beautiful objects in such a remote place, and the region's crafts slowly developed an international reputation; the craftspeople's businesses began to grow. The museum had made a major contribution to the economic regeneration of its region, and had itself gained a wide reputation and a share in the increasing prosperity.

Unit 20 Providing services: food and drink

Related Units – 18–19, 86

The type and scale of provision for selling food and drink to visitors varies widely in museums. The spectrum is a wide one. At one end of the spectrum is a refreshing drink with tables and chairs provided. At the other end is a meal in a restaurant with waiter service. Whatever your resources allow, visitors are likely to find some provision for food and drink in a museum welcome. A hot or cold drink or a snack can often encourage a longer, more relaxed and pleasurable visit.

Apart from improving customer service, food and drink in the museum, as with shops and sales points, can generate useful additional income. Catering services should therefore be designed to make a profit. As with shops, visitors should be encouraged to use the museum's catering facilities through good quality design and layout, and sensible location. If, like your museum shop, there is an opportunity for the facility to be independently accessed by visitors then this can provide the museum with an additional, competitive advantage over other catering facilities.

THEMING

Significant opportunities exist for making food and drink areas interesting places to visit by theming. There are all kinds of ways to create a special feel or theme for the catering facility, which relates to the museum's collections and services. Examples include 'period theming', where a particular historical period is evoked by decoration, layout and design of menus, foodstuffs or even staff dress; theming through special decor and fittings, for instance transport or natural history; or theming by reference to particular collections or items in the collections.

Such an approach helps to create a distinctive image for your food and drink area and a talking point for customers.

CUSTOMER CARE

However simple or elaborate, catering facilities should be well designed through-out, emphasise cleanliness and hygiene and provide good value for money in the food and drink provided. All food and drink areas should be well serviced and regularly cleaned. Service should be courteous and users should feel valued. A good experience in a museum café or restaurant can make a great deal of difference to a visitor's enjoyment of their overall visit. A bad experience can ruin enjoyment, and can create poor word-of-mouth publicity.

In most countries there are legal and licensing restrictions and requirements on catering. Compliance with statutory and religious requirements is essential. The museum manager must ensure that the museum is operating within the law at all times. In particular, laws relating to health and hygiene must be scrupulously observed.

Food and drink can be provided by the museum's own staff or through franchise, licensing or perhaps through a trading partnership. It is essential that legal advice is sought if a franchise, licensing arrangement or trading partnership is entered into. Careful records need to be kept of income and expenditure, and supplies need to be kept in clean, secure and appropriate storage, such as refrigeration. Supplies should be subject to regular inspection and stocktaking by museum management.

Food and drink in the museum may be required for special occasions like receptions, exhibition previews, evening entertainment or corporate hospitality events. The museum's own catering service may be well placed to provide for such special occasions.

Cafés, restaurants or coffee points all present good opportunities for providing visitors with information about the museum – its collections, services, and events and activities programmes. Tables can carry information cards about events programmes in the coming weeks. Slide projectors or computer screens can provide illustrations of items in the collections with checklists supplied on tables. Information about the museum can be provided on place mats or on the reverse side of a menu card. Copies of exhibition posters for sale in the museum shop may be displayed on the walls of the food and drink area. A little imagination and a flair for providing an enjoyable and different experience can provide added value to the museum visit.

STUDY EXAMPLE 20.1

A museum in a capital city with extensive social history collections piloted a series of themed dinners in the museum restaurant for tourist visitors, linked to special tours with a member of the curatorial staff. Costings were carefully evaluated, and the programme was monitored and evaluated in detail.

The dinners were organised in conjunction with a local hotel that used the programme as a training exercise for kitchen staff, under supervision of the hotel's head chef. The dinners and tours programmes were so successful that the museum established the programme as a regular event during the tourist season.

The immediate benefits were substantially increased profits for the museum's café/restaurant, additional training for the museum's own catering staff, a new partnership with a private-sector employer and increased donations from visitors attending the events. The museum thus developed a range of new expertise. Visitors were able to experience a range of regional recipes and foods, relating to the collections on view.

The series of dinners provided a different experience for visitors and it was reported on in a number of travel trade publications that resulted in increased attendances from overseas visitors.

Providing facilities for hire

Related Units – Units 18–21, 86

Many museums are able to make their facilities available to outside organisations in order to attract potential new audiences and generate additional income. Much will depend on what range of facilities your museum can provide. Display areas or lecture theatres/rooms may be booked for a variety of events ranging from education to entertainment – awards ceremonies, dance performances, conferences and seminars, lectures, meetings and gatherings, theatrical presentations, musical performances, craft fairs, corporate entertainment and many others. There are however a number of ethical and practical issues to be borne in mind, which we discuss here.

Areas outside the museum in the ownership or control of the museum – gardens, parks, archaeological sites, car parks – might also be used by external groups for historical re-enactments, fairs, craft demonstrations, transport rallies and the like.

There is a wide range of opportunity to encourage the use of museum facilities by external organisations, in accordance with a clearly defined policy, to the museum's advantage. Such activities should however be broadly relevant to the museum's mission and its educational and cultural objectives.

Every care should be taken to ensure that the museum's facilities are not hired by inappropriate or unacceptable organisations and that the museum's integrity is not in any way discredited. It is helpful to define the type of organisations deemed to be appropriate and acceptable in your policy and why, how and when they may use the museum's facilities, so that staff can take effective executive decisions.

POLICY AND PLANNING

You should consider the following points:

- The museum may be competing with other organisations in providing facilities for hire, and there may be implications for external public relations that have to be taken into account.
- The purpose for which the facilities are to be used should be acceptable to the museum's management and not put the museum's collections at any risk. Conservation, fire prevention and internal and external security requirements should be observed at all times – no smoking, no food and drink in display/exhibition spaces and adequate ventilation. Security staff should be fully briefed on the security implications of the use of the museum's facilities and the nature and size of each group using the facilities.
- The organisation(s) to which the facilities are being provided should be trustworthy and their bona fides established.

- The full cost implications should be understood. These cover additional security or staffing requirements and costs, insurance cover, depreciation costs or general wear and tear, and energy costs. Unless the museum's policy allows for certain organisations to be subsidised, museum managers should ensure that the museum does not suffer any financial loss and that the full costs of providing facilities should be recovered.
- The museum should have adequate support facilities such as cloakrooms, lavatories, car parking, to cater for external organisations using the museum's facilities.
- A clearly written contract or conditions agreement encompassing the museum's requirements should be drawn up and signed by all relevant parties; a deposit should be required.
- An acceptable form of acknowledgement to the museum should be agreed for publicity material/invitations.
- Any special legal requirements should be fully met such as licensing laws, health and hygiene laws for catering, or laws relating to the performance of recorded music.
- An internal booking system for those organisations hiring the museum's facilities should be established with staff designated to be responsible for agreed procedures.

The museum's staff should be aware of all the implications of the use of the museum's facilities by external organisations, and understand their practical needs. For example, if an organisation has booked a display area for an evening of musical performance and illustrated talks, how much time before the audience arrives will caterers require to organise their catering arrangements, or musicians require to arrange audio systems? Will these mean additional security arrangements or the display space being out of public use for a period of time? In drawing up a contract form, a checklist of questions like these will help to ensure that arrangements work smoothly for all concerned.

CONDITIONS

Here are some conditions of hiring facilities to outside organisations that need to be considered in drawing up a contract form or conditions of hire:

- Provisional bookings – how long will you allow a provisional booking to be kept open before the facility is re-let for that date?
- Deposit – if you charge a deposit when the booking is confirmed, what percentage of the booking fee will the deposit represent?
- Cancellations – a sliding scale of charges for cancellations may be appropriate. If cancellation is made less than two weeks before the agreed date, then the full booking fee is charged. If you are providing additional subcontractors such as caterers, tent erectors, extra security staff, there may need to be additional charges to cover their costs too.

- Damage to museum property – what level of charge will be made to the organisation hiring the facility if any damage occurs?
- Liability – will the museum be able to disclaim liability if personal possessions are lost or damaged?
- Responsibilities – who will be responsible for insurance, meeting legal requirements, clean-up and removal procedures, health and safety requirements, security arrangements, catering?
- Final details/numbers – when is the last date by which the hirer must provide final details of arrangements and numbers of those attending the event?

STANDARDS

Where the museum is hiring facilities for use by outside organisations, it is important to ensure that the standard of care for these organisations is of the highest order. Their audiences or members will be visiting your museum. While they may be coming to the museum to take part in another organisation's event, the quality of customer care and the standard of facilities that you provide is important for the museum's reputation and the future successful marketing of your facilities.

Having organised groups visit the museum for whatever reason always provides opportunities to promote the museum and its services, and encourage people to return to the museum on other occasions. Working with the organisation hiring your facilities to ensure a successful event is important. After all, both parties have much to gain from success. Ensuring that each other's responsibilities are clearly defined, agreed and understood is the key to that success.

STUDY EXAMPLE 21.1

A museum had regularly hired its small lecture room to a local archaeological society for its meetings for a number of years at a nominal hire charge.

The museum management wished to increase income from the use of its facilities and began a marketing campaign designed to promote its facilities to a wide range of organisations in the not-for-profit and for-profit sectors. In consequence, the archaeological society found that the hire charge for the lecture room had increased considerably and that the availability of the room was reduced.

The society therefore decided to hold its meetings at another venue, and the relationship with the museum – important in terms of its mission – was weakened.

The museum might have established a sliding scale of charges to allow for priority relationships with external organisations to be maintained, rather than impose a single charge.

Introducing interpretation

Unit 22

Related Units – Units 14, 23–37

WHAT IS 'INTERPRETATION'?

'Interpretation' usually means translating from one language to another. In the museum world, though, it has a special meaning: explaining an object and its significance. Almost everyone in the world, if shown a knife, will know roughly what it is meant to do: it is meant to cut. But if shown – say – a Tibetan prayer wheel, probably most people will not have any idea what it is, and fewer still outside Tibet will know why it is used or how it is used. To be fully understood and appreciated, it needs to be interpreted or explained.

Museums interpret things all the time. Almost every time you put an object on display, or simply take it out of its storage box and show it to a visitor, you are interpreting it. However, interpretation can be done in a huge number of different ways, some more complicated or more sophisticated than others. It is worth spending a little time thinking about the different ways museums interpret the objects in their collections, and considering which are the best techniques for interpreting different things to different people.

Interpretation, too, is not limited to museums. Indeed, the use of the term in this sense originated in North America among people responsible for the care of the National Parks and of historic sites. Many museum managers, of course, are responsible for caring for ancient sites and buildings, and for interpreting landscapes. The approach is the same, whether one is interpreting a plough, or the landscape the plough created. Interpretation may not only explain an object and its significance, it may also provide a conservation message about the object and its context.

IDENTIFYING THE AUDIENCE

To interpret something, you have to have someone to interpret it to. That person will of course come with his or her own interests, assumptions, beliefs, knowledge and curiosity. Every individual is distinct, and good interpreters, like good schoolteachers, adapt their technique to the people they are talking to. The audience for museums comes with particular goals. These may include:

- to seek inspiration;
- an eager desire to acquire knowledge;
- to educate children;
- to spend time with family or friends;

- curiosity;
- to be in the fashion;
- to fill up time;
- to shelter from bad weather;
- to examine specific items in the collection.

It has been suggested that interpretation can fail because the interpreter's goals do not match the audience's goals; when, for example, the audience's curiosity and commitment to learning are either seriously over-estimated or seriously under-estimated. The museum needs, therefore, to tailor its technique to the audience's

- education level;
- goals;
- intelligence.

In reality, it is impossible to please everyone at once, so before planning a piece of interpretation, the museum needs to decide who its target audience is to be (see Units 9–10). For example, the target audience for a lecture on Greek statues could be:

- young children;
- specialist art historians;
- sculptors;
- visitors from a foreign country.

In each case the lecture would be very different. So it is with other types of interpretation: the interpreter (in our case the museum) must be clear who is being addressed.

DECIDING THE AIMS

The next step for the museum must be to decide what the interpretation is aiming to achieve. Is it, for example, to introduce foreign visitors to Greek statuary, with enough information to enable them to enjoy it? Is it to summarise the latest research? Is it to awaken a sense of wonder, or to point out historic carving techniques? The more precisely the museum can define the aim of the interpretation, the more successful it will be.

CHOOSING THE RIGHT TECHNIQUES

Having decided what to say, and whom to address, the museum must decide what techniques to use. If you want to tell the story of farming in your particular region, is it better to create a display, publish a book, make a film or arrange lectures? If you decide a display is best, what sort of display should it be? There is a huge

---

Box 22.1 The 'communications policy'

Some museums find it helpful to adopt and publish a formal policy document, which outlines their approach to interpretation. This is often called a 'communications policy' because it covers all the ways in which the museum communicates with its visitors. The best-known example is probably *Communicating with the Museum Visitor: Guidelines for Planning of the Royal Ontario Museum*. This is a substantial book, intended to make sure that the departments of the museum achieve a consistently high standard in their communication with the visitor. It sets out the principles behind interpretation in the museum, but also goes into great detail, for example in prescribing styles of lettering, setting out procedures for commissioning audio-visual productions or laying down rules for light levels in displays.

Box 22.2 Interpretation techniques

What interpretation techniques does your museum use?
Underline the interpretation techniques (media, they are sometimes called) used in your museum in the following list. Would your visitors enjoy the displays more, or learn more, if you used a wider variety of techniques, or do you think that these are the most appropriate ones for your visitors?

Static	*Dynamic*
Objects	Live interpretation
Texts and labels	Sound-guides
Models	Guided talks and walks
Drawings	Lectures
Photographs	Film/video/slide-tape
Dioramas	Working models and animatronics
Tableaux	Computer-based interactives
Information sheets	Mechanical interactives
Guidebooks	Objects for handling
Worksheets	Drama
	Web sites

---

number and variety of techniques available, some of them more suited to some audiences, some more suited to some subjects (see Units 23–6). New techniques are being invented all the time. There is no magic way of choosing techniques.

Factors to be considered include:

- *Cost.* In some countries, electronic equipment will be formidably expensive, in others it may be cheaper than employing people.

- *Climate.* Techniques suitable for interpreting an archaeological site in the tropics are very likely not going to be suitable in the Arctic!
- *Conservation.* It is vital to consider the impact that any technique might have on the objects or site being interpreted. Sound and light presentations, for example, might require levels of light that exceed conservation standards (see Units 56–9).
- *Custom.* People learn most easily when they are relaxed. To use techniques that make people feel uncomfortable is clearly foolish. For example, computer-based techniques might not be suitable where computers are not familiar; live interpreters might be unsuitable where it is not customary to speak to strangers.
- *Participation.* Does the technique involve the audience? Does it encourage them to participate? We all learn more readily when we are actively involved in doing something than when we are simply looking or listening. Good teachers do not just lecture: they encourage their students to participate in learning through projects. The good museum tries to do the same.
- *Sustainability.* Will the technique continue to work, or can it be replaced? For example, it is unwise to rely long-term on the skills of one talented interpreter, if he/she cannot be replaced; it is equally unwise to rely on a technology likely to be expensive to maintain.

Presentation techniques: graphics

Unit

23

Related Units – 22, 24–6

Graphics can be simply defined as words and pictures. Every museum uses such presentation methods, perhaps in temporary exhibitions or together with displays of objects. The more carefully their design is planned, the more effective they will be.

One person (probably the curator) should be responsible for co-ordinating the content of the display/exhibition, and one person (ideally a qualified designer) should be responsible for its design. It is essential for them to work very closely together.

A temporary exhibition based solely on graphics, for example, might consist of a series of display panels, either fixed to the wall or fixed to screens standing on the floor. The first thing to decide, therefore, must be how many display panels will be needed. Each panel may well be devoted to one topic, and will consist of a sub-heading, some written text and one or more pictures (photographs or drawings).

The rule to obey is that all the text in one gallery should be produced in the same way, and all should be neat and clean. There is nothing worse than a museum where some text is (badly) handwritten, some is written on one typewriter, some on another and everything is untidy and faded. Text and labels should be crisp and smart. It is therefore a good rule to use equipment for producing them that will be available to produce replacements when necessary, for example a computer and laser printer.

THE DISPLAY SCREENS

Museums often need to use display screens standing on the floor to increase their wall space – sometimes they can be used together with showcases to create flexible display systems. Such screens can be bought commercially, or they can be made out of plywood or blockboard. They can be painted, or covered with cloth (see Unit 59). Choose a cloth or colour appropriate to the exhibition; for example, an exhibition of local history might use a cloth of traditional local design to cover the screens. The screens will need some sort of feet to make them stand up, or they can be joined together and so support each other. To join them together you can buy special clamps, or a local blacksmith can make hooks and rings.

THE PANELS

The designer needs to have all the pictures and text that the curator wants to have included. Normally today everything is done on computer. The pictures, if not already digital, are scanned in, and placed in their position, alongside text and motifs. When both designer and curator are happy with what they see on the screen, they simply send the design off by e-mail to the production company.

But some museums will be unable to use computers, while others may simply prefer to create exhibitions another way. In this case, the designer designs the layout of each panel in the form of a simple scale drawing, showing where the headings, text, photographs, drawings, diagrams and captions will go, and how large each will need to be. He or she will then produce text and photographs at the appropriate size, and mount them onto cardboard or softboard panels, which in turn are fixed to the screens.

TEXT

For the text, you can make a virtue of not using a computer by, for example, using sign-painting and calligraphy. Some countries still have highly skilled traditional sign-painters and calligraphers. Using painted signs and handwritten labels in the museum gives it a special character and helps preserve traditional crafts. It is also often the cheapest way! Silkscreening is still one of the best ways of preparing information panels. It is attractive and long-lasting, and can be used for both text and pictures and for a wide variety of designs. If you can really not afford any of these methods of preparing text for display, then write or type your information as clearly as possible on the best paper you can find, and fix it neatly to the display panel.

The following rules are useful to remember when designing both section panels and object labels:

- In a good light, and using conventional lettering, words can be read at a distance of the 'cap height' multiplied by 200. ('Cap height' means the height of the capital letters.) The font size 18 points is recommended for most museum labels; introductory and section text should be bigger.
- A serif font (typeface) is usually easier to read than a sans-serif font.
- *Italics* should be avoided.
- Black lettering on a white background is easiest to read.

PHOTOGRAPHS

Photographs are used in museum displays for a variety of different purposes. These include creating a mood, illustrating the present appearance of an archaeological site, illustrating comparable objects, bringing into the story buildings or large objects that could not themselves fit into a gallery, enlarging very small objects, illustrating the artist who painted pictures, and so on. Museums should avoid the temptation to use too many photos, and they should only be included if they serve a real purpose in the interpretation.

Box 23.1 Producing simple texts and labels

For most museums the easiest means to produce smaller labels is a computer with a laser or inkjet printer – borrowed, if necessary. The simpler fonts are best, and should be used consistently throughout the exhibition. Where computers are unavailable a good typewriter will be useful. Larger labels can be produced very cheaply using a photocopier.

Handwritten labels can be the best of all, but only when they are written by a real expert in traditional handwriting. Some countries still have highly skilled traditional sign-painters. Using painted signs in the museum both gives it a special character and helps preserve a traditional craft.

Lower case text (a combination of large and small letters) is easier to read than UPPER CASE TEXT, simply because it is more familiar.

Text is easiest to read for most people when placed at a height of between 1.0m and 1.5m. Text panels should be well lit and placed to avoid reflection. They should always be tested on site in advance of full commitment to production; children, people with impaired vision and people in wheelchairs should be asked to comment.

Presentation techniques: three-dimensional

Related Units – Units 22–3, 25–6

Museums use many different techniques to present their collections to visitors and to tell their stories, some of them simple, some of them very sophisticated. The following Units show a few of the techniques used in museums today. Here we examine some of the three-dimensional techniques.

Everyone likes to be able to touch as well as look at objects. Touching is an important way in which we experience things. For those with poor or no eyesight it is of course essential. Wherever possible, therefore, museums should try to allow visitors to touch exhibits, though in very many cases this will, for conservation reasons, not be possible. The museum may however wish to consider creating good-quality replicas for such purposes. Replicas, if used, should be well made, but be marked clearly to show that they are replicas.

Room settings may – in an historic building – be genuine original arrangements, or they may be modern reconstructions based on the best available evidence and research. The room setting is an effective way not only of presenting furniture or pictures in the settings for which they were originally created, but also of making historical points. For example, the living space of poor people may be contrasted with that of rich people. Visitors can be allowed into the room, into part of it, or allowed only to look in.

A *tableau* is like a reconstructed room, but includes life-size models of people arranged in a scene from history. Tableaux include figures in costume, and often furniture, decorations and even whole buildings.

Tableaux are used to show visitors how an historic building was used, to give a glimpse of life in past times or distant lands and to portray famous historic events. In museums, they can be used very effectively together with more conventional displays; one or two figures, carefully chosen to make an important point, can help greatly in a museum's interpretation scheme. Outside museums, tableaux have been used for centuries in 'waxworks' shows.

People-movers are small cars or other vehicles in which visitors ride through displays – usually through or past a series of tableaux. They enable the museum closely to control the number of visitors and what they see. People-movers are derived from fairground rides, and have been used in exhibitions for at least a hundred years. Recently, with improved technology, they have been used increasingly in 'heritage centres'. The idea of people-movers can of course be adapted to local situations. A ride in a horse and cart through the streets of an open-air museum is also a people-mover!

A *diorama* is partly a picture and partly a model. Usually there are model people or animals or landscape in the foreground, while the background is a painting; the skill of the diorama-maker lies in merging the two together in a lifelike way. Like tableaux, the diorama, too, is a technique used in museums for well over a century. Dioramas are especially effective in natural history and geology museums, used to show the habitat in which animals live or the conditions under which different rocks were created. Full-sized dioramas are also used to portray domestic life in the past or in other societies, while small-scale ones portray famous battles or archaeological sites.

Models are very widely used in museums and can be invaluable aids to interpretation. People find models fascinating, and they are much easier to understand than maps. They are especially useful in showing the development of archaeological sites or historic buildings, but they are also used to interpret historic boats, modern machinery, dinosaurs, railway engines and cars, military uniforms – in fact almost anything! Dioramas and models need to be well made and on an appropriate scale relative to the visitor, to be successful. Museums should explain the basis of evidence on which they are presented.

Presentation techniques: audio-visual and interactive

Unit

25

Related Units – Units 22–4, 26

Audio-visual techniques are very common in museums. Too often, though, musums install them without thinking hard enough about why they are using them. Even in highly developed countries audio-visual techniques are often expensive to install and both expensive and time-consuming to run. They can help the visitor to understand the museum, but the museum must be clear why it is using them and be sure that it can maintain them.

Exhibition technology is changing so fast that it is no longer possible to list (as the first edition of *Museum Basics* tried to do) the various techniques available to museum designers. Instead, we can consider how they can help the museum present its collections and tell its stories to visitors, and what planning is needed. A browse on the Internet will produce a great deal of information on the different techniques.

WHY AUDIO-VISUAL?

Audio-visual techniques enormously help museums to tell their stories and to explain their collections. They are used in four main ways:

- as an introduction to a museum or exhibition;
- to create an atmosphere in a gallery;
- to explain an object or group of objects; or
- as an exhibit, to make a particular point.

They have a variety of uses:

- Audio-visuals can create an atmosphere and can generate emotions in the visitor.
- Audio-visuals can give the context of objects, for example to show the lifestyle of the people who used a group of objects.
- Audio-visuals can explain how things were used, for example how a machine was operated, and can show parts of an object otherwise invisible.
- Audio-visuals can show how things were made or buildings and monuments were constructed.
- Audio-visuals can be interactive, and thus can involve the visitor much more than simply through looking (see Unit 14).

One of the most interesting ways audio-visuals can help the museum is by offering alternative views. Objects and labels tend just to offer the curator's view, but with audio-visuals the museum can include comments by a range of different people with different points of view.

GETTING IT DONE

With modern computer software, it is perfectly possible for an individual with a home computer to create quite sophisticated audio-visual programmes. Some museums will have staff, volunteers or supporters willing and able to do so. The dangers, of course, are that the 'expert' may not be quite so competent as he or she thinks, may not be familiar with the robust hardware needed for continuing public use, and may not always be present to maintain the system.

Some museums may be able to use the staff and students at a local college. The dangers, again, are a lack of familiarity with the demanding gallery environment, and lack of continuity.

Most museums will turn to a professional production company to design and create their audio-visuals and interactives. Choosing a production company is much like choosing a designer (see Unit 32); talk to other museums, look at a variety of audio-visuals, go and talk to potential tenderers, make sure they have experience of working in museums or similar environments, and invite three or four companies to tender. They will take charge of the whole production process (see Box 25.1).

WRITING A BRIEF

Writing a brief for an audio-visual presentation is very much like writing a brief for an exhibition designer (see Unit 32). It should include:

- Budget. How much money is available.
- Aim. Target audiences, key messages.

Box 25.1 The production process

	Who does it?
Pre-production	
Write a treatment	Writer/director or client
Storyboard/visualise	Writer/director or storyboard artist
Budget and schedule works	Production manager
Research content in image libraries and archives	Picture researcher
Researching, writing and editing a script to client approval	Writer
Finding locations for filming	Location finder
Sourcing costumes, props, sets	Stylist
Casting actors, and selecting interviewees or voice artists	Casting agent
Production	
Location or studio filming	Camera crew, director, actors, presenter, interviewees, make-up artist
Graphics and animation production	Designer/animator
Offline editing	Editor and director
Client approves offline edit	Client
On-line editing	Editor and director
Voice recording	Voice artist, sound engineer and director
Music composition	Composer
Sound mix	Sound engineer
Accessibility: adding subtitles, sign language, other language versions	Editor and director
Post-production	
Client approves on-line edit	Client
Transfer material to agreed format for replay	Facility house
Oversee installation on site, sound balancing	Sound designer
Declare all copyrighted material used	Production manager
Return all archive material to lenders	Production manager
Make back-up copies of the programme	Production manager

- Length. Shorter is better!
- Content. A summary of your ideas.
- Style. Any ideas you have already.
- Scripting. Who will write the script?
- Display and viewing conditions.
- Liaison with exhibition designer.

- Accessibility. What languages? Subtitles? Signing?
- Copyright. Do you also want to use the programme for a web site, CD, etc.?

MAINTENANCE

Continued use in an exhibition puts a very heavy load on audio-visual equipment. Continuing maintenance is essential, and should be budgeted for at the beginning of the project. The costs will include regular checking by a specialist, replacement and repair when things go wrong, and regular replacement of equipment.

Some points to remember are:

- All equipment has a lifespan, sometimes quite short (projector bulbs last 2,000 hours: about 9 months; computers are designed to last 2 years, and should then be replaced). Therefore:

  - Buy the best and most robust equipment you can afford.
  - Budget to replace it regularly.

- Everything breaks. Things accessible to the public break especially often. There is nothing more annoying to a visitor than to find audio-visuals out of order. Therefore:

  - Buy the best you can afford, but always buy standard, off-the-shelf equipment that can be replaced.
  - Avoid the latest technology; let other people discover the bugs!

Box 25.2 Cheap alternatives

Simple interactive techniques are often the best. In everyday life we are interacting all the time with other people and with objects, and the more natural the museum can be the more effective it will be. Teachers know that asking questions is one of the most useful ways of arousing interest. It is possible to design very simple displays that ask the visitor questions. One method is to show objects in a showcase, and invite the visitor to answer questions about them. The visitor has to lift a little flap to uncover the correct answer. Many science centres have developed very effective and inexpensive interactive techniques. Some history museums encourage visitors to try on replica historic costume, build simple models, assemble replica furniture, etc. The only limit to the number of simple interactive devices possible in a museum is the imagination of curator or designer.

'Pepper's Ghost' is a simple technique that, by setting two pictures or models at right angles divided by a glass screen, allows the visitor to see one merge into the other simply by switching the light from one to the other. It is an excellent technique for comparing (for example) a model of an ancient site as it is with one as it was, or comparing an archaeological object with a reproduction of its original form.

- Always have spares ready.
- Train museum staff to do the simple repairs.
- Arrange for an engineer to deal with major repairs *the same day*. This is likely to be expensive.
- Ensure that audio-visual equipment is easily accessible. Get exhibition designs checked by an audio-visual expert.
- *Always* make a back-up of every program, and document everything.

Unit
26

Presentation techniques: using people

Related Units – Units 22–5

A person talking is the oldest, most natural and most common presentation technique of all. It can also be the best, but only when the person involved is really well informed, skilled at the technique he or she is using, and in tune with the audience. Using people needs as careful planning as using any other technique.

The *guided tour* is the oldest of all interpretation techniques, and – except in the hands of a very skilful guide – probably the least successful. The guide requires a natural flair and enthusiasm for the job, considerable experience of talking to parties of people of different ages, backgrounds and interests, and a really good knowledge of the subjects being studied. A good guide can be inspiring: a poor one can quickly extinguish any spark of interest on the part of the visitor!

Many museums have commercial tour guides leading parties of tourists through the museum. Should they be allowed? Should they be (or can they be) charged a fee? The answers must depend on the local situation and local tradition, but one good solution is for the museum to license guides to use its premises, and only allow in those guides who have gone through a training course and passed an examination. This has the benefit of ensuring that the museum is exercising a degree of quality assurance for its visitors. Museums should work with the commercial tour companies to develop joint training programmes. Such partnerships are in the interests of the commercial tour companies as they can demonstrate to their customers that they are providing added value for their services.

The most interesting people are those who not only talk well, but who really know what they are talking about. Some museums – especially those concerned with recent history – encourage *local people* to come to the museum and talk about their own experiences. For example, a gallery devoted to local agriculture will come alive in a new way if visitors can meet a retired farm worker who will tell them about his or her own experience. The museum should ensure that the information provided by the guide is historically accurate and that they are appropriately briefed on the nature of the audiences with whom they will be talking. North

American museums are particularly good at training volunteers to become 'docents': museum guides. Training guides effectively is a key responsibility of the museum.

Talking to a group sitting down is very different to talking to a group walking around; it can often be much more successful. Arranging *gallery talks* on different subjects, perhaps at lunchtime or in the evenings so that local workers can attend, is an excellent way of serving people with a special interest and of making use of curators' knowledge.

The formal *lecture* is still one of the principal ways in which a museum can present its collections and its knowledge. All but the smallest museums should have a room that can be used for lectures and meetings. A lecture programme can be an effective way of communicating with visitors (see Units 15–17).

Many museums use *demonstrators* or *explainers* to bring their collections to life, sometimes in the museum gallery itself or in a separate room and sometimes outside the museum. There is almost no limit to what can be demonstrated. How something was made and how it was used can very often best be explained by a demonstration. Craftspeople are often happy to work in a museum if they can then sell what they make to visitors. It is important, though, that they have the time and skill to talk to visitors and explain what they are doing.

The use of *actors* playing the part of historical characters has revolutionised visitors' perception of some museum galleries in recent years. Sometimes the actors involve visitors in acting out scenes relevant to the displays around them, sometimes they merely greet the visitors and – speaking 'in character' as a historical person – explain the displays. As with guides, it is important that the museum monitors the accuracy of the information being presented in this way. The use of actors needs to be very carefully managed.

'Living History' or *'re-enactment'* is a popular hobby in many countries. People spend a great deal of their spare time dressing up in historic costume and re-enacting scenes from the past. In the USA, for example, American Civil War battles are very popular, as are seventeenth-century settler life, pioneer farming or early fur-trading. Living History is an exciting and imaginative way for museums to bring history to life.

A more formal use of theatrical techniques is when professional or amateur theatre companies put on small plays in the museum related to an aspect of the collections. Like Living History, this technique is increasingly used with school parties (see Units 15–17).

Unit

27

Museum lighting

Related Units – Units 29, 32, 56

Good lighting makes all the difference to a museum. How we see, perceive and understand an object is crucially affected by the character of the light falling on it.

Ideally, every display would have lighting designed by a specialist lighting consultant. In practice, this is rarely possible. But good lighting design can transform an otherwise dull display. To redesign the lighting and the labelling is often all that is needed to make an old-fashioned gallery seem renewed.

DAYLIGHT

Daylight, as a source of light for exhibits, has great advantages: it is free, it is natural and its changing qualities give the visitor a variety of impressions of the exhibits and a link with the outside world. On the other hand, daylight is difficult to control, and contains a high level of ultra-violet radiation, again difficult to eliminate (see Units 55–6). It may therefore prove an expensive form of lighting if it irrevocably damages the museum's exhibits! Further, its variability and its contrasts of light and shade may be a disadvantage in the museum, and may not correspond to the light for which the exhibits were originally designed. Greek marble for instance looks cold and flat in north European light.

Compromise is possible. Parts of a gallery can be lit by daylight, while the light falling on the exhibits themselves can be artificial and controlled, for example with the use of a diffuser panel. The danger that daylight offers to the conservation of objects, however, requires us to control it carefully (see Units 55–6).

TUNGSTEN LIGHT

The commonest form of lighting in many countries is the ordinary round tungsten light bulb or 'globe'. In addition, there is a variety of different lamps designed specially for display purposes. Tungsten lighting has many advantages: it gives a warm light that can easily be adjusted, it emits little ultra-violet radiation and it is very adaptable. Its chief disadvantages are that it gives out a lot of heat, and that its colour temperature (see Box 27.1) is difficult to control.

The first disadvantage has been met by the development of low-voltage lighting, which is also very cheap to run. This is a form of lighting which seems ideal for museums; unfortunately, it is expensive to buy, and in many countries still difficult to obtain.

FLUORESCENT LIGHTING

Fluorescent lighting is cheap to run and efficient, readily obtainable everywhere, can give varied colour temperatures and gives out little heat. However, it cannot be dimmed, is available in very few lamps suitable for use in displays, may give poor colour rendering (see Box 27.1) and emits a high proportion of ultra-violet radiation. If it is to be used to light original objects, it is essential to exclude the ultra-violet element from fluorescent light (see Unit 56).

Box 27.1 Colour temperature and colour rendering

Both the colour temperature of a light source (whether it looks cool or warm) and its colour rendering (whether it correctly reflects the true colours of an object) can be measured. Its colour temperature is measured in °K; one can say quite objectively that this lamp will distort colours, while that lamp will give no appreciable distortion.

With daylight and tungsten light there is no problem, since both give perfect colour rendering and the colour temperature cannot be altered. With fluorescent lamps, however, there are two choices to be made: fluorescent tubes are manufactured in a range of colour temperatures from cool (6,500°K) through intermediate (4,000°K) to warm (3,000°K).

In the end, the choice of colour temperature is a matter of taste. But remember that the eye adapts to its surroundings, so that in a gallery lit with a warm light a showcase lit with a cool light will look blue; the other way round and the showcase will look yellow. Objects should be presented in their true colours.

Having decided whether you want a warmer or a cooler light, you need to choose a fluorescent tube that both meets your needs and gives good colour rendering. The trouble is that manufacturers do not normally supply such information, so that it is necessary to seek advice from a specialist.

LIGHTING IN SHOWCASES

Too many showcases have bad lighting. Lighting should *never* be in the showcase itself, but always in a separate lightbox, which must be well ventilated to prevent heat building up. A new possibility though, which can be used inside showcases, is fibre optics. These give a precise beam of light without any heat.

IS IT EASY TO USE?

How easy will the lighting chosen by the museum be to maintain and use? This is the crucial question to ask when considering a museum lighting scheme. (It may be beautiful, but if it requires fifty switches to be turned every morning and evening and no-one can reach the lamps to replace them, it is no good.) Where will the switches be? Can the display lighting be turned off and the security and cleaning lighting be left on? Can all the lamps be reached so they can be replaced? Are replacements easily available, and can the museum afford to buy them? Do any showcases need to be opened in order to change lamps or adjust lighting? This should *never* be necessary.

CLEANING AND EMERGENCY LIGHTING

In many galleries, it will be necessary to have two quite separate systems of lighting in addition to the normal display lighting. The first is the cleaning lighting, needed to ensure that the cleaners can see what they are doing: often this is sets of fluorescent lights on the ceilings, screened to eliminate ultra-violet radiation and not used when the museum is open to visitors. The second system is the battery-powered emergency lighting that comes on in the event of power-failure or emergencies.

Unit
28

Museum showcases

Related Units: Units 22, 55–9

In most museums, showcases are the most important pieces of equipment, both in protecting objects and in presenting them to visitors. They have four functions:

- to protect the objects inside from theft and damage;
- to provide a micro-climate in which constant levels of relative humidity, temperature and controlled light can be maintained;
- to protect the objects inside from pollution, dust and insects; and
- to provide a 'theatre stage' on which to exhibit and interpret objects.

The perfect showcase has still not been invented; museum designers say that designing showcases is often the most difficult job they are called on to do. Whether they are built by museum technicians or bought 'off the shelf', museum showcases are too often unsatisfactory. Often they are very expensive too! In specifying showcases for the museum, there are general principles that you should bear in mind. The following is a checklist of standards that every museum showcase should meet.
Museum showcases must:

- *keep out pollutants and dust with well-sealed joints and tightly fitting doors.*
Too often one sees dust inside museum showcases. The only way in which to be certain that the showcase is free of pollution and dust is to pressurise it slightly by pumping in filtered air so that any pollution or dust is pushed out. This technique is too expensive, though, for most small museums, which must simply ensure that there are no gaps between the sides or at the top and that the door fits as tightly as possible.

• *be stable, to prevent vibration.*

Showcases often have very thin legs, for cheapness or lightness or looks. The heavier the showcase, and the more solid its base or legs, normally the better protected the objects inside will be from damage by vibration.

• *be secure, with good locks.*

The showcase is the museum's last line of defence against the thief. But most museum locks are either very easily picked or very easily forced. See how quickly you can break into one of your showcases; a thief will be able to do it very much faster. It is worth ensuring that the locking system on display cases is well designed and tested and is appropriate for the level of risk.

• *be easily opened by curators.*

If the showcase is difficult to open, it will be shaken in the process with consequent damage to the objects inside. A curator may also be tempted to leave a difficult to open showcase open 'just for a minute', with consequent security risks.

• *be made of materials which cannot damage objects.*

Many of the materials that might be used in the construction of showcases give off gases that can harm objects. Some examples are given here:

- Polyvinyl chloride (PVC) is a risk to copper.
- Felt, wool, viscose, rubber-based adhesives and certain fabric dyes should not be used with silver.
- Lead, copper, paper, parchment and leather are all affected by materials releasing acetic acid, such as paints, lacquers and some woods and wood composites, for example, cardboard, plywood, chipboard and blockboard.
- One-component silicone sealants, cellulose acetate and some polyvinyl acetate adhesive may also present a similar risk.
- Formaldehyde is emitted by the wood and resin binders in many wood composites and some adhesives.

Not all museums will be able to avoid all these materials, or even to have them tested, but all should do their best to protect their objects from these risks (see Units 55–60).

• *help maintain constant relative humidity inside.*

The showcase should help to protect the objects inside from fluctuations in relative humidity (see Unit 57). The more solidly it is constructed the better it will do so. Sometimes it is worthwhile designing a showcase that incorporates pre-conditioned silica gel, but only if the museum is then able to recondition the silica gel regularly.

• *help maintain correct light levels.*

Light levels inside showcases are often far too high for the safety of the objects. It is very important that both the light level and heat given out should be carefully controlled. Where the showcase has its own lighting, the light source and all electrical equipment must be outside the showcase itself, and must be well ventilated.

- *raise objects to a height to enable them to be seen clearly.*

Remember that your audience consists of people of different heights, and includes children and people who are in pushchairs and wheelchairs.

- *bridge the scale differences between small objects, people and the building.*

Tiny objects in a great big room can look insignificant and lost. One important function of the showcase is to give them scale and importance.

- *be constructed of appropriate materials that respect environmental concerns.*

It would be inappropriate to use wood from an endangered primary forest in a display case providing a display on ecology and conservation! Sustainability considerations should apply to the materials the museum uses for all construction purposes (see Unit 5).

- *relate to the design of the galleries.*

Showcases should be well designed, be attractive to look at and complement the design of the gallery. They should however not dominate the material that they are displaying.

Unit 29

Planning new displays and exhibitions

Related Units – Units 22, 30, 32

THE ADVANTAGES OF DISPLAY

The public is quite right to identify museums with displays. Although museums do many other things as well, and use many other techniques to communicate with the public, their unique and special method is display. Displays and temporary exhibitions have three great advantages over every other form of interpretation:

- Displays can reach a large number of different people at one time. They thus tend to be very cost-effective.
- Displays contain real objects. Visitors respond to 'the real thing' with a special respect that they do not give to the printed word, to photographs or to reproductions.
- Visitors can use displays at their own level of interest and speed.

DECIDING ON THE TARGET AUDIENCE

The museum should already know a lot about its visitors (see Unit 9). They will be very varied: adults and children, townspeople and country people, wealthy people and poor people, educated people and uneducated people, local people and tourists. It will scarcely be possible to design a display that suits everyone. The museum must start, therefore, by deciding whom the new display is mainly aimed at. It could be intended chiefly for children, or for foreign tourists, or for specialists, or for any other group of visitors.

The display will be aimed at this 'target audience', and designed to meet their needs and interests, though it should also please and interest other visitors as well. Interpreters should target their display at a particular audience or group of visitors because if they try to please everyone they may end up pleasing no-one (see Unit 22). As planning the new display goes on, we shall learn a lot about this target audience, through the process known as 'front-end evaluation' (see Unit 34).

DECIDING ON THE THEME

The number of possible themes for a new display may seem at first sight almost limitless. In fact, your choice will be limited by a number of things:

- The *mission of the museum* (see Units 80–1). Clearly any new display must serve the overall purpose of the museum. There is little point in defining the mission of the museum as 'to present the history of the Nile Valley' if you are then going to arrange displays on Buddhist art from Thailand!
- The *target audience*. Theme and audience must match; you are giving yourself unnecessary problems if you insist on presenting a display on a theme in which you know that your target audience has no interest! That said, you may feel that you want to try, and if your techniques are good enough you may succeed in giving a lot of people an inspiring new interest. If so, you are a very good interpreter.
- The *museum collections*. Probably you will want to base your display on part of your existing collection, on the results of field-collecting, on a new acquisition or on a borrowed collection.
- *Money*. A small and poor museum is unlikely to be able to arrange a display of Van Gogh paintings, or a display demonstrating the latest techniques of space research.
- *Knowledge*. It is important to choose a display theme that the museum staff (or visiting experts) have sufficient expertise to treat adequately (see Unit 30). The public looks on the museum as a source of knowledge and scholarship, and the museum therefore has an ethical responsibility to ensure through its research that what it presents in its displays is based on the most accurate and up-to-date information possible.

WHAT KIND OF DISPLAY?

Having decided on the theme of the display, the curator and the display team need to decide what kind of display it is to be. Displays in museums can be divided into six main types:

- *Contemplative display.* Here beautiful or inspiring things are put on display for the visitor to contemplate. This is the theme adopted by most art galleries, though even they often try to tell a story as well, if only by grouping paintings or statues by similar artists together.
- *Didactic display.* Here the display tries to tell a story, to teach something. The story may, for example, be the prehistory of the country, or the biology of lizards, or the folk art of the region; objects help to tell the story.
- *Reconstruction display.* In this case a genuine or imaginary scene is reconstructed. Open-air museums like Skansen in Sweden, where whole streets of historic buildings are rebuilt and refurbished, fall into this type, as do small tableaux in museum galleries (see Unit 24).
- *Grouped display.* Here groups of objects are displayed together, often with very little interpretation. Archaeological museums, for example, often have a room labelled 'Bronze Age', with many objects but very little to tell the visitor why they are important or what happened in the Bronze Age. This type of display is probably the most common type of all, and is found in museums all over the world because it is so easy to do: it requires very little thought. But it is also the least useful or interesting to visitors, except to specialists.
- *Visible storage.* Early museums used to put everything they owned on display. Then curators learned that people could enjoy a few objects well displayed and interpreted, more than hundreds of objects crowded together. Many museums put only their best things on display, and assigned the rest to storage. But now visitors are asking 'why can't we see the thousands of things you've got hidden in your stores?'. One answer is to keep the fine displays, but to open the stores to interested visitors, making only those improvements needed to protect the collections (see Unit 60).
- *Discovery displays.* This is almost the opposite of the didactic display. There are organising principles, but collections are displayed in a non-conventional way, for example not in chronological or thematic order and without labels or texts. Instead, visitors are encouraged to explore the displayed objects and make their own connections and discoveries. The museum can of course help visitors to follow their particular interests and make their own discoveries through providing different forms of interpretation, for example, booklets and sound guides (see Study example 29.1).

Can you think of any other categories into which displays could be divided? Which categories do the displays in your own museum fall into? What organising principles have you tested in the museum?

STUDY EXAMPLE 29.1

A university museum had developed its collections over some two centuries. They fell into two categories – ethnographic collections from countries that university researchers had visited mainly in the nineteenth and early twentieth centuries, and archaeology and social history collections from local and regional sites.

The museum decided to display its foreign ethnographic collections within a thematic framework based on cross-cultural issues, such as kinship, power relationships, long-distance trade, and exchange systems. The displays explained similarities and differences in the ways in which different societies in different parts of the world addressed these issues and how these were reflected in their material culture.

The archaeology and social history collections were displayed in a former library, reusing and modifying the library shelving system for display cases. The organising principle used for these collections was to arrange the collections in alphabetical order. This was partly because many objects had little associated information relating to their original discovery or acquisition, and partly because the display approach generated unusual and intriguing juxtapositions for visitors. The displays were supported by computer interactives that enabled visitors to generate chronological or thematic lists of material on display. These lists acted as gallery 'maps' or guides. Where visitors had a particular interest in a specific subject or period, they could use these to locate objects or groups of objects from the displays.

Museums can use different organising principles with their collections at different times. Such an approach helps to create change in the museum, allows the collections to be explored by curators and visitors in new and stimulating ways, examines the collections from different perspectives and helps to generate new audiences for the museum.

Unit
30

Research for displays and exhibitions

Related Units – Unit 29

No-one would consider writing a book without allowing time to do the necessary research. Yet museums quite often begin new display projects without planning who is going to do the necessary research, where they will find the necessary information and how much time they will need to do it.

There is a major distinction between research on the collections, which is a responsibility every museum carries, and research specifically for a new display. Research on the collections should be a continuous process, carried out according to a research policy and closely tied to the museum's collecting policy (see Unit 42). Research for displays is tied to the particular display that the museum is planning.

It is important first to ensure that the museum has the necessary *expertise* to research and put on a display. If the museum is thinking, for example, of arranging a new display of its collection of netsuke (Japanese carvings), does anyone working at the museum know (enough) about them? Or can an expert be brought in from outside to do the research and to supervise the arrangement of the display?

Second, the museum should ensure that the researchers have access to adequate *sources of information* – libraries and other experts. Of course, this may be more difficult for a small and poor museum in a remote place than for a large well-staffed museum with a big library and perhaps near a university. The Internet can be an important source for researchers in some subjects, though it is notorious how much sheer nonsense can be found on the Internet, alongside really valuable information! A small museum should concentrate on topics for displays it is able to research, for example local ethnography or local wildlife.

Third, it is important to make sure that enough *time* is available to carry out the research. A major exhibition in a large museum may involve two or three people researching for two or three years: a major exhibition or permanent display should be thought of like a scholarly book. Even displays for a small gallery in a small museum require some weeks' or months' research. Every new display or temporary exhibition should be based on the most accurate and up-to-date information possible, whoever the audience is to be. There is never any excuse for inaccuracy in museum displays any more than in a published book.

Finally, the people who undertake the research, if they are not also writing the brief for the designer (see Unit 32) and writing the labels (see Unit 31), must work very closely with those who do. The display must be based on well-researched, accurate and up-to-date information.

Once the display has been completed or the exhibition is over, what happens to all the information the researchers gathered? There will be lots of notes, unused pictures, drafts of text and publication, perhaps transcripts or CDs of interviews, and so on. All of this is valuable, but in the rush to complete an exhibition it too easily gets lost in the files, never to be seen again. Every museum should have a system for capturing this kind of information and making sure it is available for future researchers.

Writing text

Related Units – Units 8, 22, 32–3

Most museum visitors get their information from museum text. Yet most museum visitors read only perhaps one-tenth of the text. Even if one is very interested, it is difficult to read standing up and walking around. And while some visitors *are* very interested, and want a lot of information, others may be put off by a lot of text or complicated labels, and may be made to feel inadequate.

So writing, designing and positioning museum texts and object labels is one of the most difficult but most important tasks a museum manager has to do.

THE AIM AND AUDIENCE OF THE EXHIBITION

Whether one is planning a new display or temporary exhibition or improving an old gallery, the first question to answer is, 'what is the aim of the exhibition?'. The aim could be to tell a story, to explain a concept or simply to display fine objects.

The aim of the exhibition depends on the audience. A clear idea of whom the exhibition is aimed at is essential to exhibition planning.

THE OVERALL SCHEME

The simplest and most common text scheme in a conventional exhibition has three parts:

- An *introductory panel* explaining the purpose of the exhibition and giving its title.
- *Section panels* that – like chapter headings in a book – give background information on the objects in that showcase or that section of the exhibition.
- *Object labels* giving more detailed information about the individual objects on exhibition.

The introductory panel gives the title of the exhibition, and explains its purpose. It should encourage visitors by telling them why the objects are worth exhibiting, why visitors should be interested in the exhibition and what they can learn from it. In a larger exhibition, it should also explain briefly how the exhibition is organised, so that the visitor knows in general what he or she is going to see, and how long the visit will take.

The section panels give background information about the objects in that section of the exhibition, and should explain why they are grouped together. Each section panel should have clear headings.

The object labels explain what each object is, and why it is significant.

HOW TO WRITE TEXT

Most museum texts and labels are much too complicated. They are written by specialists who know a great deal about their subject and about the objects, and who sometimes forget that most of their visitors will know very little about either.

When many of the visitors are foreign tourists, the problem is even worse. There will be much that the curator has known and understood since childhood that to the visitor is mysterious and strange.

On the other hand, some museum labels are much too simple. A label reading 'old plough given by Hilda Beckenham' is quite useless. Most visitors can recognise a plough, but very few will have ever heard of Hilda Beckenham!

Who is it for?

As with every aspect of planning an exhibition, always keep in mind who the target audience is. Labels written for schoolchildren will be different to labels written for university professors. Find out what level of education and what knowledge of the subject your visitors are likely to have.

Consider what languages the labels should be written in. In some countries, it may be necessary to have labels written in two or three local languages and in one or two foreign languages. It depends entirely on who your visitors are likely to be. If you are getting labels translated into other languages, do try to get the translation done by a native speaker of that language; a bad translation may make your visitors laugh, but it will not help them to understand your exhibition!

Keep it short

Text on an introductory panel should have no more than 150 words; 50 words would be better.

Text on section panels should have no more than 200 words; 50 words would be better.

Object labels should have no more than 40 words. If you feel it is essential to say more than this, then put the extra information in a guidebook, or in a give-away leaflet. This is also the best solution if some visitors want more detailed information.

Keep it clear

Write simply, avoiding jargon and technical terms. Put the main point of what you want to say at the beginning. Use the language that most visitors would use. Use the active voice rather than the passive voice: 'King Ezana conquered . . .' rather than '. . . was conquered by King Ezana'. Above all, think about what might be interesting to visitors and how it could relate to something they already know.

When the panel text or the label is written, show it to three or four randomly selected visitors, and then ask them to tell you what it says in their own words. It will soon be clear whether they have understood it!

Then perhaps subject what you have written to a readability test (see Box 31.1).

It is often best to ask someone completely unconnected with the museum, ideally a writer or journalist, to write the labels, based on your information.

Use pictures instead?

It is often possible to use pictures or diagrams instead of text. For example, explaining a painting of a scene from a Greek myth would take a lot of dull-looking words – easier to use a photograph with labels pointing to the various gods and heroes.

Box 31.1 Readability and comprehension

There are a number of tests that aim to check how readable text is, including some computer ones. They rank text by 'reading age', and a museum should normally try to achieve a reading age of about 15. Opinions differ on how useful these tests are: they are usually based on the number of words and syllables in a sentence, rather than on the clarity of the sentence structure. However, one simple test that can be useful in telling whether your text is intelligible to English-speaking visitors is the Cloze Test.

The Cloze Test
1 Take several examples of your text. Type or write them out again, deleting every fifth word and replacing it with a standard-sized blank. Count the number of blanks.
2 Give copies of the retyped versions to a broad sample of visitors and ask them to fill in the blanks.
3 Score a word as correct only if it is exactly the same as the one deleted from the original (except misspellings).
4 For each response the Cloze score = number of correctly filled-in words × 100 divided by the number of blanks (deleted words).
5 Add together the total number of Cloze scores and divide by the number of responses to get the mean.
6 Mean Cloze scores above 55 are good. 57–61 means that almost everyone understood it. If the score is 35 or less the text is too difficult.

(Kentley and Negus 1989)

Box 31.2 What to say and how to say it?

Labelling objects

Writing labels is an art. The label should include all relevant details, but not be too long; it should avoid vague or inexact statements, but give some indication why the object is worthy of being displayed in the museum. Information should be verified before it is included on a label.

Examples of what *not* to include in writing a label about a sewing machine:

Sewing Machine. Believed to be a hundred years old.	A hundred years old – when? It is possible to date many historical items accurately; reference books including trade catalogues can be used.
Sewing Machine. Such machines were widely used in the early days.	The 'explanation' really adds nothing to our knowledge of the object.
Sewing Machine. This machine is unusual because it was made in America.	This label would be inadequate unless it described the only American-made machine in a collection of English-made machines. Even then information about the nature of the difference would be required.
Sewing Machine. Donated by the late Mrs Jane Smith.	In fifty years' time, most of your donors will be 'late'!

A better label, in an exhibition primarily about local history, might be:

Sewing Machine, about 1884
This machine was brought to Augusta from Ireland by Margaret Murphy in 1890. Margaret Murphy was the wife of a timber worker. Like most poorer immigrants of her generation, she made all the clothes for herself and her eight children. This machine was manufactured by the Standard Sewing Machine Company, Cleveland, Ohio.
Given in 1963 by Margaret Murphy's granddaughter, Mrs Jane Smith.

Or, in an exhibition primarily about the history of sewing machines as machines:

Standard Rotary Sewing Machine, about 1884
The Rotary was one of the most popular models produced by the Standard Sewing Machine Company of Cleveland, Ohio, USA. It was manufactured from the 1880s until about 1920.
Standard began manufacturing sewing machines in 1884. It was one of the many manufacturers set up shortly after the dissolution of the Sewing Machine Combination of Singer, Wheeler & Wilson, and Grover & Baker. The Standard Company was apparently acquired by the Osaan company around 1929 and later bought out by the Singer Manufacturing Co.

STUDY EXAMPLE 31.1

A museum realised that many local people saw it as 'distant', perhaps a bit elitist. Short of redesigning all the displays, what could be done? The museum approached a number of local people and invited them to the museum to choose one object they specially liked, and to write two or three sentences about what it meant for them. The museum then turned these short statements into labels, with a little picture of the author alongside, and displayed them beside the objects. Some of the authors were well-known locally (the town mayor, a local footballer) and some of them quite unknown (a schoolchild, a shop assistant, a factory worker). The museum did not publicise what it had done, but more and more local people dropped in to look, and the local newspaper published a story about it.

Not only did the museum get a lot of good publicity and increasing visitor numbers, but it learned an important lesson about the variety of ways in which different people can enjoy an object. Thereafter, the museum always involved local people in its exhibitions, and gave much more attention to audience research and evaluation.

Unit
32

Briefing a designer

Related Units – 22–31, 33–4

More and more museums are using their limited resources to buy the skills of professional designers. It is not always a happy relationship. When new displays prove disappointing, curators blame the designer. When new displays result in damage to objects, conservators blame the designer. When objects go missing from new displays, security officers blame the designer. When children cannot enjoy a new display, the education specialist blames the designer.

In fact, it is very probably *their* fault: they failed to make their needs clear. The design brief is the chief way in which the designer is told what the museum wants them to achieve. It is the most important part of the whole process of creating a new display.

Different designers ask their clients to provide information in different forms. This Unit, however, lists the information that every design brief should contain.

DESIGN BRIEF: PART 1

The first part of the design brief should be prepared before the designer is chosen, if an outside designer is to be employed. It describes the nature and purpose of the proposed new display. Here are some of the questions to ask and some of the points to consider. You will have more.

Why?: the purpose of the new display
What are the aims of the project – intellectual, philosophical and educational? If you can write these down in fewer than 250 words, it will demonstrate that you have thought hard about what you want to achieve.

What?: the nature of the display
Is it to be a permanent gallery or a temporary exhibition? How long is it expected to last? What sort of display is it to be: mostly graphic, mostly objects or some of each? Are the objects large or small? Will they need to be in showcases? Will they need special environmental conditions or security?

Where?: where is the display located?
Where is the new display to be? Describe and give details of the space into which it must fit. Does the space have any special restrictions such as floor loadings, ceiling heights, power supply or access?

When?: the timetable
When must the display be completed? Are there any special time constraints, such as a building programme, major events, anniversaries, availability of funds, etc.?

Who?: the target audience
Who is the target audience? It is crucial that you define your target audience at the very beginning of the project (see Units 9–10).

How much?: the budget available
If you are able to state a budget for the project at this stage, the designer will be able to assess whether it is enough to achieve your aims, the standard of finish that can be achieved and how much his or her fees and expenses are likely to be. If you are unable or unwilling to state a budget at this stage, the designer will be able to assess how much he or she would expect the project to cost. Your aspirations or your budget may then need to be revised!

DESIGN BRIEF: PART 2

The second part of the design brief is given to the designer when he or she is appointed. Its purpose is to describe in detail every single thing that is to be included in the new display.

Every single item is given a unique number, and for every item a form or computerised log is completed with the details described here.

Objects

- The title of the display.
- The title of the section of the display.
- A description of the object, with a photograph or sketch.
- Viewing proposals: how the object is to be displayed.
- Any remedial conservation required before display.
- Any special environmental conditions required while on display.
- Any special security requirements required while on display.
- Overall dimensions of the object when on display. Always use the same conventions, e.g. length × width × height (mm).
- Weight of object.
- Does the object require any special stands or supports and who will supply them?
- Where is the object now kept? Can the designer see it?
- The object's museum accession number.
- A unique number, used just for this project.

Graphic images

- The title of the display.
- The title of the section of the display.
- A description of the graphic image and a photocopy or photograph of any reference material to be used in preparing it. A sketch, however rough, will help to explain what is required.
- A list of any appropriate reference materials.
- A unique number.
- The unique number of the caption that must accompany the graphic image.
- The unique number of any objects or main text with which this graphic should be associated.

Main text

- The title of the display.
- The title of the section of the display.
- The actual text, including any title and sub-titles. The text must be *perfect*: it is not the designer's job to correct mistakes, unless you pay extra! Any corrections later will be *very* expensive. If possible the text should be typed, double-spaced or printed out from your computer printer.
- A unique number.

Captions for photographs and other images

- The title of the display.
- The title of the section of the display.

- The requirements for captions are the same as for main text. But ensure you make clear that these are *captions* – to accompany pictures, drawings, diagrams, maps or other graphic illustrations – not main text or labels.
- The unique number of the graphic to which the caption relates.
- A unique number.

Labels for objects

- The title of the display.
- The title of the section of the display.
- The requirements for labels are the same as for main text and captions. But ensure you make clear that these are *labels* – to accompany original objects, specimens and works of art – not main text or captions for photographs or other images.
- The unique number of the object to which the label refers.
- A unique number.

Audio-visual shows

These need to be treated almost as separate displays, with mini-briefs of their own (see Unit 25). Each producer will have his or her own way of working. However, the main information required will be:

- The title of the display.
- The title of the section of the display.
- Frame, shot or slide number.
- Visual description of shot or slide.
- Voice-over script.
- Special instructions to photographer or cameraperson.

Computer-driven interactives

Like audio-visuals, these need their own mini-briefs, though the design brief must refer to them so that the designer understands their role in the display (see Unit 25). The programmer will need:

- To know what the computer program is aiming to achieve. For example, is it just for fun, or is it intended to teach specific things?
- The text set out in the same format as the exhibition text.
- Illustrations of the graphic images.
- If appropriate, a network diagram of how each page of information relates to all others.

■ CONCLUSION

This Unit is based closely on notes prepared by an experienced museum designer. He concludes:

> Almost every curator I have ever worked with has baulked at the thought of filling out the many different forms which are required at the detailed design stage, with claims of lack of time, lack of resources, lack of patience. However at the end of the job every one has agreed that it has made the process of achieving a good conclusion a great deal easier.

Box 32.1 Choosing a designer

If the museum does not have its own designer, it will be necessary to use one from outside, probably a commercial designer.

The best way to start finding a suitable designer is to ask colleagues in other museums, and to look at as many recent exhibitions and museum displays as possible.

Discuss with other museum managers how well their designers managed the design project as a whole – quality of design, cost control, understanding of conservation needs, time management, quality of ideas, and so on.

Make a short list of designers whose work you like, and either interview them at their offices, or invite them to give a presentation at your museum. If you want them to give their initial ideas on your project you will need to give them the first part of your design brief (but don't expect them to prepare any designs without being paid!). Make sure that all the members of your display team are there, and that the designers send to the presentation the people who will actually be working on your project.

Unit
33

Display and exhibition design and production

Related Units – Units 29–32, 34

The organisation, design and production of a new display or temporary exhibition are complicated. The process is made more complicated by the bewildering variety of technical terms that different writers use, and the fact that most writers are discussing large projects in large museums in Western Europe or North America.

But even the smallest project has to go through the same processes. In a small project, only one or two people may be needed, whereas in a large project hundreds may be required. Whatever the scale of the project, it is still essential to plan the process logically and carefully.

This Unit illustrates the different stages that must be gone through, and the different skills that will be employed.

PLANNING

1   The original display or exhibition idea. Everyone can have good ideas: the difficulty is in persuading the museum authorities to agree and to pay for them!
2   Set up the display or exhibition team. This should ideally include curator, conservator, education specialist, security officer, perhaps administrator and (when appointed) designer. If the exhibition is to be built by the museum's own production staff, the head of production will also be a member. The team will continue to meet until after the exhibition is opened, and will be responsible for all aspects of the project. In small museums, many of these tasks will have to be undertaken by one or two people.
3   Development of the display or exhibition idea:

   - Who is the target audience?
   - What is the aim of the exhibition?
   - What collections will be exhibited?
   - What collecting/conservation work will be needed?
   - What staff will be involved?
   - When will the exhibition open?
   - How much, roughly, will it cost?

4   Permission given to go ahead, at least to next stage.
5   Feasibility study. For a small display or exhibition, this stage may be combined with step 3, but for a larger one it will be a substantial stage on its own. The feasibility study will involve significant study of:

   - the target audience, including front-end evaluation (see Unit 34);
   - the concept and theme;
   - the research required;
   - the collections;
   - the timetable/work plan;
   - the capital cost;
   - the operational cost.

6   Permission given to go ahead!
7   Research. Even the smallest new display or exhibition, if it is to be worthwhile, involves new research. All museum work depends ultimately on the quality of the scholarship that underlies it. But research is the aspect that most often gets cut short; it is vital that sufficient time is allotted to the necessary research in the exhibition planning process (see Unit 30).

8 Design brief drawn up. The design brief, which will be based very closely on the feasibility study, will probably be the most important stage of the whole process (see Unit 32).

9 Fundraising, if necessary.

PRELIMINARY DESIGN

1 Appointment of designer (see Unit 32).

2 Presentation of design brief.

3 Discussion of design brief. There is no substitute for detailed discussions between the designer(s) and the members of the exhibition team. Even in the best design brief, some important things will have been forgotten. However experienced in working with museums, the designer will need to learn a great deal about the subject of the new display if he or she is to do it justice. If (as often happens) the designer is *not* used to working in museums, the museum staff will have to do a lot of educating!

4 Site survey. The designer will obtain all necessary technical details of the site.

5 Preliminary designs. The designer prepares drawings, sketches and diagrams to show his or her initial ideas.

6 More detailed discussions between designer and exhibition team.

7 Formative evaluation. The testing on real visitors of mock-ups of displays (see Unit 34).

8 Costings. Ideas are now sufficiently developed for much more accurate estimates of cost to be made.

9 Work plan approved.

10 Approval. All concerned agree on the general character of the display.

FINAL DESIGN

1 Designer prepares final designs.

2 Conservation programme underway on objects to be displayed.

3 Script writer drafts all text for panels, labels and catalogues.

4 Audio-visual specialists create programmes.

5 The display or exhibition team meets regularly during this phase to monitor progress and to iron out difficulties. As designs develop in their final form, conservator, security officer, fire officer, education officer and curators all ensure that their own concerns and requirements will be met by the finished design. The administrator keeps a close watch on the budget.

6 Final designs presented and agreed by the display or exhibition team and – if necessary – by the museum authorities. This is the second most important stage of the whole process, and is very demanding for the members of the exhibition team. They will each have to check very carefully every aspect of the design and specifications. The education officer must check, for example, that the text can be understood by children and adults, and the objects viewable from a wheelchair. The fire officer must check that the materials specified are fire-resistant and the electrical systems designed to minimise fire risk. The

security officer must check that there are no places for a thief to hide, and that the showcases are secure. The conservator must check that relative humidity will be controlled. The curator must check that the exhibition will achieve what he or she originally wanted it to do.

7 Final text approved.

8 Final choice of objects agreed.

9 Timetable for production and opening date agreed.

CONTRACTS

1 Contracts for work not being done by museum staff are drawn up and put out to tender:

- exhibition construction;
- production of text and graphics;
- production of audio-visual installations and programmes;
- installation of lighting scheme;
- floor covering and other furniture.

2 Designs modified, if necessary, to meet budget.

3 Contracts awarded.

CONSTRUCTION AND INSTALLATION OF DISPLAY OR EXHIBITION

1 Construction and installation of:

- painting;
- exhibition carcass and showcases;
- floor covering;
- lighting;
- text panels and graphics;
- showcase linings and fittings;
- environmental control equipment;
- security installations.

2 Catalogues and other print such as posters, invitations to opening ceremony, information sheets, and education packs are sent for publication.

CASE-DRESSING

1 Case-dressing. This phase, the installation of the objects themselves, is the third most important stage of the whole process. It is extremely important that enough time is allowed for this stage, and that – if the construction phase is delayed – it does not get shortened or hurried. It is a time of great danger for the objects, when breakages and thefts can occur. The curator, conservator and security officer will be chiefly involved.

2 Testing of conservation conditions.

3 Adjustment of lighting and other minor adjustments.

▌ PUBLICITY AND OPENING TO PUBLIC

1 Publicity. The publicity for the new display or exhibition will have been planned from an early stage, and will have been building up in parallel with the development of the display.
2 Appointment and training of any extra warding, interpretation or sales staff required for the new display or exhibition.
3 Press previews and private views arranged.
4 Opening ceremony!
5 Display or exhibition opens to the public.

▌ AFTER THE OPENING

1 Maintenance begins, and the maintenance programme is adjusted in the light of experience.
2 Summative evaluation begins (see Unit 34).
3 All administrative matters completed, bills paid, etc.
4 Display or exhibition team carries out a review of success and failure leading to:
5 Redesign and adjustments. There will inevitably be things that have gone wrong: mistakes shown up by the summative evaluation, maintenance difficulties, and conservation problems. It is important that this is expected from the very beginning of the process, and money and time are set aside to make the necessary corrections.

The work plan – also called the 'critical path' or 'Gantt chart' – shows exactly who should be working on what, and when. For those museums with computers, software is available for work planning purposes. Many activities cannot be started until other activities are completed, so it is very important that everyone involved in the new display or exhibition takes the work plan very seriously, and that if there are delays the work plan is corrected.

Unit
34

Evaluating displays and exhibitions

Related Units – 29–33

'Evaluation' in museums is the technique of measuring the success of museum exhibitions and displays. Museums spend a great deal of time and money in creating and maintaining exhibitions to inform and inspire visitors, but how successful are they? Do visitors go away understanding more than when they came? Can we learn to create more successful exhibitions?

There are three principal types of evaluation, to which specialists have given the terms:

- 'front-end' evaluation (at the beginning);
- 'formative' evaluation (in the middle);
- 'summative' evaluation (at the end).

These clumsy jargon terms have been taken from the literature of educational research. Formal evaluation in museums is developing surprisingly slowly, but the techniques we use now will no doubt seem very crude in years to come.

BEGINNING ('FRONT-END') EVALUATION

Front-end evaluation is carried out before any exhibitions have been produced, or even designed. It is the testing of ideas and proposals for exhibitions, and its purpose is to avoid mistakes by collecting relevant information before the exhibition is designed.

The first step, as always, must be to decide the *purpose* of the exhibition, including whom it is chiefly intended for (see Unit 29). For example, a temporary exhibition on painting may be intended chiefly for people who themselves paint as a hobby, or a museum may arrange an exhibition chiefly to appeal to a local minority group. This is the 'target audience'.

The second step is to find ten to twenty representatives of that target audience, and to discuss in detail with them your ideas for the display. The aim is to find out the needs and interests of the target audience. Their comments will probably change your ideas considerably!

At the same time, discussions can be held with two other groups. The first is the subject experts. Thus if you are preparing an exhibition on seventeenth-century Chinese ceramics, it is very sensible to listen to the views of *other* specialists before your ideas for the exhibition become too firm. If you are planning an exhibition on the history of a town, it is essential to hold detailed talks with a wide variety of groups in that town before ideas for the exhibition become fixed.

Another group with which to discuss your ideas is your fellow professionals. Museum curators, designers, journalists, teachers and advertisers are all specialists in conveying information and ideas to the public. Their suggestions and comments on your ideas may prove very valuable.

MIDDLE ('FORMATIVE') EVALUATION

Formative evaluation is the name given to techniques for testing the effectiveness of exhibitions as they are being produced. The purpose is to try out design ideas and, if they do not work well, to modify them.

The usual way of doing this is to build a mock-up of the exhibition (or part of it), using cheap materials, handwritten text and so on. The mock-up display is then shown to a small sample of visitors (about twenty or thirty), and their reactions are obtained by observing them, by interviewing them in detail and by questionnaires. As comments and criticisms are received, weaknesses discovered and improvements suggested, the mock-up exhibition is modified bit by bit until it seems to be successful.

END ('SUMMATIVE') EVALUATION

Summative evaluation is the type of evaluation study that is carried out on the completed exhibition once it has been built and opened. The aim is to discover whether the exhibition works: whether it actually achieves the aims its designers intended. Every curator likes to think that his or her new exhibition is a success. But the only way to get answers to the questions 'does it work?', 'can it be improved?', 'do people like it?', is to carry out a summative evaluation. There are three main techniques.

The first technique is systematically to *watch* or *track* visitors, and to note the direction they take, and how long they spend in front of each display or showcase. You can then draw a map showing the routes taken by visitors, and a chart of how long individual displays are looked at. These will help show whether the layout of the exhibition is successful and which parts are most popular. The disadvantages of this technique are obvious. First, it may be difficult to watch visitors without them noticing and becoming nervous: some museums have used hidden watchers or even cameras for this reason. Second, you learn nothing of *why* visitors are attracted to one section rather than another.

The second technique is to *interview* a fairly large random sample of visitors. The questions will have to be carefully devised to make sure that they find out the information you need. A number of different approaches are possible:

- to find out what the visitors learned by asking them questions about the exhibitions they have been looking at;
- to ask the visitors which sections they found most interesting or stimulating, and if they can explain why; and
- to ask the visitors what improvements and changes they would suggest.

Summative evaluation techniques are limited in what they can achieve. If the aim of the exhibition was to give the visitor certain pieces of information – for example, to explain the history of a region – then it is comparatively simple to design an evaluation technique that will discover what the visitor has learned.

But it is important to remember that a museum is not a school. Visitors to museums may be seeking inspiration and understanding rather than information.

The techniques must be used sensitively. You can learn from them whether the visitor has acquired extra knowledge, which are the most popular exhibits, whether the display could be better arranged, how much of the text is read and so on. What you cannot learn is whether the exhibition has lit that spark of imagination in one visitor's mind, started a new enthusiasm or opened the door to a new understanding.

> The child who is fascinated by shadows on a wall of the Exploratorium [a Science Centre in San Francisco] as they shift and merge in every colour of the rainbow cannot tell you what he or she has learned. But years later the teacher who explains how colours combine to make white light will find it a little easier, and the student will find it a little less intimidating.
>
> (Tressel 1984)

The third summative evaluation technique is *critical appraisal*. This means simply inviting an outside expert to prepare a detailed critique of the completed exhibition. The value of critical appraisal lies in having a sensitive expert, one who can identify problems applying skills that the museum professional does not have. This approach can be particularly useful when an exhibition that has been in existence for a number of years is due to be modernised. The aim is to learn about the strengths and weaknesses of the exhibition as it stands now so that strengths can be built on and weaknesses overcome when the exhibition is redeveloped.

STUDY EXAMPLE 34.1

A natural history museum was planning an exhibition aimed chiefly at amateur naturalists. Front-end evaluation was intended to find out what the target audience wanted from the exhibition.

At first, the museum curators thought a taxonomic display of specimens would be best. But perhaps, since amateur naturalists normally concentrate on fieldwork, a habitat approach would be more acceptable?

It was decided that a small number of qualitative interviews would be better than a large number of short questionnaires. Fourteen visitors who met the criteria of 'amateur naturalist' were given interviews of between thirty and forty-five minutes each.

None of the visitors interviewed thought that the exhibition should just present specimens in a taxonomic display. Several stressed that they did not want to see butterflies pinned up in rows. So the curators accepted that there was a convincing consensus in favour of a habitat approach, and that is how the exhibition was created.

Front-end evaluation was used here to ensure that the exhibition met the needs of the target market and that resources were effectively used.

STUDY EXAMPLE 34.2

A city museum service was planning a new museum. Called 'The People's Story', it was to be a museum devoted to the lives and work and struggles of the ordinary working people of the city. The question was: how to ensure that the displays really did reflect the lives of the city's people, not just in the distant past, but up to the present day?

The museum staff linked up with an organisation that already ran education programmes in the city. Together they set up a project – called *Memories and Things* – which brought together local history and reminiscence groups from different parts of the city to handle and talk about everyday objects from the past.

The groups met weekly, and members brought in family photographs and objects, which helped stimulate discussion on themes such as budgeting, days out, unemployment, customs, food, living conditions, shopping, and so on. The sessions were all tape-recorded, and the group members were given transcripts of the tapes.

Out of these discussions grew the new museum's displays. Group members agreed on the main themes that should be presented and helped find appropriate objects. The displays used many quotations from group members.

As a result 'The People's Story' reflects the life of the people of the city in a way few museums achieve.

Formative evaluation was used to test the effectiveness of the displays as they were produced.

Unit
35

Information services

Related Units – Unit 37

Museums provide information to their users in a wide variety of ways – through exhibitions, publications, telephone enquiry services, web sites, posters and leaflets, reception desks, identification services, lectures and talk programmes, correspondence and many more.

Information about your museum is also provided by other people outside the museum – tourist information officers, trustees or governors, volunteers and Friends, corporate supporters and visitors. However information is provided by the museum, it is important that it is accurate, clearly presented and communicated, and is in accordance with the museum's mission and communications policy.

Remember that significant numbers of visitors may not be able to read because of factors such as poor education or visual impairment, or because they are unfamiliar with the language in which information is given. We outline a number of ways in which information can be effectively provided by the museum.

RECEPTION DESKS

For the visitor, the museum reception or enquiry desk is often the first point of contact with the museum. Information provided there normally covers the following areas:

- admission charges and discounts;
- times of opening and closing;
- activities allowed or not allowed (e.g. smoking);
- general information about the museum and its collections;
- the range of facilities and their location in the museum;
- the range of services and their availability;
- events and activities programme(s);
- advice on identification procedures for items.

First impressions are important. It is essential that staff at reception desks are appropriately trained to welcome visitors and respond accurately and courteously to their enquiries, in the languages of the principal user groups. It helps staff and visitors if basic information, for example about admission charges, times of opening or closing, regulations about smoking, animals, prams and children's pushchairs and so on, is clearly and logically displayed, preferably using signs and symbols to reduce the number of times the same question is asked.

While basic information about the museum and its collections is best provided in leaflet or publication form, and on interactive screens where possible, visitors may nevertheless welcome the opportunity to talk about the museum and its collections with staff in more detail. User services staff should be trained in the principal languages of their users to provide basic information about the museum and its collections, but refer more detailed enquiries to study centres or curatorial staff.

Printed information about the museum's facilities provided at reception desks needs to be clearly related to the signposting system used in the museum. It is important to guard against printing in an expensive format information that is liable to go out of date. Much better to carry such information on well designed, but cheaper forms of publicity/information material.

Information about events and activities programmes should be provided in a variety of formats targeted at different audiences in order to encourage take-up: leaflets, posters, advertising in newspapers or broadcasting media all help to create a sense of immediacy and vitality for the museum. The reception desk should be conceived of as a key 'point of sale' for the museum.

User services staff at the reception desk should be aware of the range of information about the museum being provided and be fully briefed about any changes to published information or details. It is important that they are trained to be consistent and proactive – recognising opportunities to provide information to visitors and promote events and activities – rather than being simply passive. The reception desk can be effectively used to promote services and facilities, and events and activities programmes, and user services staff should be aware of the important role they have in supporting the museum and its work.

IDENTIFICATION OF OBJECTS

Reception desks are often the first point of contact for visitors bringing items into the museum for identification. Items brought to be seen later by curatorial staff should be recorded on a standard entry form, assigned an entry number, passed to a secure area and processed according to written guidelines developed by curatorial staff (see Unit 49).

Where a visitor is unable to leave an item in the museum for identification/ enquiry, a simple enquiry form should be completed for any later follow-up needed. Visitors with items for identification should be provided with a written report on the item, but not a valuation. It is possible that items that are first brought in as enquiries for identification may be acquired later for the collections. Courteous, prompt, accurate and friendly service can often help to secure items for collections at a later date.

TELEPHONE ENQUIRIES AND CORRESPONDENCE

Museums receive numerous enquiries by telephone or by letter. Staff should be trained to respond effectively in both forms of response. The wider availability of computers is now making it easier to develop standard replies that can be tailored to meet the specific needs of the enquirer. Standardising forms, letters and information sheets about different categories of objects can help to reduce staff time. Be aware, however, that a personalised response to an enquirer can help to develop a long-term relationship between the museum and the enquirer.

INFORMATION AND MARKETING MATERIALS

The leaflet and the poster are perhaps the commonest forms of information vehicle used by museums, although museum web sites are becoming increasingly important as information providers. There is every reason to ensure that marketing materials are well designed and well printed, and carry the museum's logo or brand identity. Good design is not necessarily expensive, and it is often possible to obtain advice on leaflet and poster design and layout from art colleges, schools or design companies at no cost. It is well worth collecting examples of leaflets and posters from other museums and cultural institutions for comparative purposes.

It is critical however not to waste hard-earned resources on marketing materials carrying information about the museum that are not clearly targeted and effectively distributed. As part of the museum's overall communications policy, information is only useful if it is successfully and appropriately communicated to the museum's different market sectors. Distribution patterns of leaflets and posters need to be carefully monitored by the museum and evaluation of the impact of its marketing materials regularly undertaken to ensure value for money.

RESEARCH ENQUIRIES

All museums have to provide information for researchers, whether these are school-children carrying out classroom projects or academics undertaking postgraduate or scholarly research. It is important to ensure that answers are given promptly, and at an appropriate level. Regular enquiries can often be answered through specially prepared information sheets or web-based information, but enquiries can often be time-consuming for museum staff. Well-organised filing systems, museum libraries, databases and information retrieval systems can save valuable staff time. Care also needs to be taken to ensure that the museum is properly acknowledged for any research input that staff make in this way. Museums should be appropriately acknowledged and credited for their contributions to publications and research programmes.

Museum managers should be aware that the forms in which information is provided to visitors and users are a key part of the way in which the museum's brand and reputation are promoted and reinforced. Your museum needs to develop a clear communications policy within which the museum's information services have a defined role.

STUDY EXAMPLE 35.1

One method of tracking the impact of a marketing leaflet is the discount voucher. The leaflet carries a tear-off voucher providing the visitor with a discount on admission or for purchases in the shop or café.

If the print-run of leaflets – say 10,000 – has been numbered sequentially on the discount voucher, and the museum keeps track of where numbered sequences of leaflets have been distributed, it is then possible to monitor the impact of the promotion when visitors hand in their vouchers.

For example if the first 1,000 leaflets have been distributed through tourist information offices, and 250 discount vouchers are returned, then a minimum of one in four visitors received their information through the tourist information offices. If 5,000 leaflets were distributed to schools, and only 100 vouchers are returned then the impact of the leaflet here – translating information into visitation – is much less successful.

Building up knowledge in this way helps to ensure appropriate and cost-effective methods of marketing and promotion are used for the future.

Publications

Unit
36

Related Units – Units 35, 37, 86

Publications based on the museum's collections and produced by or for the museum form an important permanent information resource for visitors/users. They reflect the role of the museum in contributing to knowledge and play an important part in placing the museum's collections in a wider context. Publications may be produced and published by the museum itself, produced by the museum and published by a publishing house for the museum, or produced and published by an independent author and publishing house.

They can take a wide variety of forms, ranging from scholarly catalogues of collections to popular guidebooks, to articles in specialist academic journals to children's activity books. They can also include CDs, audio-tapes, videos and web-based materials that can be downloaded from the museum's web site. The various approaches to be taken will depend on a number of factors, including the following:

- the museum's communications policy;
- funding;
- availability of expertise;
- time;
- market potential;
- marketing and distribution systems.

EXISTING POLICY AND PRACTICE

Publications should reflect the purpose and objectives of the museum. They should conform to the museum's communications policy, and seek to provide information relating to the museum's collections and their context. Museum managers should be careful to ensure that time is not spent by staff on the production of publications that have limited or marginal relevance to the museum and its mission.

Museum managers should also be aware that copyright is now a vital consideration with new international legislation in force.

FINANCES

Developing a range of in-house publications – at whatever level(s) – can be expensive. The museum has to decide whether the necessary investment in research and author time/costs, and design and publication costs, is worthwhile in terms of the rate of return through sales on the capital invested. The museum may decide that a subsidy can be justified in order to make information about its collections more widely available. It may seek sponsorship or grants to help reduce the unit cost or to keep the retail price at a lower level. Whatever the case, it is important to:

- analyse the full costs of publications in advance of commitment;
- consider the real costs of author time required for researching and writing;
- ensure that firm cost quotations for design, typesetting and printing are obtained from relevant individuals/organisations;
- consider additional costs of marketing, distribution, discounts for bulk sales and storage.

EXPERTISE

Writing for publication carries with it substantial responsibility on the part of the author to ensure accuracy. All publication carries with it the need for research. In some cases, this may be extremely time-consuming and complex; in other cases, it is more straightforward.

Commitment to publication carries with it commitment to dedicating sufficient time for research. Whatever the publication – promotional leaflet, guidebook, article, information sheet, web pages, collections catalogue – it is important that museum managers ensure that authors with sufficient and appropriate expertise are employed for research and writing. Editors (who may be the same people as the authors) should be capable of seeing a publication through the full publication process.

Marketing and selling also require expertise. It is of no value to the museum to produce large quantities of publications at great expense if they then languish in store because their market has been poorly researched or too few retail outlets are available to stock them.

TIME

It is easy to underestimate the amount of time needed to produce publications. Research, writing, typescript/word processing, editing, proof-reading, picture research and selection, liaising with designers, typesetters and printers, marketing, publicity, publication launches, stock control and audit, all of these stages and activities represent time, and therefore costs to the museum. It follows that in determining a publications strategy for the museum, the scheduling of publications (as well as their costs) needs careful consideration.

MARKET POTENTIAL

The value of publications is related to their markets. As we noted in Units 5–6, the services that a museum provides must be related to its various market segments. Publications are no different in this respect, and publications should be produced on the basis of the museum's understanding of its markets. The museum's publications policy should seek to service as much of its market as possible. It is important to investigate the marketability of different types of publication by comparing what other museum shops produce and sell, and their prices.

MARKETING AND DISTRIBUTION SYSTEMS

The development of a publications programme for the museum must take into consideration the marketing and distribution systems needed for publications. Do not assume that everyone will beat a path to your door to buy your publications! There is plenty of competition, and the success of the museum's publications will depend on good publicity and promotion within and outside the museum.

Museum publications can be sold through many outlets – not just the museum shop or web site. Mail order is only one method of extending the museum's sales reach. For example, use your existing mailing lists to your supporters' groups as a basis for marketing publications. If the museum is in partnership with a publishing house, the strengths of their marketing team and existing distribution network will be able to support the museum's publications programme.

OTHER PUBLICATIONS

The museum may wish to stock publications produced by other authors/organisations in its shop, on its web site or through its mail order catalogue. The principles outlined earlier should also apply to material bought in for resale.

STUDY EXAMPLE 36.1

A museums service composed of four museums under one management developed a series of attractive information sheets exploring aspects of the area's cultural and natural history. Topics chosen were based on a questionnaire to museum visitors about their particular areas of interest over the period of a year, and a questionnaire distributed to schoolteachers asking about the needs of their syllabus.

Each information sheet was produced to the same format with a standardised heading carrying the museums service's logo. The museums organised a small exhibition and a standard illustrated lecture and workshop on each of the information sheets that could be given by a number of different staff.

The information sheets were printed locally in small print-runs of 200, stock and capital therefore being kept to a minimum. Additional copies were ordered when the stock fell to a specified level. As the series developed, the information sheets became a useful method of providing information to answer questions on topics that were regularly enquired about.

One of the benefits of the series was that it demonstrated the range of expertise within the museum staff. This helped to increase the status and standing of the museums service within the area.

Museum web sites

Unit **37**

Related Units – Units 10, 35

Museums have been quick to respond to the opportunities that the new range of communications technologies have brought to their work. Museums of all types and sizes have established web sites, making use of the World Wide Web to disseminate information about their sites and collections and market their services. Museum web sites have become increasingly innovative and inventive in terms of content and design.

However, information provision is only one aspect of web site provision. Museums have also recognised the enormous potential that the new interactive technologies provide for engaging users with their collections and allowing them to explore them at different levels of engagement in a myriad ways. Museum web sites can now enable users to access and manipulate web-based resources to suit their personal learning and research needs.

At the same time, museums have also recognised that they can create communication channels with individuals and groups to allow them to make a direct contribution to the museum's work. This may be for example through providing research or field data, information about collections or creative products for re-presentation in the museum or on the museum's web site.

The power of web sites is that they extend the reach of even the smallest museum far beyond its normal marketing area and enable people, who may or may not be able to visit it conventionally, to engage with the museum in new and innovative ways. Indeed, many people using a museum's web site for different services, for example web-based temporary exhibitions, on-line shopping, collections research, on-line conferencing or learning resources, may never actually visit the museum in person. Museum web sites therefore have the potential to reach and develop new 'virtual' audiences in parallel with the museum's physical visitors.

However, web site development and management also brings with it important considerations. In professional terms, museums must be concerned not only with questions about how to capture, store and present the virtual, but critically also how to present it in ways that enhance rather than supplant the authority of the real object. Market demand analysis and the identification of audience requirements for web sites must play an important part in considering how virtual museums and services can ensure that they match product to market appropriately.

In terms of museum planning, two main questions need to be answered – *does the museum know what is to be communicated through its web site?* and *how will the museum assess its effectiveness?* These are important questions because they both need to be explored from a number of perspectives. The first question, for example, raises issues around objectives, research and prioritisation. The second question raises issues around design, access and evaluation.

The 'virtual museum' is opening up a rich seam of new thinking in museum work – thinking about the nature of authenticity, approaches to the presentation and interpretation of collections and associated information, accessibility in physical, intellectual and cultural terms, and empowerment of the individual visitor.

In developing a web site, the museum should take professional advice on its design and management and consider carefully how it will be maintained for the long term. Web sites that are not effectively designed and maintained and become out of date are of little value and can damage rather than enhance a museum's reputation.

AIMS

The aims of a virtual museum fall into two main areas. During the development (or redevelopment) of a museum, the aims of the virtual museum or web site will be to:

- ensure that the mission and objectives of the museum are clearly explained and described for the visitor and user;
- reinforce the brand identity of the museum;
- enhance potential visitors' understanding of the museum by providing virtual 'surrogate' visit experiences;
- help potential visitors and the community keep up to date with the museum's progress;
- provide a community forum for the generation, discussion and exchange of ideas relating to the development, content and future use of the museum, thereby creating a sense of participation and ownership;
- serve as an effective marketing tool for the museum, helping create a committed user and visitor base in advance of the opening date.

At the time of the opening of the museum and beyond, the aims of the virtual museum or web site will be to:

- continue all of the above functions, but with the emphasis on complementing the actual visit experience rather than providing surrogate experiences;
- exploit and provide access to the results of development projects currently being undertaken to create digital content;
- establish the site as a provider of unique, high-quality content and integrate it into the resources being developed by the museum in its particular subject areas;
- develop additional 'layers of access' designed to create high-quality, lifelong learning resources and a reliable source of formal education resources;
- provide links to international gateways (e.g. ICOM) and local and regional tourist sites.

Public relations and the media

Related Units – Units 10, 39

The museum's status and standing in the eyes of the public depend on a number of factors both in and outside your control. Managing the relationship between the museum and its public is critical to success (see Unit 7). How can this be successfully achieved?

In all relations with the public – direct and indirect – it is important to promote a positive image of the museum based on success and achievement in the different aspects of its work. This is the museum's reputation. Contact comes in a variety of ways, some of which we have explored in units elsewhere in this book. They include:

- reception services;
- retail outlets;
- displays;
- exhibitions;
- visitor facilities;
- education services;
- information services;
- advisory and consulting services;
- web sites;
- publications;
- identification services;
- buildings;
- events and activities programmes;
- marketing materials.

Success in managing the museum's reputation with individuals and groups coming into contact with the museum depends on care and attention to detail. All museums need a strong brand identity that is reinforced through the museum's products and services and that reflects the museum's mission. A brand identity or logo is a recognition signal, but the true identity of a museum is in its personality and character. These are forged out of a number of factors:

- the quality of the services the museum provides;
- the quality of the relationships it has with its public;
- the understanding and appreciation on the part of the museum's staff of the importance of first-class public relations; and
- what makes your museum unique from the next, its collections.

Building a museum's reputation has to be worked at, and reputation has to be earned. Bad publicity or poor experience on the part of the museum's visitors or users can damage the museum's reputation sometimes out of all proportion to the event itself. Contrary to popular wisdom, all publicity is not good publicity. *All* staff have to be involved in building a museum's reputation. Museum managers have therefore a key role in ensuring that staff are trained to build a good relationship with the museum's public in all its forms.

The most effective form of publicity is good word-of-mouth publicity. A satisfied user is infinitely preferable to a dissatisfied user who can damage your museum's reputation without your knowledge.

Satisfied users are your best advertising agents.

THE MEDIA

The news and broadcasting media have an important part to play in helping a museum develop its reputation. News or features stories about the museum can reach substantial numbers of readers. It is however important to remember that the museum does not have control over what journalists write. Their role is to sell news, not to promote your museum. It is therefore useful to develop good working relationships with the news and broadcasting media so that mutual understanding of each other's requirements is created. Careful programming and scheduling of press and media information about the museum's work can be a positive help in building the museum's reputation.

Press releases, photocalls, interviews with journalists, staff appearances on radio and television, should all seek to emphasise positive success and achievement out of the museum's policies and programmes.

Collect and file copies of the museum's press coverage and circulate these to your staff and governing committees for them to read. Many museums have a noticeboard in public areas with news items about their work are pinned up and changed on a regular basis. Make news coverage work for you in building good public relations.

The museum's staff should be alert to the opportunities for good news coverage. So ask all staff to contribute their ideas for news stories on a regular basis and give individuals the opportunity to 'front' a news story if they have been responsible for the idea.

CHECKLIST FOR PRESS/RADIO/TELEVISION RELEASES

- Think of the person at the receiving end of the release.
- Make the release easy to read and handle.
- Use the best paper available, ideally good-quality white paper, in the standard typing paper size used in your country.
- The letterhead should include the name, address, telephone, e-mail and fax number, the museum's web site address and the museum's logo.
- Head the release 'News', 'Press Information' or 'Information'.
- Ensure you include the date and time of the release.

- Use one side of the page.
- Leave wide margins.
- Type the text using double-spacing.
- Staple papers together; do not use pins or paper clips.
- At the end of each page write 'MORE' or 'MORE FOLLOWS'.
- At the end of the release write 'ENDS'.
- Add 'For further information, contact . . .' and include one or two contacts with their addresses, daytime and evening telephone numbers, and e-mail addresses.
- Fold the release outwards with the heading of the release showing in the envelope.
- Make the heading of the release short and to the point.
- Make the first paragraph of the release the most important.
- Remember the five W's: What? Who? Where? When? Why?
- What's happening? Who's doing it? Where is it happening? When is it happening? Why is it happening?
- In subsequent paragraphs, expand on the introduction.
- Give more detail in descending order of importance.
- Concentrate on facts; do not use superlatives.
- Keep the release to two or three pages at maximum.
- Use direct reported speech in quotation marks to add a personal note to the story.
- Remember the media are always looking for absolutes – first, last, smallest, oldest, etc.
- Keep your style clear, digestible, terse and economical.
- Keep sentences short and avoid jargon. Explain any unusual words.
- Be positive.
- Time the release to suit your most important outlets.
- Follow up the release with a telephone call or e-mail to selected media if you need to add extra emphasis.
- Be ready to respond appropriately to requests for comments, interviews, photographs or film coverage.

▊ STUDY EXAMPLE 38.1

A museum with a particularly large collection of local photographs needed help to identify the individuals shown in a number of group photographs. Discussions with the editor of one of the local newspapers led to the paper featuring one photograph each week over a two-year period, and inviting readers to write in with any identifications/information about the individuals and locations featured in the photographs.

In this way, the museum mobilised a very large number of people to help it in its work – far larger than the number of its visitors; raised interest in

continued

the museum's photographic collections; encouraged new donations (of which there were many); and developed a significant audience for a range of photographic exhibitions it later mounted from this work. The newspaper had gained an easy source of interest – and hence sales – for its readers.

The museum had established a mutually beneficial partnership with the news media that then led to further joint projects.

Unit 39

Working with Friends' and membership groups

Related Units – Units 7–10, 38

No museum is an island. All museums have to work with other organisations in a variety of ways. These may include other museums or museum organisations, tourist organisations, educational organisations, special interest societies and clubs, groups with special needs, hospitals, arts organisations, learned societies, businesses – the list is endless. The value of working with other organisations is that of mutual benefit and developing and maintaining partnerships is an important and essential part of museum work.

Co-operation and collaboration with other organisations on programmes or projects can represent a valuable method of achieving results that might not be possible by the museum working in isolation. Few museums in the world are able to have access to all the resources that they would like in order to carry out their work. Museums therefore have to seek out active partners to progress their forward planning and development programmes.

In dealing with organisations outside the museum, professional standards should be observed at all times. We have seen in Unit 38 that the museum's reputation depends to a large extent on how people perceive and experience the museum. Working formally with organisations carries with it even greater responsibility than dealing with individuals. Organisational relationships can often be stronger and longer lasting. In all dealings with external organisations, the museum should seek to provide a high quality and professional service, emphasise the positive aspects of the museum's work and build up support for the museum in as broad a sense as possible (see Unit 10).

Where formal co-operation occurs, for example on a joint exhibition or field project, it is sensible to ensure that formal agreement is reached on the respective roles and responsibilities of the parties. It is helpful to put such agreements in writing, or if necessary in contractual terms, so that responsibilities are clearly defined, and results appropriately acknowledged. Lack of clarity can lead to confusion and upset, and damage to relationships can easily occur. This is true for all forms of relationship that a museum has with outside bodies such as project partners, sponsors or funding bodies as well as with contractors such as designers and architects.

Where the museum is providing services on behalf of a funding body, for example a local authority or a government agency, it is useful to draw up a Service Level Agreement identifying the nature and extent of the services that the museum will provide for the funding body's investment. In this way, it is possible for the museum to demonstrate how it is meeting the funding body's requirements and expectations and providing it with high-quality services and good value for money in return for its financial support.

SUPPORTERS' GROUPS

Supporters' groups can take different forms. Here we discuss Friends' organisations and volunteer groups.

The key difference between Friends' organisations and volunteer groups lies in the type of support they each provide. While volunteers provide practical, 'hands-on' support – work *in the museum*, Friends' organisations provide support in kind – work *for the museum*. Both can be invaluable in their contribution to the museum's work, provided that their aims and objectives are clear and their work adds value to that of the museum.

FRIENDS' ORGANISATIONS AND MEMBERSHIP PROGRAMMES

A Friends' organisation helps to create public interest in the museum by supporting it financially and politically. For example, Friends' organisations may provide funds for new acquisitions or conservation programmes, host social occasions or fund temporary exhibitions. They represent an important constituency of dedicated support that continues from year to year.

However, a museum should guard against its Friends' organisation becoming an exclusive club or clique. It should ideally reflect all sections of the community and be as socially inclusive as possible.

The sort of benefits that Friends may derive from their membership of a Friends' organisation include:

- social events and activities organised for their benefit;
- informal educational events and activities, e.g. lectures and study visits;
- discounts on publications or events;
- free tickets for exhibition previews;
- a dedicated newsletter or journal;
- a special area or room in the museum; and
- a sense of participation in and contribution to the life of the museum.

Friends' organisations need to be established on a formal footing. They require a formal constitution and clear lines of accountability for finances, marketing, etc. Some Friends will wish to become more actively involved in aspects of the museum's work and may also work as volunteers.

Internationally, Friends' organisations play an increasingly important part in museums of all sizes and all types. Information and assistance on establishing a group can be obtained from the World Federation of Friends of Museums (see Unit 100). It is well worth considering establishing such a group, but advice should be taken first to ensure that it is set up on appropriate lines.

VOLUNTEER GROUPS

Volunteer groups can provide helpful support to professional museum staff. Volunteers should not be thought of as a substitute for paid staff; their work should complement, not duplicate, that of paid staff. Volunteers can bring many skills and wide-ranging expertise and experience to a museum. It is important, however, that volunteers are carefully selected and trained for their duties, and that museum management provides clear line management and job descriptions for them. Volunteers should be carefully briefed on their role and responsibilities and should only work under formal supervision within the museum's policy framework. Their involvement with the museum should be decided as a matter of policy by the museum's governing body.

In museums with paid staff, it is inappropriate for volunteers to undertake core responsibilities such as entry documentation or security. Alternative tasks should be found for them. Remember, however, that volunteers are giving their time free to the museum; they should be afforded every courtesy, made to feel welcome in the museum and appropriately thanked for their support. Volunteers should also understand how their work relates to the museum's forward planning, and it is necessary that progress on their work and that of the museum should be reported to them on a regular basis (see Unit 89).

STUDY EXAMPLE 39.1

A museum with an active Friends' organisation established a Fund for Conservation through the Friends' fundraising events. The Fund was able to attract additional matching grants for specific conservation projects from government agencies and private-sector sponsorship.

At the end of a five-year period, a major exhibition was mounted to demonstrate the value of the Friends' support for a wide range of conservation projects, both preventive and remedial. The information presented was reused as the basis of a display illustrating the role of the museum in caring for its collections.

The new display allowed the museum to focus on a key aspect of its responsibilities and the museum was able to explain the conservation process as well as the end product. The display encouraged visitors to give additional donations to its Fund for Conservation for further projects.

The overall project involved both its Friends and its visitors in an important aspect of museum work that is often carried out behind the scenes and rarely given enough attention in museum galleries.

Without the Friends' support, the museum would not have had sufficient funds to meet its responsibilities for the care of its collections.

Unit
40 # Researchers as users

Related Units – Units 30, 50

Research on the museum's collections helps to provide new information about those collections for many different types of museum user – from the specialist scholar to the schoolchild undertaking a project, from the university research student to the general visitor – whether they are engaging with the museum on-site or off-site, through published work or the broadcast media or on-line.

One of the fundamental tasks of all museums, large or small, is to add to knowledge by undertaking or facilitating research. This may be directly through field and research programmes undertaken by or led by staff and made available through publications on aspects of the museum's collections, through papers on the museum's collections and programmes given to conferences or through web sites. Museum managers should help and encourage their staff to undertake research on their collections and publish or make available their findings, wherever possible.

Museum managers should also facilitate research on their collections by others from outside the museum (see Unit 50). This may be done on a proactive or reactive basis.

For example, a museum may have an important coin collection, but no specialist numismatists on the museum's staff to research the collection. An invitation to an appropriate specialist, perhaps from a national or university museum, to review the collection and provide a report and guidance for its future care and management would provide the museum with a useful basis for the future. At the same time, opportunities to publish the collection or parts of it could be discussed. Such a proactive approach enables the museum staff to identify those parts of their overall collections that require external assessment and ensures that they deepen their understanding of the significance of their collections.

Museums also have to react to external requests to undertake research on their collections. Such research may provide valuable new insights into aspects of the collections and allow the museum to extend the range of information about the collections that it can make available to its visitors and users. The museum should however take especial care with requests of this type and ensure that the bona fides of researchers are fully established and cross-checked for security reasons before they are allowed direct access to collections for purposes of research (see Unit 67–8).

Depending on the museum's resources, researchers should be provided with appropriate facilities to undertake research, especially where this requires handling original material. Every care needs to be taken to ensure that appropriate handling procedures are employed and access to collections is suitably monitored and controlled by curatorial staff (see Unit 68).

The museum should require the researcher to provide a copy of any written material arising from their work for reference purposes, e.g. publications, doctoral thesis. Opportunities now exist to disseminate research findings more widely than ever before through the new communications technologies. These are enabling museums to make data about their collections more generally available and in turn encouraging other research programmes to include this information.

STUDY EXAMPLE 40.1

An important collection of coins was donated to a museum as part of a bequest, including early coinage that had been minted locally. The importance of the gift enabled the museum to raise funds for a specialist research programme to be undertaken to study and catalogue the collection, and subsequently for the development of a specially designed coin gallery to house the collection. As a consequence of the research programme, a series of detailed catalogues were published jointly with the museum and these were then used to inform the interpretation of the coins on display in the gallery and support a series of associated formal and informal education programmes.

In this case, research was used on a number of levels to inform different audiences of the significance of the collection.

Section 3
The development and care of the museum's collections

Unit

41

Types of collections

Related Units – Units 2–3, 42–8

The history of collecting and the formation and management of collections is a fascinating and complex field of study. Collections have been formed in countries throughout the world for many centuries, and collecting as a human endeavour takes place for many reasons in and outside of museums. It is possible, however, to detect general underlying trends in collecting at different periods, and to analyse collecting in a variety of ways.

Understanding the history and nature of collecting, and change and continuity in attitudes to collections, is an important aspect of museum work. Museum directors should be well versed in the history of collections formation in their own museum, and how in this respect their museum fits into a more general context of collecting. (Past collecting – perhaps during a different political regime or just under outdated ideas – may today seem very wrong. But it is still part of human history, and the museum has a duty to preserve and record past policies.)

Here we examine collections in four ways – by intellectual rationale, by method of acquisition, by discipline and by material categories.

■ INTELLECTUAL RATIONALE

People have developed and used collections through time and space for many reasons and for personal as well as public benefit. Private collections have been built up for reasons of social or political status, for academic or scientific interest, for commercial benefit and for personal 'hobbyist' interest. In many cases, personal collections that have been developed out of a particular interest are ultimately acquired in whole or in part by museums. In some cases, museums are built specifically to accommodate personal collections and serve as memorials to their collectors.

Collections may be developed in a haphazard way, based on the souvenir or 'curiosity' approach to collecting where items hold personal interest and meaning for the collector. They may be based on a 'fetishist' approach to collecting, where the collector is concerned to acquire many examples of similar artefacts or natural history specimens. They may be 'organised' collections where they are used to demonstrate or illustrate a particular intellectual argument or standpoint. They may be based on 'systematic' collecting in which collections are built up in a comprehensive way based on sound disciplinary approaches.

Whatever intellectual rationale underlies collecting, collecting in its widest sense is a powerful human trait, which has greatly influenced the development and philosophy of museums and their work. Collecting and disposal policies for museums reflect more general attitudes to collecting, and this has been true since museums began to be developed.

METHOD OF ACQUISITION

Museums acquire material for their collections in a variety of ways, which are described in greater detail in Units 42–8. We describe five main ways here – by donation, by purchase, by field-collecting, by exchange and by loan:

1   Many museum collections have been built up almost exclusively on the basis of donations. Donations take different forms and can vary in scale and importance. Items may be brought into the museum for identification and then offered to the museum, or may be left as bequests. In many cases, major collections have been left to public museums as bequests by private collectors (see Unit 44).
2   Opportunities to purchase items will be constrained by available finance for most museums. Purchase normally takes place to complement existing collections (see Unit 44).
3   Field-collecting as part of a defined research programme allows for a systematic approach to collecting in line with the museum's overall collecting policy (see Unit 45). It is essentially a proactive approach to collecting, rather than the responsive approach to collecting that characterises donations and purchases.
4   Exchange of items or collections between museums is another method of collections development. Here collections are transferred to or exchanged with museums that can provide appropriate resources and skills to look after them (see Units 44 and 51).
5   Loans are a method of providing the public with an opportunity to see material in public or private collections that may not otherwise be accessible to the museum's users (see Unit 44).

However, collections are built up over time, the museum has a responsibility to collect in the context of a defined collecting policy. It is the collecting policy that provides the framework within which collections are developed and acquired (see Units 42–3).

DISCIPLINE

Collections can also be analysed by subject or discipline. Museum collections have been traditionally divided into a range of disciplines such as archaeology and anthropology, natural sciences, fine art, decorative arts, social history or technology. Such disciplines reflect academic training and approaches to the subject, and structures within higher education.

Collections analysed in this way may restrict opportunities for more interdisciplinary presentation and interpretation in displays and exhibitions. The opportunities to use collections in a variety of ways and to view them from different standpoints can be lost through compartmentalisation. While academic study of collections using techniques appropriate for each discipline is necessary, it should not preclude alternative ways of using and interpreting collections for the public.

MATERIAL CATEGORIES

Collections can also be analysed in terms of the material of which they are composed, such as stone, wood, feathers, leather, bone, ceramics or metals. All organic and inorganic materials have different requirements in terms of collections management and preventive conservation (see Unit 55). It follows that collections may be housed or stored by material category, even though they may fall within different subject disciplines. They may also be displayed by material category in cross-disciplinary displays or exhibitions.

Understanding the nature of collecting, its historical development and its impact on museum development is an important requirement for museum staff. It provides a context within which to view your museum's collections and the history of their development. It gives insights into the changing ways in which people have used and presented collections in museums, and above all makes people think about and question the approaches they use in their work. Museums can no longer claim to be the only source of knowledge, meaning or understanding about collections. They do, however, represent a significant body of expertise in the formation and use of collections. They can help users explore collections in many different ways and a good understanding of types of collections and their development is a valuable and necessary basis for their work.

Unit

Policies for collecting

Related Units – Units 44–51

What should we collect? That is probably the most important question any museum has to decide; every aspect of the museum's work will be affected by the museum's collecting policy.

Every museum should have a written collecting policy formally agreed by its governing body. This written policy will be part of the museum's collections management policy and its forward plan that sets out the museum's intentions for all aspects of its work (see Unit 81).

What should be in it? The collecting policy should include the following points:

- *What will the museum collect?* This should describe in some detail the areas in which the museum intends to collect. For a large general museum this will be quite a long, complicated description; it should always be sufficiently detailed to enable a curator to decide whether or not to acquire an object.
- *Where will the museum collect?* A regional museum will probably collect only items relating to its region, and mostly in the region itself. An art gallery,

however, may buy paintings or accept donations from many different countries. A natural history museum may send expeditions to research and collect in biologically interesting parts of the world.

- *How will the museum collect?* Will it collect through fieldwork? Will it purchase objects? Will it actively encourage members of the public to donate or bequeath things to it? Will it accept items on long loan? All these are policy decisions.
- *Why does the museum collect in these fields?* The collecting policy should explain why the museum collects particular groups or collects in particular areas. It should clearly justify the museum's collecting policy, explaining how it fits into the museum's overall policy, and describing the historical collections held by the museum.
- *When, or in what circumstances, would the museum consider disposing of items?* It is very important to ensure that no curator ever disposes of anything from the museum collection without strictly following the written procedure approved by the museum's governing body and set down in its collecting and disposal policy.

The *What* section should set out clearly the restrictions on collecting imposed by both law and ethics. Many of these restrictions will be peculiar to the country or even the museum concerned, but every museum should include in its collecting policy the principles set out in ICOM's *Code of Ethics for Museums* (see Unit 6). Some of the most important are:

- Objects or specimens will be acquired only if the museum is satisfied it can obtain valid title.
- The museum will not acquire objects where their recovery may have involved the unauthorised, unscientific or intentional destruction or damage of monuments, archaeological or geological sites, or species and natural habitats.
- Collections of human remains and material of sacred significance will be acquired only if they can be housed securely and cared for respectfully.
- The museums will not acquire biological or geological specimens that have been collected, sold or otherwise transferred in contravention of local, national, regional or international law or treaty relating to wildlife protection or natural history conservation.
- Every effort must be made before acquisition to ensure that the object has not been illegally transferred from another country.

The collecting policy may be a quite brief document, or it may be highly detailed; each museum should decide what it needs. Some museums have two documents: a brief policy that is formally approved by the museum's governing body, and a much more detailed version to be used by the museum staff. The policy should be reviewed on a regular basis in the light of the success of the museum's collecting programme.

Policies for disposal

Related Units – Units 6, 42

When a museum acquires an object – whether by purchase, donation or fieldwork – it acquires it in order to preserve it forever for the benefit of the public.

Even so, there are reasons why a museum might want to get rid of an object, and some of these are good reasons and some are bad:

• *because the object has decayed so badly that it is now quite useless.*
Are you *sure* it is useless? There are many examples of important scientific collections being destroyed by people who did not understand their value. Such a decision should never be taken without consulting at least two specialists.

• *because it has been discovered to be a fake, or was wrongly identified.*
But it may still be of interest and importance: many fakes have played an important part in art history, and comparing real and false will help future curators to learn. And if an object can be wrongly identified once, perhaps it can twice. Every museum contains examples of objects whose importance has been realised long after they came to the museum.

• *because it does not fit into the museum's collecting policy.*
At first sight, this seems a very good reason for disposal, but beware! However hard we try to be rational and to be good planners, the fact is that collecting policies are influenced by fashion. In the 1960s many British museums, which used to try to collect everything, adopted policies of collecting only items of local and regional interest. Now they deeply regret disposing of foreign ethnographical material, which could illuminate the connections of their regions with foreign countries, or illustrate the cultural background of immigrant communities.

• *in order to sell it, and buy a better example.*
This is a very dangerous practice indeed, and is contrary to the principles that govern museums throughout the world; only a few large North American art museums regularly try to build up their collections by selling and buying. The practice is dangerous because it betrays the trust of those members of the public who give objects to museums, and because we can never be sure that our judgement will be approved by our successors. Many of the most treasured objects in museums today were once regarded as worthless.

• *in order to make an exchange with another museum.*
Exchange is full of dangers, for the reasons given above, but at least it ensures that the object remains in a public museum.

- *because the museum already has many examples of this object.*

This is sometimes a strong argument for disposing of an object, especially where the other examples are in better condition, or have more information associated with them. But it is still open to the criticism that donors may feel betrayed, and the danger that information relating to that object may turn up. Duplicates may, however, be used for different interpretative purposes; for example in handling boxes or loan boxes for School Loan Services.

- *because the museum is ordered by state authorities to do so.*

There are sadly many examples, from all sorts of regimes, of museums being ordered by state authorities to surrender objects so that they can be given as presents to visiting dignitaries, or (for example) used to decorate a presidential palace. In such a situation there is little the museum can do to resist: really this is not so much disposal as theft.

- *in order to return the object to its country or people or region of origin.*

Campaigns for cultural restitution have resulted in many museums returning to their country of origin items of special significance to that country. A number of museums, too, have returned human bones or religious items to groups to whom they are deeply significant. This is an area of intense debate (see Unit 51).

There are two aspects to disposal: *law* and *ethics*. All museums are of course subject to the law of their countries. In many countries whether a museum can sell, exchange, destroy or give away objects from its collections is controlled by law: either the general law that applies to all public bodies, or specific laws that govern museums or one particular museum. It is the responsibility of every museum manager – curators, administrators and members of governing bodies – to ensure that they are familiar with the laws that apply to their museum, and to ensure that those laws are obeyed.

So far as the ethics of disposal are concerned, there is general agreement among museum workers worldwide that the principal function of a museum is to acquire objects and specimens for the public benefit and to keep them for posterity. There must be a strong presumption against the disposal of any items in the collection of a museum. Very occasionally, however, disposal is the right thing to do. In that case:

- Any object being considered for disposal must be considered by at least two curators, one of whom should be from another museum, and their views should be given to the museum's governing body. Contact with a second curator may need to be made by post or email.
- Any decision to dispose of an object must be made by the governing body of the museum and the curator, not by either alone.
- Any donor, or anyone who contributed to the purchase of the object, must be – wherever possible – consulted.
- When the decision to dispose has been made, the object should be offered, by gift (preferably), sale or exchange, to other museums. Usually an announcement will be made in whatever journal or newsletter is most widely read in the country's museums.

- Complete records must be kept of disposals and the objects involved.
- Any monies made from sale of objects must be used solely for the purpose of buying new objects for the collections. They should not be used for offsetting operating or capital expenditure.
- Museum personnel, the governing body, or their families or close associates, should never be permitted to purchase objects from a collection for which they are responsible.

Of course, a curator of an open-air museum of farming faced with a pile of rotting wooden tools may find it hard to take such a lengthy, complicated and formal procedure seriously. How much easier simply to wait until the museum is closed and set fire to the pile – end of problem! But that is exactly how many of the most important collections in our museums have disappeared. It is a betrayal of the trust that society places in its museums and their curators.

The best way of ensuring that a formal procedure for disposal is taken seriously is for the museum's governing body to adopt a formal disposal policy, incorporating the points listed earlier. Such a procedure is set out in ICOM's *Code of Ethics for Museums* (see Unit 6). All museum governing bodies should formally adopt the relevant parts of this Code, and all museum workers should follow it.

Unit 44

Donations, purchases and loans

Related Units – 42–3, 45–50

The development of a museum's collections needs to take place in a systematic way, with appropriate documentation procedures. Acquisitions may be through donations by members of the public, purchases by the museum, or loans for different periods of time.

Here is a checklist of steps that need to be carried out in acquiring objects for the museum through these three methods.

DONATIONS

1 The museum hears about the offer of a donation. A note is made on an Offer Card (see Box 44.1).
2 The offer is investigated. The manager responsible for the collection speaks to the prospective donor, arranges to inspect the object and records the offer on the Offer Card.

3 The object is examined. The museum manager examines the object, and records all the information available about it (see Box 44.2).

4 The object is checked against the museum's collecting policy. Does it fall within the museum's collecting area? Are resources available to care for and use it? Does it contravene any ethical constraints (see Units 6, 42 and 51)?

5 Formal acceptance or refusal. Whoever is responsible for taking decisions on accepting objects formally decides, in the light of the collecting policy and the existing collections, whether to accept the object. Normally such decisions are the responsibility of the manager of the collection concerned. If the offer is to be refused, the donor must be thanked, usually both in person and by letter; refusing a gift tactfully is often the most difficult job in museum work! A manager may wish to suggest another museum to which the item could be offered.

6 Taking possession. The point at which the museum takes possession of the object may be the last opportunity to gather information about it from the donor.

7 Thank-you letter. The writing of a formal letter of thanks to donors should be a normal part of the acquisitions procedure of the museum. It may be helpful to explain in the letter that an object acquired may not necessarily be placed on display but will be used by the museum for a variety of purposes. This avoids disappointment if the donor visits the museum at a later date expecting to see their object on display only to find that it is in store.

8 Entry documentation. The entry documentation for the object is completed (see Unit 49).

9 Inspection and treatment/conservation. Any necessary preliminary treatment, for example for insect or fungal infestation, and any remedial conservation, is carried out.

Box 44.1 The Offer Card

The Offer Card is a system of recording objects known to the museum that *might* come into its collections. Whatever system is chosen, it is important to have a method of recording objects when they are first heard about, and that will record contacts with their owners until they are given, lent or sold to the museum.

A simple system consists of cards of a distinctive colour kept in a file that ensures that they are checked through at regular intervals.

The Offer Card should be kept very simple, but should include:

- name of object;
- name and address of owner;
- name and address of contact;
- where object is now;
- nature of offer: gift/loan/sale;
- dates of contacts.

A simple computer database would work in just the same way.

Box 44.2 Recording information with objects

Social history and ethnography collections have little use or significance if their objects are not accompanied by information on where they came from, how they were used, who used them, their role in the value-systems of their society and so on.

Yet when museums acquire objects, they too often miss the unique opportunity to ask the right questions to record this information. Here is a list of the questions the curator could ask when talking to the donor, lender or vendor of an object being acquired for the museum.

Name

- What do you call the object?
- What did the maker call the object?
- Do you know any other names for it?

Materials

- What is the object made of?
- Where did the materials come from originally?
- How did the maker obtain them?

Manufacture

- When (as nearly as possible) was it made? How do you know?
- Where was it made?
- Who made it? Please give the maker's name, address, occupation, age.
- In what circumstances did he/she make it (e.g. in his/her workshop, in his/her spare time, at home)?
- Can you describe briefly how, and with what tools, it was made?

History

- Who was it made for originally?
- Did the maker sell it to them? How much for?
- Did they resell it? How much for?
- Were many such objects made by the maker, or by other local makers?
- Please can you list the successive owners, and how each obtained it?

Use

- How was the object originally used?
- Who was it used by?
- Was it used regularly, or occasionally?
- Where was it generally kept?
- When was it last used?
- Has it been used for any other purpose?

Box 44.2 continued

Description

- Has the object been altered at any time? Is it broken?
- Are there any parts missing?
- In what colours was it originally painted?
- Does the object bear any name, initials, numbers or symbols? Can you explain them?

The donor

- Please give your name, address, occupation and age.
- May we contact you by telephone or e-mail?
- How did you acquire the object?
- What is your relationship, if any, to the object's maker or user?
- What is your relationship, if any, to the subsequent owners?

Documentation

- Have you any photos or drawings showing this or a similar object, or of the makers or owners?
- Have you any documents or papers – letter, deeds, accounts, notebooks, etc. – relating to the object, its maker or owners?

The object now goes to be accessioned, and then goes into store or on display. Temporary displays of recently acquired objects are an effective way of saying thank-you to the donor and also encouraging other donations to be made to the museum.

PURCHASES

1   The museum hears about the object. Whoever first hears about the object completes an Offer Card (see Box 44.1).
2   The object is examined. The museum manager responsible for the collection examines the object, and records all the information available about it (see Box 44.2).
3   The object is checked against the museum's approved collecting policy. Does it fall within the museum's collecting area? Are resources available to care for and use it? Does it contravene any ethical constraints (see Units 6, 42 and 51)?
4   A price is negotiated. In negotiating a price with the vendor, it is important to remember the ethical considerations involved.
5   Decision on purchase. Whoever has authority to purchase objects (usually the manager up to a certain price, and the governing body above that) decides both whether the object is appropriate to the museum's collections, and whether the price is right.

6 Fundraising. For more expensive acquisitions, many museums will have to raise the necessary funds from a public appeal or other type of fundraising campaign (see Unit 87).

7 Purchase made. The sale is formally agreed between vendor and museum. When the sale is made by auction, the auctioneer's standard conditions of sale apply.

8 Taking possession. This may be another opportunity to find out more information about it from the person selling it to the museum (see Box 44.2).

9 Payment. Payment is made.

10 Documentation. The entry documentation for the object is completed (see Unit 49).

11 Inspection and treatment/conservation. Any necessary preliminary treatment, for example for insect or fungal infestation, and any first-aid conservation, is carried out.

The object now goes to be accessioned, and then goes into store or onto display.

LOANS

The procedure for loans should be the same as that for donations. Too often museums accept items on loan much more readily and informally than they accept donations. This is a mistake, because the museum can become responsible for an embarrassing number of loans that it does not really need, but that it has the cost and responsibility of looking after. Loans should be for a finite period of time and for a specific purpose, for example a temporary exhibition. Long-term loans should be avoided.

Agreement must be reached between lender and museum, *before* the object is collected, on all aspects of the insurance. These will include who is responsible for insuring, the sum insured for and the risks covered. The arrangements for the loan, how long it is for and any conditions, must be carefully set out in the Loan In Form completed as part of the entry documentation (see Unit 49).

Unit **45**

Collecting and field documentation

Related Units – Units 41–4, 46–50

COLLECTING

Museum collecting, to be successful, must be *systematic* and *active*. It is not enough to draw up an impressive collecting policy and then to sit back and do nothing: every museum should also draw up an active collecting *programme* so that the policy can be implemented.

This collecting programme should not be overly ambitious, but it must not be so vague that no-one takes any notice of it. Too often museums leave collecting and fieldwork to the initiative of individual managers. The enthusiastic managers spend a great deal of time out of the museum, perhaps neglecting their other duties such as documentation and display. The less enthusiastic ones find all their time taken up inside the museum, and the result is a static collection. Most museums can find evidence of both faults somewhere in their history. There may have been periods when a great deal was collected and a backlog of documentation was allowed to build up, and periods when nothing seems to have been collected. Good museum managers will ensure that their museum carries out a collecting programme that actively implements its formal collecting policy.

In drawing up such a programme, the museum will consider what *staff time* and *money* are available for collecting. Who will be involved in the collecting programme, and how much time can they devote to it? Are funds available to meet the programme's costs? It is easy to forget, when considering an acquisition, the cost that one is demanding that future generations pay to look after it. The programme must be realistic, otherwise it will soon fail.

Then the museum must identify the *gaps* in its collections. The collecting policy will have identified the broad areas in which the museum needs to collect, but within those areas there will be some gaps that need filling more urgently than others.

One reason for collecting may be *rescue*. Objects the museum would like to acquire may be disappearing for one reason or another, and if the museum does not collect them now there may never be another chance. One example might be tribal or folk art or crafts in a region where old values are changing and dealers are buying up for export every historic item they can.

Another reason may be the museum's *display needs*. A planned exhibition may give an urgent requirement for a collecting programme.

Yet another reason may be to take part in a joint collecting and research programme with other museums, or with archaeological organisations, universities and other partners. Museums can be very much more successful when they co-operate in their collecting and fieldwork programmes.

Finally, collecting programmes should be carefully planned and structured, so that everyone involved can understand who is expected to do what and when.

FIELD DOCUMENTATION

The collecting techniques the museum uses will of course vary greatly according to what is being collected: collecting local ethnography will demand quite different approaches and quite different equipment to collecting – say – entomology.

But one thing every type of collecting in the field does require is rigorous *field documentation*. Many museums, sadly, can show examples of collections acquired in the past that are much less useful than they should be. This is because the museum failed to record all the information it could have recorded about the object or specimen when it was collecting in the field.

It is a vital part of the collecting programme to lay down precise procedures for field documentation. The museum managers must insist that all staff follow the procedures precisely, and they should also ensure that younger members of their staff are so well trained in field documentation that it becomes second nature to them. ICOM's *Code of Ethics for Museums* provides additional guidance (see Unit 6).

The actual techniques of field documentation will, like the techniques of collecting, vary from discipline to discipline. Geology fieldwork will require different techniques to fieldwork in – say – industrial history. In many fields – particularly in archaeology and biology – there are standards set by professional bodies, to which the museum should keep. Such standards often extend to how the resulting information and finds are preserved, and museums need to work to reconcile them with their internal procedures.

At the core of many fieldwork techniques is the field notebook. Every museum worker should be trained to keep a field notebook and to enter it up every day in the field. The notebook should include sketches and diagrams as well as written notes: not everyone can be a great artist, but even the crudest drawing will preserve information that cannot be expressed in words.

Photography is another essential technique in every kind of fieldwork, and all museum workers should use a camera as naturally as they use a notebook (see Unit 47). The tape-recorder and video-camera will also be valuable tools for many museum field-workers.

Finally, the museum must ensure that the field documentation is kept safely – for it is as important as the collections themselves. It should be linked to the collections so that in years to come a researcher studying a group of objects can easily find the records made in the field by those persons who collected them.

Remember: field documentation belongs to the museum and not to the curator or manager!

Unit

46

Fieldwork and record centres

Related Units – Units 41–5, 47–50

Fieldwork is a major part of the work of many museums, whether in archaeology, social history, ethnography, biology or geology. Museums are also often required to store and to make available the results of fieldwork by others. Museums, for example, care for the finds and records from archaeological collections, the collections and notes of geologists, the sketches, tapes and photographs of ethnographers. In many cases museums collaborate with one another in this area because associated records are often held by more than one museum. Researchers may well combine material from many museums to create a whole picture of the topic being studied.

In addition to systematic programmes of fieldwork, the museum staff will acquire a great deal of casual information as part of their everyday work. For example, a museum manager giving a lecture to a local community group might be told about the history of an old house, about the sighting of rare animals, about traditional local customs or about a geological formation briefly exposed by engineering work.

Finally, a great deal of information will be acquired along with the acquisition of artefacts and specimens (see Unit 44).

RECORDING INFORMATION

Each of these types of information must be recorded, but how?

The first step must be to formulate a policy for fieldwork and environmental recording, which should be summarised in the museum's forward plan (see Units 42 and 82). What level of responsibility does the museum intend to take?

At the highest level, the museum would maintain an Environmental Record for its area, seeking to gather information on all aspects of the environment, including land-use, ecology, geology, historic buildings, archaeological finds and sites, and perhaps customs and traditions as well. A museum attempting this level of environmental recording will require considerable resources, and a sophisticated computerised database. Even a simple Sites and Monuments Record will need staff qualified in information management as well as in archaeology to maintain it. A full Environmental Record will also include geological site records, species records and biological site records, as well, perhaps, as a record of historic buildings and industrial monuments and even of activities and events of ethnographic or sociological interest. Such a Record would need specialist staff in all these areas.

At the lowest level the museum would not maintain any Environmental Records itself, but would simply make arrangements for any information that came its way to be passed on to another, more appropriate, museum. Thus an art gallery might learn about a newly discovered archaeological site, or a history museum might be told of a threat to an important scientific site. Such museums should have formal arrangements to pass such information on, and all staff and volunteers, whatever their own specialism, should be able to recognise the importance of such information.

Most museums, though, will fall between these two extremes. They will need to devise ways of recording the information they need in an accessible form.

A common method used by rural museums is to maintain files for each village in their area, into which everything is put, from photographs to field notes. Museums in towns often arrange their files by street. No arrangement is entirely satisfactory, and only if the museum maintains computerised indexes to all its information will it always be possible to find all the information the museum or an enquirer needs.

It is essential, therefore, for every museum to decide what information it will need to record, and what questions that information will most often be expected to answer. Then the museums should devise a system that will best meet those needs, but is not too complicated: a system that is simple but works is very much more useful than a system that is logical and intellectually elegant, but is so complicated that no-one uses it!

STUDY EXAMPLE 46.1

A museum with responsibility for an area that covered 100 villages developed a system of 'village files'. Each file contained a range of standard information, which included:

- a list of all archaeological finds from its area and their present location;
- a list of other finds/objects in its collections;
- a list of finds/objects from the village held in other museums;
- a list of all the architecturally significant buildings;
- location maps;
- aerial photographs;
- photographs of field monuments;
- photographs of significant buildings;
- lists and photocopies of relevant historical publications and other bibliographical material of relevance, including press cuttings;
- transcripts of interviews held with local people; and so on.

Information was put into the files as it occurred. They formed a valuable and developing information resource for research and reference purposes. Without recording information over time and developing appropriate filing systems, the museum would have been unable to respond effectively to enquiries or to develop other forms of service such as exhibitions, publications and teaching resources.

Unit

47

Photography, film and video

Related Units – Units 38, 39, 41

Photography, film and video are used by museums in five ways:

- as recording techniques, for fieldwork and collecting;
- as original records, themselves forming part of the collections;

- as display techniques, to help interpret and present the museum's collections to the public;
- on the museum's web site;
- for commercial and marketing purposes.

In this Unit we look at the first way: using photography, film and video, like a notepad and sketchbook, as techniques for field recording.

PHOTOGRAPHY

In almost every country, photography is now commonplace, and cheap but reliable cameras are widely available. Museums should all have cameras. Staff should carry cameras with them everywhere, especially whenever they are undertaking fieldwork. The camera should become as familiar as a pencil and notebook, and be used in the same way. Photography is a wonderful technique for field recording, and all collecting should be accompanied by the taking of photographs. Though high-quality photography is still a specialist skill, anyone can take adequate photographs with a modern camera, and all museum workers should be able to achieve adequate results.

As technology develops, museums are faced with more and more difficult decisions on which technology to adopt. At the time of writing, digital cameras are replacing film cameras very fast, and they mean that images can be easily edited, put onto the Internet, incorporated into the museum's documentation, incorporated into computer-driven audio-visual displays, and sent by e-mail. But using digital technology means that the museum must be able to rely on always – long into the future – having easy access to computers on which to store the images, and the resources always to be able to transfer files as technology changes. Many museums will not be confident of always having these resources. The advice must be to use the technology for which resources are easily available locally.

Museum directors should make sure that all their staff, who undertake fieldwork or work with the collections, receive regular training in photography. They should have access to a camera and to facilities to develop and print film or upload digital images to a reliable database.

Wherever possible museum workers should use 35mm Single Lens Reflex cameras, or even a larger format. They should have a wide-angle lens (35mm or 28mm) as well as the standard 50mm lens, so that they can take photographs indoors or in restricted spaces. Not all museums, of course, will be able to afford this, and the rule must be simply to use the best camera you can afford.

Electronic flash may be useful, but museum workers should learn to take photographs in available light as far as possible, and should have a tripod. The ability to take better pictures in poor light is one of the great advantages of digital photography.

An invariable rule must be to make a note of every photograph you take at the time. Record where it was taken, who took it, when it was taken and what it shows. Once back at the museum, film should be processed as soon as possible, ideally in a darkroom at the museum.

All museum workers should learn to develop and print black and white film, but in many museums it will be more efficient to get the processing done by someone else, perhaps a commercial studio, especially for colour film. Make sure that the technician doing the processing understands the special techniques of 'archival processing' needed to ensure that the negatives and prints last. This involves fixing film and paper adequately to remove unexposed silver halides, washing appropriately to remove excess fixer, and preferably treatment with some sort of toning or sequestering solution to prevent the emulsion silver from oxidising in the presence of environmental pollutants. Digital images should be uploaded to the database or disks on which they are to be permanently stored, and renamed.

Finally, the museum must set up a method of storing and documenting photographs that ensures both that they are kept in the best possible conditions, and that any particular image can be found when required. The best method is to keep the negatives and one print in unique number order, and to have a series of indexes such as people, places, classified by subject to enable them to be found. It is wise to keep a file of prints of digital photos, too, linked to the originals on their database or disks.

FILM

Few museums will want to use film for fieldwork nowadays, but a surprising number of museums have in their collections old documentary film – for example of ethnographic scenes, of local wildlife or of archaeological excavations – of immense historic interest. Any museum that holds old films should get specialist advice on how to look after them, but the following points should be considered.

- Have you any film on nitrate stock? A cellulose nitrate base was used for most 35mm film stock up to the early 1950s. It is *very dangerous* because it is highly inflammable and can spontaneously explode. Any nitrate-base films should be copied and the originals kept in a special fireproof building.
- All films should be stored in a cool dry place, in the dark.
- Every time a film is projected it is in danger of damage. Try to get historic film copied on to video so that the originals do not have to be used. But keep the originals safely, because video is never of such good quality as film.

VIDEO

So far museums have used video more in displays (see Unit 20) than for fieldwork records. Video is, however, cheap, flexible and easy to use, and, although few museum workers are likely to achieve professional standards, it offers museums an invaluable recording technique. For recording activities and processes video is invaluable. Nothing else could record so effectively the working of a machine, a craft technique, a dance or a ceremony.

Unit

48

Oral history and audio recording

Related Units – Units 42–7, 49–50

ORAL HISTORY

In societies where most people do not regularly read and write, storytelling and the oral tradition remain of immense importance. Sadly, it seems that as literacy becomes more widespread, many of the traditions based on memory and word-of-mouth get forgotten, and oral tradition becomes despised by those for whom only what is written on paper or on disk is important.

Happily, in the last twenty years the widespread use of tape-recorders has led to a revival in respect for the oral tradition, and to a worldwide movement in favour of oral history. Alex Haley's famous book *Roots* showed how a family could preserve some of its memories from its roots in The Gambia, through the terrible experiences of slavery, to the modern urban world of the United States. His book showed, too, how oral history techniques could be combined with the evidence of historic documents to bring to life a past apparently lost forever.

Oral history is a technique and a hobby that has enlisted the enthusiasm of all sorts of people, from schoolchildren to professional historians. It is something

---

Box 48.1 Hints on oral history work

The best place to interview someone is where they feel most comfortable. Often this will be in their own home. Drawing any window curtains may improve the acoustics. Place the recorder beside you, keep the notes on your lap and sit facing the interviewee at a comfortable distance; the microphone should be between you and the person you are interviewing.

It is important to recognise that interviewing individuals especially about the past can generate a powerful emotional response from the interviewee. Interviewers need therefore to be careful not to intrude into areas of personal life that might cause unease or anxiety on the part of those being interviewed.

The more interviewing you do, the more skilful you will become at extracting valuable historical information from people.

Technology is changing too fast for it to be possible to suggest what equipment might be most effective. Museums planning to do recording should find out what technology and equipment offers the best quality and seems likely to last longest, and buy the best they can afford.

Box 48.2 Preserving the recordings

A museum undertaking even a few oral history interviews will need to give thought to how they are to be preserved and made available to users.

Whether the museum is preserving magnetic tapes or computer files, the first thing to create is a record system. This will probably comprise a card system or computer database similar to the museum catalogue. There will be a record for each tape that should include:

- date of interview;
- name of interviewer;
- name of interviewee;
- age, occupation and brief family details of interviewee;
- where interview took place;
- what equipment was used;
- copyright details and any restriction on use of the recording.

The record card should also ideally contain a summary of the topics covered, preferably with a note of where on the tape they come, as indicated by the index-counter.

What indexes are required? Some sort of classified index is probably necessary, though for a small collection of recordings it may be a very simple one.

Recordings, whatever their media, should be kept in a dry, cool atmosphere. Reel-to-reel and cassette tapes should be kept as far as possible away from any iron, and ideally in a cupboard with brass rather than ferrous-metal hinges, in order to avoid electromagnetic sources that can affect the tape. Experts have disagreed over whether tapes should be regularly played to keep them in good condition. Most now seem to think that this is unnecessary.

To transcribe every recording is hugely time-consuming, and should probably only be done where the interviewee was promised a transcript or where the transcript is to be published. There is, however, value in making a transcript that can be annotated by the interviewer. Much is hidden from view in an audio-recording, and the interviewer is the one person who can 'interpret' the spoken word effectively because he/she was present at the interview.

Like photography, digital recording technology is evolving very fast indeed, driven by the music industry. The danger is always that, in a few years time or longer, the technology will no longer be available to listen to the recordings, in just the same way that the equipment to listen to nineteenth-century recording cylinders is now very rare. Experts suggest that CDs may last for a good while, but there is no escaping the responsibility to transfer recordings from one medium to the next as technology develops. Museums must keep up with progress, and make sure that they plan and budget for copying their oral history recordings as it becomes necessary.

everyone can get involved in, it can illuminate almost any aspect of life, it can create a valuable permanent record and it gives great enjoyment and satisfaction to all involved.

Many museums become involved in oral history work. Many museums are the base for groups of volunteer enthusiasts undertaking oral history work, while museum managers and researchers use oral history techniques as one of their research tools when researching books or exhibitions, or simply when researching the background of objects in the museum's collections.

Oral history can thus provide a valuable dimension to museum documentation and interpretation.

AUDIO-RECORDING

Tape-recording is also used to record the sound of activities, processes and music. Although perhaps not so good as video (see Unit 47), audio-recording will help to capture the sound and atmosphere of a huge variety of human activities, and can later be used in conjunction with photographs, written descriptions and orig-inal artefacts both for research and in the museum gallery. Examples might include the work of fishermen at sea, ploughmen in the field, ironworkers in the factory or stall-holders in the marketplace.

Audio-recording is a technique of interest to all sorts of museums, not just to history museums. Art museums can record artists talking about their work, and the environment and activities that inspired it, or can record the different views of art historians and critics. Natural history museums can record the sounds of ani-mals, insects or birds. Industrial museums can record the sounds of machinery and the reminiscences of their operators. Musical museums can bring their instruments to life with recordings; audio-recording has revolutionised the study of folk-song.

Unit
49

Documentation systems

Related Units – Units 41–8, 50

There is nowadays a standard documentation system for museums, increasingly agreed by museum workers throughout the world. In many countries it is formalised in a set of standards, adopted by almost all museums; in the UK, for example, it is published as *SPECTRUM*. This documentation system has seven parts.

ENTRY

Every object or group of objects coming into a museum – whether as a gift, purchase, loan or enquiry – is recorded on a numbered *entry form*, which is completed (clearly, in ink) in the presence of the donor or vendor who then signs it to certify that it is a correct record. If possible three copies are made:

- one is given to the donor or lender, as a receipt;
- one stays with the object(s) until initial processing is complete, when it goes into a supplementary information file or into a short-term loans and enquiries file;
- one is filed permanently in an entry file arranged in entry number order.

The purpose of the entry form (sometimes called a deposit form) is both to acknowledge receipt of the object(s) and to ensure that information from the donor is not lost before a full record is made (see also Unit 44). For what the form should include, see Box 49.3.

A *temporary label* is tied to the object or objects, bearing the number from the entry form.

ACCESSIONING

Accessioning is the formal acceptance of all acquisitions (whether by gift, purchase or bequest), into the museum collection.

Each object, or group of objects, to be kept by the museum (whether gift, purchase, bequest or long loan) is entered in the *accessions register*. This register is the most important part of the documentation system. It has three main functions:

- it assigns a unique number to each object;
- it describes each object;
- it gives the history and provenance of each object.

The register must be a bound book of good-quality paper. Each page should be numbered consecutively. The register must be kept in a safe place, preferably in a fireproof cabinet, and a copy must be kept in another building. Entries must be written in permanent black ink only.

Each *group of objects* received at the same time and from the same source is given a permanent *accession number*. This may consist of the year of accession, a point and the next number available in the accessions register (e.g. 2005.28).

Each object in the group is then numbered separately (e.g. 2005.28.3). The whole is known as the *identity number* and is unique to that particular object.

The advantage of this two-part numbering system is that a large collection can be recorded as a group immediately, while its individual objects may have to wait for attention. Some museums use a running number system – every object entering the collection is given a unique number in sequence.

Most objects (except for coins) should be marked neatly and unobtrusively in permanent black ink; paper items should be marked in pencil. Coins should be kept in coin envelopes and details of the coin, including its accession number, should be written in permanent black ink on the envelope.

To make doubly sure, each object has a *permanent label* attached, bearing the permanent identity number. The temporary label is removed.

The permanent accession number is also written on the entry form.

Wherever possible or practical, the object should be photographed at this stage for record purposes.

It is polite to write to every donor to thank them for their gift, and to tell them that the object has been formally accepted by the museum (see Unit 44).

If the object has been given to the museum, it is a good idea to ask the donor to sign a *transfer of title form*. The top copy goes into the supplementary information file, while the donor is given the second copy, signed by the museum director. The purpose of the transfer of title form (sometimes called a donation form) is to ensure that the museum could – in the event of a dispute – prove its legal ownership of the object. The wording of the form must therefore be in accordance with the laws of the country.

LOANS

Loans in should be accepted only for specific purposes and for a specific period – usually for a maximum of three years (see Unit 44). They are recorded in the same way as donations, using the entry form. They should not be accessioned, but should be recorded in a separate loans book.

CATALOGUING

The *catalogue* entry is then completed. The catalogue is a complete record of everything that is known about every object in the museum's collections. It can be either held on a card catalogue, or on a computer program.

A card catalogue consists of individual cards, usually pre-printed, kept in identity number order in a metal card-drawer, ideally in a fireproof lockable cabinet.

Eight types of information will be present on each card:

- name of museum;
- accession number;
- name of object – classification;
- entry method (donation, find, purchase);
- source of entry (donor, vendor);
- date of entry;
- history of object;
- location.

Other types of information may be useful as well, but the above are usually considered essential.

The cards should be filed in identity number order. (It is almost always a mistake to file them in any other way.)

A *supplementary information file* (sometimes called an object history file) contains all the documentation relevant to the object. It will contain the entry form and transfer of title form for each object, and may also contain invoices, receipts, letters, newspaper cuttings, conservator's report, photographs, excavator's notes, etc.

To avoid confusion, terms used in documentation should be standard ones. Thus the *name of the object* should always be a standard one, and every museum needs to develop a *thesaurus* of standard terms. Increasingly these are being developed internationally, and many museums will be able to use an existing thesaurus.

INDEXING AND RETRIEVAL

Indexes enable the manager to find information in a card catalogue without reading every single card, and in a computer catalogue to retrieve particular types of object. The museum must decide what questions are most often asked, and therefore what indexes are needed. The most commonly used indexes are:

- names and details of donor;
- classification;
- location;
- provenance;
- artist.

In a manual system, there will need to be a separate set of cards for each index. A computer system will permit vastly more sophisticated indexing.

MOVEMENT CONTROL

Movement control means the recording of movements of objects from the collections, both within and in and out of the museum. The bigger the collections, the more important it is for the museum to have a good movement control system.

In the simplest system, every time an object is moved permanently, or for a long period, a note is made on its catalogue card or file, showing the date it was moved, who by and where to. Every time it is moved temporarily, for a short time, a *proxy card* is left in its usual place, showing when it was moved, who by and where to.

EXIT DOCUMENTATION

Exit documentation records every movement of an object out of the museum building.

A good system to use is an exit form similar to the entry form. One copy of the form is kept in a loans out file until the object comes back, when it is put permanently in the supplementary information file. The second copy goes to the borrower or recipient. For what it should contain, see Box 49.4.

Box 49.1 Materials needed for documentation

- entry forms;
- exit forms;
- transfer of title forms;
- accession register;
- labels;
- supplementary information file;
- permanent black ink;
- pens;
- catalogue cards;
- index cards;
- card cabinets;
- fireproof safe.

Box 49.2 Computerisation

Computerising the museum's documentation will save the museum neither money nor time. It will certainly cost rather more than a purely manual system, and will almost certainly need as much staff time to manage.

A poorly designed or badly managed documentation system will not be improved by being computerised.

What computerisation *will* do is to allow the museum staff to achieve far more than they could achieve with a manual system. If well planned and well managed, it will give the museum much greater control over its collections and its information.

Remember that there are many additional costs involved in managing computers, which require software, disks and other 'consumables' as well as regular maintenance. They will also require a reliable power supply, and will only operate within a specific temperature range, usually 50°F to 104°F (10°C to 40°C). If the range in your museum is outside this range, you may need specially prepared equipment.

How can a museum computerise its documentation? The first step must be to ensure that the museum's basic manual documentation is efficient, well designed and to modern standards. Computerising will quickly show up problems in the basic system.

The second step must be to seek advice. If at all possible, initial advice should be from someone who understands both computers and museum documentation. Many museums have run into problems because their adviser understood computers, but did not really understand the requirements of museum documentation. Computerising museum documentation and classification is a highly complex field.

If good advice is not available locally, CIDOC, the ICOM International Committee for Documentation may be able to help.

Box 49.3 Entry forms

Entry forms should contain the following information:

- entry number;
- name, address and telephone number of the current owner (and depositor if different);
- entry date;
- condition and completeness;
- brief description, including any accompanying information concerning production, usage, etc.;
- entry reason;
- entry method;
- number of objects deposited;
- any conditions;
- agreed return date;
- signature of the owner (or depositor if different);
- name and signature of the museum staff member who receives the object;
- insurance details (including a previously agreed valuation);
- note of packing materials if necessary (they may be an integral part of the object);
- any field-collection information;
- any additional information about the object.

Box 49.4 Exit forms

Exit forms should contain the following information:

- accession/object or entry number;
- brief description;
- person responsible;
- condition;
- valuation if required for insurance;
- authorised signature of the museum the object is leaving;
- destination name, address and telephone number;
- reason for exit;
- signature of person receiving the object;
- date of exit;
- date of delivery;
- anticipated return date and method;
- reference to appropriate file containing additional details.

The role of collections in research

Related Units – 42–9

All types of museum collections have a vital role to play in research. Indeed, one of the primary justifications for collecting material for museum collections is that it forms a permanent body of research material for future generations. Hence it is of critical importance that collecting is not carried out in an arbitrary or aimless way. It must be done within the framework of a carefully considered collecting and disposal policy and through well-organised collecting programmes.

Managing collections effectively and efficiently, and making the necessary invest-ment in them over time, will ensure that the collections are available for research purposes in the future. It is often the case that in the light of new scientific tech-niques, new discoveries or new methodologies, researchers will be able to approach and use museum collections in ways that had not previously been considered. The recent advances in the analysis of human and animal bone housed in museums for the recovery of DNA is a contemporary example.

In considering the role of collections in research, it is also necessary to remember that researchers will often be examining classes of material held in more than one museum. Your museum may be one of a number managing, for example, archae-ological material or geological material. In such cases, the body of material as a whole – the sum of the parts – may be of interest. If some of those parts have been poorly managed and have suffered neglect or degradation, research will be impaired. Collections in a museum therefore should not be thought of in isola-tion from other collections in museums elsewhere. It is essential that the museum is able to compare and contrast its own collections with the wider resource and this is one of the benefits of active research programmes.

In Unit 78, we discuss the opportunities for museums to work with other organ-isations. In the field of research, museums have good opportunities to create joint research programmes with other museums or allied institutions known to be collecting or to hold collections in the same subject areas. Collections research projects of this type can often lead to improved understanding and awareness of the importance of particular holdings, throw new light on collections through documentary research and lead to joint publications, exhibitions and associated collecting and research projects. Study example 50.1 is based on a large-scale, national research programme, but the principles could be applied for any subject area with relatively small numbers of museums at local or regional level.

Carrying out research on collections in-house, or making collections available to outside organisations or individuals for research purposes, underlines the importance of effective documentation in collections management. Without high-quality records, updated to include the results of relevant research, the usefulness of museum collections is substantially reduced. The museum should create information systems and documentation procedures that allow for data about items/specimens to be kept and maintained systematically. Whenever researchers have used information or collections held by the museum, the provision of copies of their work for the museum should be made a condition of access.

STUDY EXAMPLE 50.1

A two-year collections research programme was established to record all natural history collections held in museums in one European country. Some 300 museums were surveyed by postal questionnaire, and study visits were made to 100 museums over the two-year period to record selected collections in more detail. The results of the project were recorded on computer, and a report and digest published.

The computer database was used to 'reassemble' collections that had been fragmented across a number of museums and to throw more light on the natural historians of the nineteenth century who had initiated many of the collections. The research programme was also able to identify how to improve collections management for the collections, in particular storage and documentation. A number of museums used the recommendations of the report to generate funding to mount new displays on their natural history collections.

Collaboration in assessing a national resource provided the basis for developing long-term strategies for research and conservation.

Unit

51 Ethical considerations and repatriation

Related Units – Units 42–3

All museums should be aware of the issues surrounding the return and restitution of cultural property to its country or place of origin, or to its original owners. This has become of increasing importance in recent years, particularly as countries have recognised the significance of their cultural property to national identity and statehood and as international law has developed around the restitution of cultural property of all types.

The principles on which museums need to consider the return and restitution of cultural property are enshrined in two key documents – UNESCO's *Convention on the Means of Prohibiting and Preventing the Illicit Import, Export and Transfer of Ownership of Cultural Property 1970* and the UNIDROIT *Convention on Stolen and Illegally Exported Cultural Objects 1995* (see Unit 101). Every museum should integrate the principles of these Conventions into its collecting and disposal policies (see Units 42–3).

A museum should take every step to co-operate in the return of an object or specimen (in its collections or on offer to it) if it can be shown to have been an integral part of a country's cultural or natural heritage and exported or otherwise transferred from that country, in contravention of the principles of these two Conventions.

Where a request for the return of cultural property to the country or people of origin, for example a minority ethnic culture within a country, is made formally, a museum should where possible initiate discussions from a professional perspective rather than taking action at governmental or political level. Because there may be complex legal arguments and precedents involved in repatriation cases, museums are advised to seek professional legal advice in repatriation and restitution cases.

Some museums may hold material from other countries in their collections and wish to engage in international programmes. While a wide range of potential partnerships exist, there are interesting possibilities for developing partnerships and exchanges with museums in those countries that have lost a significant part of their cultural or natural heritage through destruction or theft. Touring exhibitions, for example, that return a country's cultural or natural heritage to it for a limited period may do much to build and foster longer lasting relationships between museums and their countries.

An allied convention to the UNESCO and UNIDROIT Conventions is *The Hague Convention for the Protection of Cultural Property in the Event of Armed Conflict* (The Hague Convention, First Protocol 1954 and Second Protocol 1999). Under the principles of this Convention, a museum should not purchase, appropriate or acquire cultural objects from any country that is occupied by the armed forces of another country.

Unit

52

Museum archives and museum history

Related Unit – Unit 49

Documentation about the museum's collections is considered in Unit 49. In this Unit, we consider documentation about the museum's historical development and what materials the museum should consider keeping in its institutional archives to help record and illustrate the history of the museum and its work.

The museum's archives serve as *the institutional memory* of the museum. Members of the governing body and staff will come and go, but the museum may be in existence for centuries. Governing bodies thus have a responsibility to ensure that the museum retains and safeguards key documents that reflect its work and progress as a cultural institution through time. These documents provide an important strand of evidence for charting the historical development of the museum and also constitute an important source of reference on the museum's history for museum staff and researchers.

A clear policy and programme for developing and maintaining the museum's archives are required. The policy will need to be reviewed on a regular basis, but it should aim to provide for consistency and continuity of approach in selecting and retaining material for the museum's archives. There are no set rules for what material to retain for archive purposes. However, the checklist here will provide some suggestions. As with the management of the museum's collections and associated documentation, information relevant to the museum's archive will be recorded on a wide variety of materials, for example paper, photographs, computer disks, tape, film and video. Every care needs to be taken in ensuring that such records are preserved in appropriate conditions (see Unit 55).

Museum archive checklist:

- agendas and minutes of board meetings;
- agendas and minutes of committee meetings;
- board papers;
- policy papers;
- accounts and other financial records;
- forward plans;
- annual reports;
- press releases;
- press cuttings;
- copies of museum publications;
- reviews of museum activity;
- CVs of members of the governing body;
- CVs of museum staff and volunteers;
- letters to and from the museum;
- photographs;
- moving image;
- transcripts of TV and radio broadcasts;
- transcripts of lectures.

It is helpful for the museum to maintain an up-to-date account of its historical development. This is useful for background for funding applications, in induction programmes and manuals for staff, volunteers and members of the governing body, and for briefing purposes for external bodies. It is also useful in informing visitors, for example through displays and exhibitions or the museum's web site, how the museum has developed through time and what its achievements have been. This helps to strengthen understanding and appreciation of the museum's mission and objectives, and reinforces its status and reputation in the public mind.

Conservation planning

Related Units – Units 54–68

Conservation is only one aspect of managing museums and collections, but it is in many ways the most important.

The collections in the care of the museum form the principal resource from which all other activities flow. The museum's responsibilities to its collections should be paramount above all others. Without collections, there is no museum. The duty of care for the collections is thus central to the museum's work and should be implicit in the museum's mission statement and its organisational objectives.

This book has emphasised throughout that you should first establish policies for the different aspects of your museum's work (*what we should do*), and then draw up a management or forward plan to help you implement those policies (*how we are going to do it*). A key component of the museum's overall management or forward plan is a conservation plan that forms an integral part of the museum's collections management strategy. A conservation plan will help to provide a framework for establishing and maintaining appropriate standards of collections care and for setting priorities for both preventive and remedial conservation work. What steps do you need to take to draw up a conservation plan and what should be its contents?

A conservation plan will cover a range of matters, for example:

- regular conservation assessments of the museum's collections by trained conservators;
- procedures for monitoring environmental conditions in collections stores and displays;
- buildings inspection and maintenance programmes;
- documentation procedures for remedial conservation programmes;
- a strategy for dealing with disasters and emergencies like fire, flood, civil unrest, war, earthquakes (see Unit 65);
- conservation guidelines within your museum's policies on loans.

What steps do you need to take to draw up a conservation plan? The following checklist provides some guidelines that can be adapted to suit different museums:

- First of all, ensure that the conservation plan is drawn up taking into account the museum's policies towards its collections.
- The museum manager then commissions a written assessment of the state of the museum building(s) from a building surveyor.
- The building surveyor reports on the structural condition of the museum building(s) and the implications for the museum environment, makes recommendations for any improvements and provides indicative capital costs.
- In the light of this report, the museum manager commissions a written report on the collections in the care of the museum from a conservator.

- The conservator looks at the situation overall and reports on:

  - environmental conditions in display and storage areas, following a pro-gramme of monitoring relative humidity, temperature, pest activity and particulate pollution;
  - the state of preservation of the objects or specimens in the collections;
  - the approaches to storage and materials used for storing collections;
  - the approaches to display and the materials used for displaying collections.

  He or she then makes recommendations in a written report to the museum manager on the current state and the necessary steps to improve conditions. The report indicates costs and sources of supply, and identifies any additional specialist conservation advice that may be needed to supplement the general collections report for particular items or specimens or categories of material.

- Additional specialist conservation advice is then commissioned, as required.
- The museum manager then co-ordinates a curatorial assessment of objects or specimens within the collections to ensure that the museum is aware of the historical or scientific significance of the material held in its care. This may also necessitate bringing in specialist curatorial advice to the museum from individuals in other museums or institutions to complement that of the museum staff (see Unit 50).
- In the light of all this information, the museum manager prepares an overall statement of conservation policy for the museum, relating this to other policy statements, for example, the museum's collecting and disposal policy.
- The museum manager then prepares a conservation plan which covers the following areas:

  - the specific improvements necessary to the fabric or structure of the building(s);
  - the specific improvements needing to be made in preventive conservation and storage, and the priority order in which these should be carried out;
  - the establishment of effective monitoring procedures for buildings mainte-nance purposes, for environmental conditions in storage and display areas and for the control of artefacts in the care of the museum;
  - priorities for remedial conservation of items/specimens in the collections, in the light of the conservation and curatorial assessments;
  - arrangements for training staff in the care of collections, for example, handling, storage control, documentation, environmental monitoring.

- The museum manager includes estimates of costs in the plan and indicates the timescale over which the different elements of the work will be carried out.
- The museum manager in consultation with the museum's governing body seeks the requisite funds to carry out the necessary work over a defined period.
- The museum manager produces a procedure manual for staff engaged in preven-tive and remedial conservation to ensure that they are aware of the museum's policies and adhere to agreed management procedures and standards.

You will note from the checklist on pp. 163–4 that the museum manager has a central role in this work. It is the manager's overall responsibility to ensure the long-term safekeeping and safeguarding of the museum's collections. A conservation plan is a powerful method of achieving this objective.

Working with conservators

Related Units – Units 53, 55–68

Few small- to medium-sized museums have conservators on their staff. Many have to rely on contracting conservators to carry out environmental assessments, collections surveys and reports, and remedial conservation work on collections. The number and availability of trained and experienced conservators working in different disciplines vary from country to country. Consequently, museums have to decide how most effectively to obtain and use available professional conservation services to meet their needs.

The process of conservation planning and the role of conservators are discussed in Unit 53. Wherever possible, conservators should be employed to undertake environmental assessments of storage and display areas. However, with effective staff training programmes and appropriate equipment other staff can be used to carry these out and undertake monitoring programmes. A conservator should nonetheless assess their work on an agreed schedule.

Collections surveys and reports should also be carried out wherever possible by trained conservators, either generalists or specialists in their fields. Other staff, following appropriate training, may carry out general surveys and condition reports on collections where conservators are not easily available. Museum managers should use conservators to help train staff in preventive conservation methods (see Unit 55).

However, remedial conservation is another matter. Here it is essential to use trained conservators to conserve or restore items. Irreparable damage can be caused by well-intentioned, but unskilled or inappropriate, 'conservation methods'. Some categories of artefact may be cleaned and protected under the supervision of a trained conservator, but in general, unless appropriate guidance and supervision are readily available, this is not recommended. Conservators should be asked to identify the sort of practical, remedial conservation work that can be legitimately carried out under supervision by trained museum staff and volunteers.

Conservators therefore have an important and continuing role to play in the museum, and establishing good working relationships with professional conservators is vital. They are skilled professionals and their work, advice and expertise should be highly regarded by the museum. They should be involved wherever possible or practicable in discussing or planning for exhibitions, displays, storage facilities and new buildings: wherever collections are to be used or housed. Their advice should also be sought by the museum in developing information resources on conservation, i.e. relevant books/journals about conservation, suppliers of materials for storage or display, suppliers of conservation equipment, names/addresses of other specialist conservators and sources of training for staff.

In establishing work programmes for in-house or contract conservators, a detailed, written brief should be developed by the museum manager or curator, together with a schedule for the work programme. The programme should be an outcome of the wider conservation planning discussed in Unit 53. Both parties should agree the brief and schedule, and work should be undertaken within this contractual framework.

STUDY EXAMPLE 54.1

A museum manager, newly appointed to a museum, contracted a professional conservator to visit the museum for a week. The conservator worked in a large urban museum and was able to visit the museum as part of a recently established support programme for small museums. The first day was taken up with an assessment of environmental conditions and an assessment of current preventive conservation measures, and necessary improvements; the remaining four days examined four priority collections and their storage in detail.

Each lunchtime, different groups of staff and volunteers underwent a training session in preventive conservation methods led by the conservator, with a special focus on methods of handling collections and their storage. The conservator provided the museum manager with a detailed report on the necessary improvements to preventive conservation – new blinds and shutters in the windows, environmental monitoring systems, handling procedures – and to collections storage – packaging materials, shelving systems, cleaning regimes – together with special reports on remedial conservation for items in the four priority collections and their special storage requirements.

The reports then formed part of the museum's collections management plan and ultimately the museum's forward plan. The reports also included recommendations on a new training programme for museum staff and volunteers in the principles and practice of preventive conservation, and refresher courses for senior staff.

The museum's governing body recognised the quality and value of the external advice from the conservator and provided additional resources to implement the recommendations in the reports.

Preventive conservation: principles

Related Units – Units 53–4, 56–68

Effective preventive conservation should reduce the need for remedial conservation. Preventive conservation is about ensuring that the museum's collections are displayed, handled, stored and maintained in ways that do not lead to damage or deterioration. Remedial conservation is about repairing damage or decay to collections, using techniques that are reversible.

Preventive conservation seeks to ensure that expensive and complex remedial conservation is not required for the future and is an important aspect of sustainability. It can therefore be seen as a form of insurance policy against incurring costs in the future. Preventive conservation and security go hand-in-hand in ensuring the long-term well-being and safeguarding of collections.

In many cases, preventive conservation is a matter of basic common sense. We explore different aspects of preventive conservation in the succeeding Units. It is important to recognise however that preventive conservation is first and foremost about meeting the museum's fundamental responsibility to care for its collections.

This is a key duty of the museum's governing body; its members must be made aware of the benefits of preventive conservation and its role in terms of sustainability. The museum manager will need to exercise skilled diplomacy to persuade and to encourage the museum's governors to give priority to this aspect of collections management.

Investment in preventive conservation is now seen as a key priority for museums of all types and sizes internationally. The growing recognition that effective and efficient care reduces long-term costs for a museum provides museum managers with a valuable argument in their case-for-support for investment (see Unit 5).

Different types of collections of course need different forms of care. What is appropriate for example for the storage of metallic objects is not necessarily appropriate for textiles or photographic collections. Museum managers and staff with responsibility for collections care and use should therefore be trained in understanding the special needs of different types of collection. In particular, they should be aware of the effects of different materials used in storage and display on museum collections and the special requirements in terms of light, temperature and relative humidity levels that different collections need.

Museum staff should be particularly trained in the appropriate handling of items in their collections. Poor handling, packing and transport is a major source of damage to collections, and there can be no excuse for museum staff damaging material in the collections through lack of care in these areas.

Common-sense precautions include:

- ensuring all staff understand the principles and practice of preventive conservation;

- ensuring that relative humidity and temperature are kept stable in storage and display areas and at an appropriate level for objects and specimens;
- ensuring that light levels are at an appropriate level for items on display;
- checking that materials used in storage and display – wood, fabrics, paints, adhesives, plastics and rubber – are not harmful to objects and specimens;
- keeping storage areas clean, tidy and uncluttered;
- providing sufficient space in storage containers to avoid crushing or abrasion of items;
- not storing items on top of or inside one another;
- raising stored items and storage containers off the floor of storage areas in case of flooding;
- keeping storage areas unlit when access is not required;
- making sure that collections are stored in secure areas;
- cleaning items only following expert advice;
- checking collections on a regular basis, for example to guard against pest infestation;
- avoiding handling wherever possible, and then only using cotton gloves;
- providing appropriate facilities for examining collections for research and study purposes by staff or visiting researchers;
- limiting the number of individuals with authority to handle collections;
- not smoking, eating or drinking anywhere in the vicinity of collections.

Key word

Preventive conservation – the processes by which a museum's collections are stored, handled, displayed and maintained in ways that do not lead to deterioration and the need for remedial conservation.

STUDY EXAMPLE 55.1

As part of its administrative handbook (see Unit 98), a regional museum established a range of induction procedures for all new staff. Included in these procedures was a two-day course on preventive conservation. As a basis for this in-house course, a training manual was developed in association with a professional conservator so that the course tutor(s) could ensure a consistent and standardised approach to the training. Use was made of existing publications, videos and conservation reports to illustrate the course.

All staff in the museum were also required to undertake a one-day refresher course each year on preventive conservation techniques to keep them up to date with new developments. The training manual was extended to include the refresher course.

The training manual and the courses were so successful that they became used on a regular basis by a number of small museums in the area. This was a good example of a regional museum providing services to a number of museums in its area and maximising the value of the investment made in the training programme.

Environmental monitoring and control: light

Related Units – 53–5, 57–68

Light can cause serious damage to museum collections and is one of the greatest threats to the long-term care of collections. Light is a form of energy and can cause colour fading as well as deterioration in the materials from which museum objects are made. All museum objects are to a greater or lesser extent affected by light, although metals and ceramics are not affected to the same extent as other materials. Some materials are extremely sensitive to light and every care needs to be taken to reduce their exposure levels. Special care should be taken to protect museum items made of more than one type of material.

While damage from light can never be completely eliminated, it can be reduced by:

*   reducing the amount of time an object is illuminated;
*   reducing illumination to a level necessary for comfortable viewing by visitors;
*   eliminating ultra-violet (UV) radiation.

LIGHT LEVELS

Any light, however strong or weak, causes damage. A strong light produces approximately the same amount of damage in one year as a weak light one-tenth the strength will produce in ten years. The intensity of light is measured by a *light meter* using units of measurements known as *lux units*. Recommended maximum levels of illumination range from 50–200 lux. The following levels should not be exceeded for the categories of material shown:

*   200 lux – oil/tempera paintings, undyed leather, lacquer, wood, horn, bone and ivory, stone.

- 50 lux – costume, textiles, watercolour paintings, tapestries, furniture, prints and drawings, postage stamps, manuscripts, ephemera, miniatures, wallpaper, dyed leather and most natural history and ethnographic items.

Light levels should be regularly monitored in all areas where collections are displayed or kept. Staff should be trained to measure light levels using appropriate equipment and records of the measurements should be kept to analyse trends. All museums should own light meters for regular use.

It is difficult to reduce the level of illumination to 200 lux when the museum's gallery displays are lit by daylight. For a value of 50 lux, daylight is too variable and artificial light will be needed for museum displays containing items that need to be lit at or below that level.

Display and exhibition galleries need to be designed and used with light levels firmly in mind. A combination of artificial light and daylight, which can be controlled by a variety of methods, depending on the nature of the material to be displayed, will provide the flexibility a museum needs. The museum has to reach a compromise between the needs of the object (total darkness!) and the needs of the visitor (enough light to see the object comfortably!).

There are a number of methods to reduce light levels that can be used singly or in combination by a museum:

Simple and cheap methods

- installing curtains, blinds with horizontal or vertical louvres, or shutters, and closing them when the museum is closed to the public;
- moving items on display away from window areas;
- siting display cases/display screens out of strong daylight zones;
- fitting screens or covers to display cases;
- reducing the number and wattage of light bulbs;
- fitting dimmer or cut-out switches to room/case lights;
- cutting out illumination when the museum is closed to the public;
- blocking out windows.

More sophisticated and expensive methods

- installing photocells to control blinds automatically;
- fitting time switches to case lights;
- fitting diffuser panels over lighting systems;
- installing 'grey' or light sensitive glass in windows.

UV LIGHT

The ultra-violet component of light is particularly damaging, and must be eliminated by using UV-absorbent filters. Daylight and fluorescent lamps emit high levels of UV radiation. Tungsten incandescent lamps do not need UV filters, but tungsten halogen (quartz iodine) lamps should only be used with ordinary glass filters to eliminate short-wavelength UV.

UV levels are measured by a *UV-monitor*, which measures the proportion of UV falling on an object. Levels over 75 microwatts per lumen (uw/lm) are considered excessive for light-sensitive objects and the UV light must be screened out by UV-absorbent film or glass in one of the following ways:

- laminated glass UV filter;
- acrylic/polycarbonate sheets;
- UV varnish applied to window or display case glass;
- polyester film applied to window or display case glass;
- plastic filter sleeves for fluorescent lamp tubes.

Advice should be sought from conservators and manufacturers as to the most appropriate form of protective material for the museum. Check for life expectancy and length of manufacturers' guarantees.

RADIANT HEAT FROM LIGHTS

Most lights emit heat. Museums should guard against mounting tungsten light fittings too near to museum objects. Heat build-up from tungsten lights can have an adverse affect on the moisture content of sensitive materials, and surface heating can create cracking and splitting. Light fittings of all types should therefore be mounted outside display cases wherever possible to avoid radiant heat problems.

Beware, too, of shining spotlights directly on light-sensitive materials as this can cause localised heat build-up and damage.

STUDY EXAMPLE 56.1

A museum wishing to display a large collection of postage stamps developed a system of horizontal sliding display units made by a local joiner using materials that were specified by the museum's conservator. The display units slid into a cabinet that provided protection from light when the stamps were not being examined, and the unit could also be locked for additional security when the museum was closed. Visitors wishing to see the stamp collection simply slid out each of the twenty display units, which were glazed on both sides, for viewing, and slid them back after study.

The technique described is suitable for a variety of light-sensitive paper items, such as engravings, watercolours and drawings or flat textiles.

Museum display and storage units of this type can be copied or adapted by other museums. A neighbouring museum adopted a similar system to store sheets of music.

Unit 57

Environmental monitoring and control: temperature and humidity

Related Units – Units 53–6, 58–68

Humidity and temperature are key agents of deterioration in museum collections. As with light (see Unit 56), their control is essential to ensure the long-term safe-keeping of collections. These two agents affect different categories of material in different ways and museum managers must ensure that appropriate conditions for collections on display and in storage are maintained.

RELATIVE HUMIDITY

Relative humidity (RH) is the ratio of water vapour in the air to the amount that it could hold if fully saturated; it is expressed as a percentage. Low levels of relative humidity imply dry conditions since the air is then capable of taking up moisture. High values are recorded when the air is already humid and unable to take up much more moisture, for example in humid or wet weather. RH is measured with a *hygrometer*.

Stable RH is critical for museum objects. Changes in RH create dimensional changes in organic museum objects, e.g. wood, leather, textiles, ivory, bone, paper, etc. These changes can cause expansion and contraction of materials and irreparable damage can result. Organic materials are also liable to attack from moulds/fungi if conditions are humid, over 65 per cent RH (see Units 58, 60–1). Metallic objects can also be adversely affected by high levels of RH, which encourage corrosion. RH needs to be as low as possible for all metallic objects.

Museums should aim to have a constant RH all year round in storage and display areas. Ideally, it should not rise above 60 per cent or fall below 40 per cent, and should be stabilised at 50–5 per cent for a mixed collection. In older buildings, where condensation can occur at this level, 45–50 per cent RH is an effective compromise.

It is perfectly possible of course – and may be a practical solution in many small museums in tropical climates – to provide micro-environments or more controlled areas for special categories of material in the collection. This is an effective approach where it is difficult to maintain appropriate levels of RH throughout the museum buildings.

Museums should be aware that in certain countries items that have adjusted over a long period of time to particular environmental conditions may be irreparably damaged if introduced into a controlled museum environment too rapidly. This is of particular importance when considering loans to other museums.

TEMPERATURE

Temperature is measured with a *thermometer*. Temperature is an important factor in RH because the ability of air to hold water vapour increases with higher temperatures and decreases with lower temperatures. Change in temperature in a storage or display area can therefore affect levels of RH. Changing temperature can also speed up the rate of biological/chemical deterioration.

Museum collections do not require high temperatures. A temperature of 18°C (+/–2°C) is an acceptable temperature for the display of a mixed collection; a temperature of 15°C is adequate for storage areas. Beware of localised high temperatures created by heaters or spotlights.

MEASURING ENVIRONMENTAL CONDITIONS

Relative humidity and temperature must be recorded on a regular basis to build up a picture of environmental conditions and any problems in the museum. A hygrometer and a thermometer should be installed in those locations where environmental conditions need to be checked. Ideally, an *electronic hygrometer* can be used for taking spot checks on conditions and for calibrating continuous recording instruments. These are called *recording thermohygrographs* and record temperature and humidity levels on a weekly or monthly chart. They should be sited in all areas of display and storage where conditions need to be measured. Small case meters or recording strips can also be used to monitor conditions within display cases.

More sophisticated monitoring systems for display and storage areas that can be linked to a central computer are now available. Associated software can provide sophisticated analyses of trends in levels of RH and temperature over time.

However, the museum manager should recognise that monitoring systems and procedures, however basic or sophisticated, are not ends in themselves. They are the basis for any necessary action to be taken to improve environmental conditions in the museum. They provide objective evidence that can be used in the case-for-support for any necessary improvements.

PREVENTIVE MEASURES

Equipment

Various methods of controlling RH conditions exist. Specialised equipment can be used to humidify or dehumidify areas operated by a humidistat. Seasonal changes can radically affect conditions. In some countries, a high priority may be to install a permanent heating or cooling system so that constant temperature conditions can be maintained throughout the year. The system can be fitted with individual thermostats allowing for adjustments to suit collections in different areas of the museum.

Standards of environmental control will vary from museum to museum depending on resources. At a minimum, museums should aim to eliminate too high or too low levels of RH and should avoid all sudden changes in humidity. A higher standard will require constant RH control throughout the year. It may not be possible to control humidity levels simply by a heating system. Free-standing units – *humidifiers* where conditions are too dry or *dehumidifiers* where conditions are too damp – may need to be used. An optimum approach is to use a full air-conditioning system, but this will be too expensive for many smaller museums to contemplate.

Control measures

The museum will need to improvise where money is limited. Windows may be opened in good weather to help ventilate the indoor climate and to introduce warm air into damp or cold rooms, but avoid periods of high atmospheric pollution especially in urban environments or desert areas. Fans may also be used to circulate air and artificial heat can be used to dry out damp environments. Oil or paraffin burners should *not* be used as their gases are harmful to collections. If humidity levels are too low, introduce trays of wet cotton wool and fungicide in different parts of the display or storage areas.

Other basic precautions

Other basic precautions may include:

- specifying individuals to be responsible for monitoring and reporting on environmental conditions in display and storage areas;
- maintaining equipment and environmental control systems on a regular maintenance schedule;
- keeping all objects off floors in case of dampness;
- keeping all objects away from external walls in case of condensation;
- providing sufficient space for free air-flow and adequate ventilation;
- ensuring that the museum has control over heating systems in use in storage and display areas. Sometimes where a museum is in a building shared with one or more organisations, lack of control can be a problem;
- not introducing amounts of water into display and storage areas, e.g. for cleaning purposes, without due care and control.

Environmental monitoring and control: air pollution/insect and pest attack

Related Units – Units 53–7, 59–68

Air pollution and insects and pests are agents of deterioration in museum collections. As with light and RH (see Units 56–7), it is essential to control them to ensure the long-term safekeeping of collections. Museum managers must be aware of their potential to damage collections and ensure that conditions in display and storage areas are regularly monitored.

AIR POLLUTION

Air pollution is mainly associated with urban areas and industry and is mostly caused by the burning of fuels. Dirt particles move in the air, vary in weight and therefore settle in different ways and in different densities.

Particles of dirt in the air outside the museum include sooty and tarry material. They are usually acid from having absorbed sulphur dioxide, especially where fuels have been burnt in power stations or in vehicle engines. They can contain traces of metals, for example iron, which can create deterioration in collections. Dust and dirt particles absorb moisture and acids from the air. Once they are in contact with museum objects, they set up undesirable chemical reactions. Where the air is polluted, the corrosion of metals is a particular difficulty. In rural and desert regions, dust or sand storms are an additional hazard.

Other forms of air pollution derive from salt in the air in coastal regions, which can cause severe deterioration in metalwork; gaseous pollution, which, like particulate pollution, is caused by burning fuel in factories, cars, machinery, power stations and chemical plants; and even furnishing materials such as carpets and curtains in the museum. A typical city atmosphere includes:

- 20 per cent oxygen – O_2;
- 78 per cent nitrogen – N_2;
- carbon dioxide – CO_2;
- water vapour – H_2O;
- argon – Ar;
- contaminant gases.

The worst contaminant gases are:

- sulphur dioxide – SO_2;
- sulphur trioxide – SO_3;

- ozone – O^3;
- nitrous oxides – NO_1, NO_2, NC_2O_3.

Sulphur is released by burning petrol. Sulphur plus oxygen gives sulphur dioxide; sulphur dioxide plus oxygen gives sulphur trioxide; sulphur trioxide plus water gives sulphuric acid. In a similar reaction, ozone and nitrous oxides produce nitric acid. Both acids are strong and powerful, and attack many materials including stone, metal and organic materials.

For museums in towns or industrial areas, or in areas that are at risk in other ways, museums should ideally invest in air-filtering or air-conditioning systems. This is expensive, and for many museums not a possibility. The problems of dirt and dust must therefore be minimised in other ways. Dirt on museum objects not only looks unsightly, but also requires to be cleaned off to avoid the object suffering deterioration. Cleaning carries with it certain dangers and risks if it is not carried out appropriately. Objects should never be dusted.

Guidance on cleaning from professional conservators should be integrated into the museum's conservation and collections management plans and should inform the museum's staff training programme.

Basic precautions include:

- avoiding putting objects on open display;
- using well-made, dust-resistant display cases;
- keeping objects wrapped in acid-free tissue paper in closed storage units or in boxes with lids;
- using dust covers for large objects;
- keeping doors and windows shut and sealed where possible or desirable;
- ensuring public and staff areas of the museum are kept as clean as possible;
- cleaning museum areas with vacuum cleaners, not dusters.

INSECT/PEST ATTACK

Pest attack, especially by rodents, can be a particular problem for museums. The control of rodents is relatively simple, although the assistance of commercial companies may be needed to protect against the problem or eradicate nests, etc. Advice should be sought on safe and appropriate methods. Do not disregard traditional methods of controlling pests and insects. For example, the museum cat can be a cheap and simple method of reducing rodent problems! Rodents can not only damage museum items, especially where these are made of organic materials or are natural history specimens, but will also chew through packaging materials, files, and electrical wiring circuits. Storage areas in particular should be regularly checked for any signs of rodent presence.

The control of insects is a more complicated matter. All organic material, especially wood, entering the museum should be first inspected for insect infestation. Insects are notoriously difficult to kill, especially where they have to be controlled in areas such as public display galleries where only 'safe' measures can be taken.

The normal life cycle of insects passes through three stages: egg, larva and adult. It is often the larva that damages items, but cannot always be detected until the adult stage is reached. Signs of attack vary from insect to insect. Active wood-worm, for example, produces little piles of sawdust, while insect attack on natural history specimens will produce disturbance of bird feathers or fallen hair in mammals. Termites are a particular menace in many countries. Professional advice needs to be taken and a regular control programme established.

Various proprietary brands of chemical treatment against beetles and moths are available, which can be absorbed on to inert pads and put into showcases and storage areas as a preventive measure. Fumigation of items, which may be necessary to kill eggs or larvae, is a hazardous procedure, and appropriate equipment and safeguards are essential. In all cases, health and safety measures should be closely observed (see Unit 97).

Vigilance and regular inspection are required to avoid damage to collections. As with all conservation, prevention is better and more cost-effective than cure.

Unit
59

Materials testing

Related Units – Units 53–8, 60–8

The choice of materials to be used for display or storage purposes needs particular care. They may be convenient to use or look attractive, but may cause serious physical or chemical damage to museum collections. All materials used for display cases and storage containers/shelves should be inert, especially as these may be reused for different objects at a later date. Seek professional advice from a conservator if in doubt.

CHEMICAL DAMAGE

One of the main causes of chemical damage in museums is from materials that release compounds into the air in vapour form. We have already noted in Units 55–8 how dangerous such gaseous pollution can be to collections. In confined spaces, such as display cases or storage cupboards, vapours generated from materials can build up to a serious level very rapidly and severely affect items.

Metals are particularly liable to attack and can corrode very quickly. For example, organic acids can act as a catalyst for the reaction between lead and carbon dioxide. The reaction causes the surface of lead to be covered by a white powdery layer of lead carbonate. If the reaction is allowed to continue, loss of surface detail and ultimately disintegration will follow. While this type of damage is easy to see, other types of decay such as the effect of formaldehyde on leather, which makes it brittle, are not always obvious.

Materials should therefore be checked and tested before use, and manufacturers asked to guarantee the suitability of their products for the use(s) intended by the museum. Money can be wasted if inappropriate materials are used, and collections can be put at risk or suffer irreparable damage. Take care to ensure that manufacturers have not changed the composition of their products without notification since previous testing.

It is important to note that problems associated with chemical damage can be more acute in high temperatures or high relative humidity (see Unit 57).

PROBLEMS TO BE AWARE OF

Wood

All woods produce vapours harmful to objects; some are worse than others. Unseasoned wood produces more than seasoned wood. Least harmful woods include mahogany, obeche and well-seasoned softwoods; most harmful include oak, chestnut and Douglas fir.

Composite boards – chipboard, plywood and hardboard – emit organic acid vapour, as well as producing vapours from their bonding adhesives. These are usually formaldehyde-based resins, which can tarnish metals, and damage materials containing protein – leather, wool, fur and bone. Marine and exterior plywood are usually bonded by adhesives that release lower forms of formaldehyde and are therefore safer to use.

To minimise the dangers from wood/resin vapours, wood should be sealed with suitable paints, varnishes or lacquers. These cannot stop the emission of vapours completely, and impermeable membranes such as aluminium foil can be used to supplement sealants. Remember to seal the edges of composite boards which emit vapours at a higher rate than surfaces.

Fabrics

Woollen textiles and felts contain sulphur compounds and can tarnish metals. They can also take up moisture in the air. Cellulose-based materials – cotton, linen, hessian – do not create this problem and are safe to use. However, where cellulose-based materials have been dyed, it is worth having the material tested by a conservator before use as some dyes have sulphur in them.

Paints

Oil-based paints will produce organic acid vapour as they dry, so ensure that these paints are dry before use and the smell has disappeared. Allow plenty of time for emulsion paints to dry before use. It is preferable to use as little paint within display cases as possible. Seal wood and cover it with a safe fabric where possible.

Adhesives

Many synthetic adhesives have complex chemical formulae and should be avoided near objects. Advice needs to be taken from professional conservators before their use.

Plastics/rubber

Some poly-foam and poly-sheeting is stable and can be used as lining boards and display mounts in display cases. Stable forms of polyester are used for envelopes for archival material and packing tissue.

Polyurethane or rubber-based materials should be avoided. Rubber is not a stable material and can perish under adverse conditions.

Materials in contact with objects

- Never use 'Plasticine' or proprietary putty-like substances for fixing objects or paper. Staining and tarnishing can result.
- Never use rubber bands for attaching labels or mounting objects. Rubber tends to age and stick to objects.
- Never use metal pins or wire in contact with metal objects as corrosion will occur. Use Perspex rods or nylon wire or thread.
- Never use metal pins in contact with textile, leather, bone or organic moisture-holding materials as the pins corrode and stain objects and materials.

If in doubt, contact a conservator and the manufacturer/supplier. Where possible, carry out tests to ensure that appropriate materials are used at all times.

STUDY EXAMPLE 59.1

A museum had used 'drawing pins' or 'thumb-tacks' to fasten a number of original photographs to a display board covered by felt. Because the RH in the display room was high, the felt had absorbed moisture and the pins gradually rusted. The rust damaged and discoloured the corners of the photographs through which the pins had been pushed: a practice to be avoided at all times!

The photographs had been lent for a special exhibition, and when the lender saw the way in which the museum had not cared for the photographs properly, she withdrew them from the exhibition. The photographs had been the central feature of the exhibition.

The museum had demonstrated that it was not able to look after collections responsibly, and its reputation was severely affected by the subsequent embarrassment.

Storage: principles

Unit

60

Related Units – Units 53–9, 61–8

In many museums, the bulk of the collections is likely to be in store rather than on display and more space for storage is likely to be needed than for display. There is no set prescription for storage facilities, as much will depend on the nature and mix of a museum's collections and the museum's policy towards their display, exhibition and use.

This Unit looks at the general principles of storing collections of all types. Unit 61 examines in more detail the practice of storing different types of collections.

The storage of collections in museums is often poorly considered and inappropriate. A key responsibility of museum managers is to ensure that appropriate storage facilities and methods are provided for the museum and all its collections in line with the museum's collections management policy. The same standards of care need to be exercised for material in store as on display.

High-quality storage, well organised and well managed, enhances the museum's overall efficiency and in the long term saves money. It ensures that the collections are kept safely and securely and that access to them by staff is cost-efficient and cost-effective (see Unit 5).

▌STORAGE FACILITIES AND SYSTEMS

- Storage facilities of all types need to be housed in secure and suitable buildings, whether these are custom-built for storage purposes or appropriately adapted from former uses.
- Space needs to be sufficient for the movement of people and collections. In general terms, storage facilities need to maximise space without overcrowding or creating hazards for the movement of objects or people.
- Space for expansion needs to be provided to allow more items to enter the collections in line with the museum's collecting policy and programme.
- Environmental conditions need to be controlled to suit the categories of collections stored there (see Units 56–8), and monitored on a regular basis.
- Documentation systems and procedures need to be developed for the entry, location and exit of all items, and for audit and stocktaking (see Unit 49).
- Procedures for the safe handling and movement of objects should be developed in line with health and safety requirements (see Units 62 and 97).
- Regular conservation and security assessment needs to be undertaken (see Unit 55). Unauthorised personnel should never be allowed in storage facilities.
- Written procedures for logging staff and accompanied visitors in and out of storage areas, and for ensuring that equipment such as humidifiers or thermohygrographs are maintained on a regular schedule, should be established.

- Racking systems and cupboards need to be of an adequate size to cope with the collections and should have adjustable shelving to allow for changes in use.
- Racking/shelving systems can be built as free-standing units, or in roller systems to maximise limited space and to allow for increased security.
- It is helpful to have lists of items in any one storage container – box, shelf, cupboard, roller racking – attached to the outside of the storage container for ease of reference and security checking. These help to prevent unnecessary searching for items that may lead to damage and can form part of the documentation systems for entry, location and exit, as well as helping in audit and stocktaking.

OPENING UP ACCESS TO STORED COLLECTIONS

Increasingly, museums are exploring ways to make their reserve collections in store more accessible to their visitors in line with their access policies. Different approaches and combinations of approaches are being developed in different countries. Some of these are noted below:

- The advent of the new information and communications technologies means that museums are digitising their reserve collections in order to make them available on-line in different ways (see Units 49 and 99).
- Museums are using events and activities programmes to provide participants with controlled access to their stores to show them how the museum cares for its collections and explain the ways in which reserve collections are used for study, research and exhibition purposes (see Unit 17).
- New museum stores are being designed so that a percentage of the reserve collections can be presented to visitors on an 'open access' basis. Different approaches to their design and presentation provide a contrast to gallery displays and temporary exhibitions. This approach shows visitors the 'raw material' that is used to create displays and exhibitions and helps them understand the different ways that collections are used for research purposes.
- Selected objects from the museum's reserve collections are being housed in 'object-rich' study centres where they can be studied and handled by visitors, either engaged in formal or informal learning programmes or on general museum visits.
- New museum displays are providing a greater density of objects drawn from the reserve collections and making use of new forms of computer-based interpretation to provide information about them to the visitor.
- Museums are reconsidering the balance between display and temporary exhibition areas and putting increased emphasis on temporary and touring exhibitions to allow for more of their reserve collections to be seen on a regular basis.
- Selections of objects from the reserve collections packaged up into '*study boxes*' or '*reminiscence boxes*' are provided to organisations outside the museum for study and reminiscence purposes. These may include schools, old people's homes, hospitals, etc. and help to develop new audiences for the museum (see Unit 16).

- Groups of museums are co-operating to create touring exhibitions based on their reserve collections. In some cases, the objects for these exhibitions are being selected by members of the public invited into the stores to explore the museums' reserve collections and identify items for exhibition.

All these approaches reflect the ways in which museums are making their reserve collections more accessible to their different users. Museums always need to be able to justify the costs associated with managing and maintaining reserve collections. Increasing their public use in such ways can strengthen their case and clearly demonstrate the value of collecting and collections.

Storage: practice

Unit
61

Related Units – Units 53–60, 62–8

LARGE AND HEAVY ITEMS

Key points

As with all collections storage, the following points should be considered for the storage of large and heavy items:

- a suitably secure building is required, purpose-built or adapted;
- environmental conditions need to be monitored and controllable;
- systems and procedures need to be developed for documenting the entry, exit and location of items, and for audit and stocktaking;
- handling procedures need to be developed and suitable equipment provided for lifting and moving;
- regular conservation assessment needs to be undertaken; and
- physical access and accessibility need to be assured through its design and layout.

However, large and heavy items have a range of special considerations that are discussed below.

Storage buildings

Buildings used for the storage of large or heavy items – industrial and agricultural collections, transport collections, monumental or architectural items – or the bulk storage of collections, such as excavated bone or ceramics, should be secure, weatherproof, well lit and adequately provided with an electricity supply.

Most museum objects are likely to be accommodated in a building with a head-room of 5–6 metres, suitable for a lorry to be unloaded with the aid of a mobile crane or fork-lift truck. If the building has columns, a spacing of c.4 metres is likely to be the minimum acceptable. The main access door should be the full height of the building and not less than c.4 metres wide.

For unloading and moving purposes, there should be a concrete platform or apron outside the main access at floor level. Heavier items can then be unloaded outside the building and pulled or winched inside. It is helpful to have anchor points set into the floor for attaching pulling devices. Large items that have to be stored outdoors, should be protected with tarpaulins or covers. Wherever possible, and in whatever climate, it is preferable to store all items inside the storage building. Even large items of machinery that have been working in the open can deteriorate if left stored open to the elements.

Environmental conditions

Creating appropriate environments for stores holding large items is complicated. Sufficient heating or dehumidification must be provided to ensure that condensa-tion is avoided, otherwise even with the application of preservatives metalwork will rust. With large items made of wood, or a range of materials, too low a level of humidity or fluctuating relative humidity will cause damage. A stable environ-ment should be aimed at with an RH level of 50–5 per cent (see Units 56–8).

As we noted in Unit 60, stores should be kept as clean as possible at all times. Concrete floors should be sealed to avoid concrete dust being thrown up. Items should be covered with dust sheets. Polythene sheeting, however, should not be used as it can easily cause condensation.

Care of collections

Equipment needed for the storage of large and heavy items includes a variety of mechanical handling systems. Where possible, items should be put on wooden pallets, stored on heavy duty racking and moved with a fork-lift truck or hydraulic lift. Special care should be taken at all times in terms of health and safety. The lifting and manipulation of heavy items should be very carefully planned and carried out to avoid any injury to museum staff (see Unit 97).

It is worthwhile reassembling industrial items or machinery wherever possible. It is easier to store a machine in a made-up form, than in many component parts. It is very easy for machine parts, for example, to be muddled up or to be damaged. Many large and heavy items can be severely damaged by poor handling. Just because they are large and heavy does not mean that they are robust! Large stone items in particular can be much more fragile than they look. Every care should be taken in handling and storage not to put stress on weak parts.

Large and heavy items being stored or moved within a museum building – machinery, stone, sculpture, paintings, mummy cases, furniture – need very careful handling and support (see Unit 62).

SMALL AND LIGHT OBJECTS

Key points

In storing small and light objects, the following points need to be covered:

- a suitably secure building is required, purpose-built or adapted;
- physical access and accessibility need to be assured through its design and layout;
- handling procedures need to be developed and training for staff made available as required;
- appropriate moving equipment, for example trolleys, needs to be provided;
- environmental conditions need to be monitored and controlled to meet appropriate standards;
- regular conservation assessment needs to be undertaken;
- systems and procedures need to be developed for documenting the entry, location and exit of items, and for audit and stocktaking.

Metallic objects

Iron objects should ideally be stored at an RH of 40 per cent or less, although for mixed material objects or mixed collections an RH of 50–5 per cent is acceptable. Iron will corrode if RH levels are too high, and every effort should be made to create adequate conditions for storage by providing suitable micro-environments within general storage areas.

Iron objects from archaeological excavations on land or underwater can often be unrecognisable and it is only through x-ray that their function or form becomes apparent. It is therefore essential that all iron is treated carefully. It should be stored in inert containers with acid-free tissue or packaging materials such as inert foam to avoid movement within the storage container.

As with iron objects, copper alloy or bronze items should be kept in conditions of low RH, at 40 per cent RH or less where possible, to avoid corrosion. Other metal objects, silver, lead, gold should be stored in inert plastic or metal cabinets or containers. Dry silica gel, a desiccant agent, can be used in storage containers to help provide localised control of RH. It absorbs moisture from the air and helps to achieve a balanced environment. The manufacturer will supply details of the amount of gel needed to provide good protection for the objects.

Ceramic collections

All ceramics should be handled as little as possible and with great care, and should be stored in their normal upright position in secure, dust-free cupboards, one row deep on a shelf. If space does not allow, store smaller items in front of larger ones. Never overcrowd ceramics in store, and always see that there is sufficient clearance for withdrawal or when closing the door. Never stack cups and bowls inside one another, and never stack too many plates in a pile. Where plates are stacked, use folded tissue paper or insert foam or paper between them. Wherever possible, store ceramics on lightly padded shelves to minimise the shock of any vibration or movement, and make sure that lateral movement is minimised by padding.

Ethnographic collections

Ethnographic collections include complex objects that are often made from organic materials, for example leather, hide, skin, grass, wood, fur, feathers or shells. All of these materials are sensitive to RH fluctuation and prone to insect and pest attack (see Units 57–8). Storage conditions should be 50–5 per cent RH wherever possible. Where storing items on shelving, aim for a free movement of air around the object to inhibit possible mould growth and a dust-free environment. The best packing material for most ethnographic collections is acid-free tissue paper, used in conjunction with acid-free storage boxes.

Paintings

In general, problems with the storage of paintings occur with overcrowding, stacking of paintings on top of each other and inadequate space for movement. Strong, secure racking, using wood or metal, should be padded to reduce the danger of frames being chipped or damaged. Care should be taken to ensure that the surfaces of paintings are not in contact with glass or Perspex. Sliding storage racks on which paintings or frames can be hung, while expensive, provide a good solution to storage, provided that paintings are securely fastened to the racking and are well supported.

Watercolours, prints and drawings are particularly sensitive to environmental changes and light. They are best stored flat in boxes or drawers with acid-free tissue used as padding. Acid-free storage boxes specially designed for these items should be used. Watercolours, prints and drawings should be stored out of their frames wherever possible.

Natural history collections

As with paintings, care should be taken to avoid overcrowding or stacking in storage containers, on shelves or in cupboards. Damage can too easily occur in these conditions. Sufficient space therefore needs to be given to mounted specimens of birds or animals on shelving, and where stored in boxes sufficient acid-free tissue paper should be used to pad the specimen enclosed.

Study collections of insects, butterflies or moths need specialised storage and advice should be sought from a trained natural history conservator in their care. Special care needs to be taken to check natural history specimens regularly for pest and insect infestation in storage areas.

Textile collections

Textile collections can be divided into two groups – flat and three-dimensional. Flat textiles include: tapestries, wall hangings, carpets, household linens, bed covers, curtains, flags and banners, embroideries and lace. Three-dimensional textiles include costume, accessories and upholstery.

Flat textiles should be stored flat in trays or acid-free boxes interleaved with acid-free tissue. If the objects are too large, they can be rolled onto cardboard or plastic tubes. Cardboard tubes are acidic and should be first protected by wrapping them in aluminium foil and acid-free tissue paper. Once rolled onto the tube, the textile should be wrapped in pre-washed calico or closely woven cotton fabric and tied with wide tapes. Tubes should be stored suspended in racking, and rolled textiles should never be stacked on top of each other.

Three-dimensional textile items should be hung on prepared and padded hangers and well spaced in cupboards with protective cotton covers, where the item is robust enough. For more delicate items, as well as costume accessories, storage in boxes with acid-free tissue padding is recommended. Upholstered items such as chairs, sofas, screens should be covered with pre-washed closely woven cotton to protect them from dust and dirt. Textile conservation is extremely time-consuming and therefore expensive, and good storage will help to prevent damage occurring and remedial conservation being required.

Photographic collections

Photographic prints and negatives should be enclosed in archival quality, acid-free paper sleeves, envelopes or wrappers, placed within a box and sited on a shelf or cabinet. Slides are best stored in acid-free paper sleeves in a hanging file in a cabinet. Glass plate negatives should be stored individually in neutral paper enclosures, and put vertically in strong acid-free boxes.

Electronic media

Computer disks, audio and videotapes should be stored away from sources of electro-magnetic radiation.

Glass collections

As with ceramics, never overcrowd storage shelves and never let glass objects touch one another. Never place small objects inside larger ones, and always place smaller items at the front of shelves where more than one row of objects has to be stored. Glass fragments should be stored in boxes with supportive padding made from acid-free tissue or foam plastic. Great care should be taken when handling or moving glass, especially fragments.

Geological collections

Materials to be used in storage containers for geological collections should be tested in advance of their use. It is commonly and mistakenly thought that geological collections are stable. This is by no means true. Oak cabinets will release organic acid vapour that affects carbonate specimens. Lead specimens can be corroded by acetic and formic acid from composite boards and boxes. Specimens should therefore be stored with due care to their packing.

Poor handling or inadequate packing is often the cause of damage to geological specimens. Specimens should be placed in trays or in acetate topped boxes so that they are held gently but firmly, and cannot knock or rub against each other. Acid-free tissue paper can be used for additional packing. Drawers in cabinets should be of a size that allows them to be easily lifted when full of specimens.

Don't forget: geological specimens can be heavy!

Unit

62

Handling, packing and moving collections

Related Units – Units 53–61, 63–8

Most damage to museum collections comes about through careless handling and transport, or poor storage. Apart from the damage handling itself can do to artefacts, they are exposed to many more risks when handled and moved. Handling or moving artefacts or specimens of all types and of all sizes in the museum's primary collections should therefore be kept to a minimum at all times.

It is important to think ahead and plan before handling, packing and moving artefacts. The checklists here are designed to help raise as well as answer questions that are relevant to handling, packing and moving collections of all types.

GENERAL POINTS TO REMEMBER

- Understand the special needs of different types of artefact before handling or moving.
- If an artefact needs to be handled for study, transit, restorage, display, etc., only allow designated, responsible persons to handle it.
- Never let other persons handle collections, for example students or researchers, without express guidance and supervision at all times.
- Ensure that documentation procedures are followed when moving objects from one location to another.
- Use lint-free cotton gloves when handling artefacts to avoid leaving any residue from your fingers or hands.
- Concentrate when handling or moving objects; do not carry on conversations, attempt to write or type with one hand, or answer the telephone.
- Special care should be taken when handling certain types of object, for example, old bird or animal mounts that may have been treated with arsenic, or radioactive materials. Appropriate gloves, masks, goggles and protective clothing are required.
- Wear protective clothing and footwear where necessary, for example, a cotton laboratory coat, overalls or steel-toed work boots, when handling or moving items.
- Use pencils, not ink, in the vicinity of artefacts or natural history specimens.
- Never eat, drink or smoke in the vicinity of an artefact or natural history specimen.
- Know and carry out all relevant health and safety requirements.

WHEN STUDYING

- When working with items, work on a clean, uncluttered table or desk or in a clean area. You may need to pad work surfaces for certain types of artefact.
- Ensure that light levels are appropriate for the categories of collections being studied.
- Never reach across artefacts or move or carry one artefact across another in case of accidents.
- Never pile objects or specimens on top of other objects or specimens.
- Remember that lightweight items, e.g. glass or ceramics, can be easily knocked over. Take necessary precautions to provide cushioning wherever possible.
- Never leave objects out of storage containers, for example on a table, for any length of time unattended.
- Never lift fragile objects by weak points such as the rim or handle, but use both hands to cradle the item.
- Do not use flash photography with light-sensitive objects.

IN THE STORES

- Keep stores uncluttered, tidy and clean to avoid accidents when objects are being carried or moved.
- Make sure that doors are opened for you if required, rather than trying to open a door while carrying objects or putting objects temporarily on the floor to open the door.
- Never put objects down in a location where collections are not normally located.
- Make sure that you have enough people to help, or appropriate equipment, for example trolleys, hydraulic lifting apparatus, carrying straps, or glass-lifters to assist.
- Use trolleys in stores where possible or practical to avoid carrying.
- Do not overload drawers, storage boxes or containers; too much weight can create difficulties in lifting or sliding.
- In storage areas, on racking and in boxes and containers, ensure objects are well spaced to avoid items rubbing against each other.
- Ensure that objects are relocated in the correct position, following study or display, when they are brought back to the stores.
- Use both hands to lift objects.
- Carry one object, drawer or box at a time.
- Do not carry objects stacked on top of other objects.
- When carrying smaller items, use a padded container or basket.

PACKING AND TRANSIT

- Pack or store objects wherever possible using inert, tested materials such as acid-free tissue paper or acid-free storage boxes.
- Packing for transit implies movement, vibration and shock, and objects need to be carefully protected and cushioned. Use experienced and trained technicians where possible or ask for advice if uncertain.
- When moving a three-dimensional artefact, make sure its rear and sides are well protected.
- When moving items, make certain that corners are well protected.
- Label all objects in transit with FRAGILE/THIS WAY UP notices and put red warnings on vulnerable parts.

There are a number of useful publications on the transport of museum collections and special packing systems. Museum managers should be fully aware of all the risks inherent in the handling, movement and transport of collections.

With careful forward planning and effective preparation, risks can be minimised. Without due care and attention, and consideration, museum collections are at their most vulnerable when being handled or moved. Museum managers must make certain that all staff designated to handle collections are fully aware of procedures and risks, and training should be provided in this crucially important area.

Remedial conservation: principles

Related Units – Units 53–62, 64–8

This Unit examines the definition and principles of remedial conservation. Unit 64 explains the practice of remedial conservation. Both Units illustrate the relationship between remedial and preventive conservation.

Remedial conservation is the process by which the deterioration of an object is halted and its survival in a stable condition is assured. Conservators are highly skilled individuals and will have, or will develop through training, a close understanding of the make-up of an object and its physical condition. It is their job to analyse the needs of an object using all available means and to treat it in an appropriate way. Wherever possible, the conservator will use materials and employ methods of treatment that can be reversed at a later date if required.

Different materials require different conservation treatments and remedial conservation can often be a very time-consuming and costly matter. New, often highly sophisticated, scientific techniques are now employed by conservators to examine and analyse objects before treatment. It follows that items that have undergone often-expensive remedial conservation must be returned to conditions of display or storage that will ensure their survival in the long term. Remedial and preventive conservation therefore go hand in hand.

Where a museum has identified a programme of remedial conservation (see Unit 64), the conservator should provide the museum with estimates of time and money for the necessary work to be carried out. While these estimates may need to be revised once work in the studio or laboratory begins and the conservator can examine the object(s) in appropriate conditions, they provide a basis on which the museum can plan and budget for the conservation programme.

Detailed records, including photographs, should be taken of all the remedial work carried out on the objects, and copies should be returned to the museum with the conserved items. If in the future more work is required, these records provide a valuable part of the 'conservation history' of the object. Cross-references should be established to the museum's collections documentation system, so that a record of all work that has been carried out is easily accessible.

Curator and conservator should work closely together in the remedial conservation process. The conservator will benefit from having detailed information about the object to be treated, and the curatorial staff should take an informed interest in the work that the conservator carries out on the object. The remedial conservation process at all stages may reveal a good deal about the nature and history of an object, which can significantly enhance curatorial understanding.

CONSERVATION OR RESTORATION?

The difference between the terms 'conservation' and 'restoration' is an important one for museum staff to understand. In some countries, the processes are barely distinguished from each other. But the distinction is important. While remedial conservation seeks to halt deterioration and stabilise an object, restoration aims to return an object to as near its original position as possible. In museum work, restoration may follow from conservation if there is a recognised need, for example, for the object to be meaningfully displayed.

Different objects will require different approaches. If restoration work is carried out, it should be undertaken with the same attention to detail as remedial conservation. Over-restoring an object can damage its historical and aesthetic value. Restoration will require often detailed comparative research with other objects of similar type, and the processes used must always be capable of reversal if at some future time new techniques or new research findings demand modification or alteration to the restored object. Detailed records of the approaches and the processes used in any restoration must be fully documented, and supplied to the museum when the work is completed.

The balance between conservation and restoration is often a difficult matter. Some objects, such as vehicles, for example, may need to be fully restored if they are to be displayed in working condition or used for demonstration purposes. It is essential for conservators, restorers and museums alike to be able to identify and explain to the public the extent of restoration on a museum object.

Conservators have undergone intensive professional training and work within the framework of professional codes of ethics. No remedial conservation should be undertaken by unsupervised museum staff, as such work always causes damage to collections. Always take guidance from a professional conservator.

If your museum does not employ conservation staff, and you wish to have specialist remedial conservation carried out, select conservators on the basis of their experience, qualifications and the type of work they have carried out previously. Ask colleagues in other museums what quality of service they have received, and visit conservators at their workplace to discuss their work and the range of documentation or photography they will provide.

Developing a good working relationship with the conservator will be of the utmost importance in any conservation programme that you undertake.

Key word

Remedial conservation – the processes involved in repairing damage to collections, using specialist conservation techniques that are reversible. The need for remedial conservation is often due to poor collections management and inadequate preventive conservation measures.

Unit

64

Remedial conservation: practice

Related Units – Units 53–63, 65–8

This Unit explains the practice of remedial conservation. Unit 63 examines the definition and principles of remedial conservation. Both Units illustrate the relationship between remedial and preventive conservation.

In general terms, only experienced and professionally trained conservators should carry out remedial conservation on museum collections (see Unit 63). An enormous amount of damage can occur to objects of all types and sizes if untrained or unsupervised individuals attempt to carry out remedial conservation. Museum managers should guard against this happening. It is often the case that well-meaning intentions can lead to irreversible damage to museum items. Inappropriate cleaning techniques or materials may be used, adhesives may affect material adversely because of their chemical composition or physical damage may occur that cannot be undone.

In practice, museum collections are extraordinarily wide-ranging. Different types of objects and different types of material have different types of needs (see Units 60–1). It is this range of need that requires expert knowledge, and few conservators can be expected to have expert knowledge across all specialist areas. However, conservators can advise on what not to do in a general sense, or help create a programme within which remedial conservation can be carried out (see Unit 53).

The key element is skill. In many areas, highly skilled traditional craft workers (with, say, textiles or wooden objects) may be the best people to undertake the actual work of conservation or restoration, but this should always be under the supervision of the conservator and the museum manager.

Some limited basic conservation, or repair and restoration (see Unit 63) can be carried out on museum collections by people who are not trained conservators. However, the museum manager must always work with conservators to define precisely what can and what can not be done by untrained people. They must, of course, be fully briefed as to what are the limits of their work; and they should be reassured that it is always better to ask for advice from the museum manager than to make a mistake with a museum object. Once the museum manager has established these procedures, it may be possible, under skilled supervision and guidance, for much useful work to be carried out in this way.

There are risks, even with good procedures, in using untrained workers or volunteers. In particular, delicate objects such as textiles, ceramics, glass objects, clocks and watches or paintings can be irreversibly damaged if treated in an inappropriate way. Many 'amateur' conservators will not necessarily appreciate the damage they can cause. What on the surface of things may appear a straightforward process to the untutored eye, such as cleaning and polishing, can have long-term damaging effects on museum objects unless suitable materials and techniques are always used. Constant support and guidance are needed, and regular discussions with museum staff should be held, as methods can and do change, and they need to be kept fully informed.

Techniques, methods and materials in conservation vary through time. A professional conservator will be able to keep the museum manager up to date and advise on the best possible way to approach the collections in line with the museum's collections management plan (see Unit 53).

Museums have a key responsibility to care for their collections. Never attempt to conserve or restore an item without guidance from a professionally trained conservator.

Unit

65

Disaster planning

Related Units – Units 53–64, 66–8

Disasters can and do occur at any time and in any place. As recent history shows, museums are not immune to fire or flooding, earthquakes or explosions, civil unrest, vandalism or war damage. The disaster may be small or large scale, due to neglect, error, human agency or the forces of nature. How can museums cope with disasters?

First, any disaster requires a speedy reaction to reduce or limit damage to collections, buildings/equipment or people. Controlling a disaster is only likely to be effective if systems and procedures to mitigate its effects have already been put in place. This means planning ahead for possible eventualities and producing a *Disaster Control Plan* for the museum. Where possible, the museum should ensure that its Disaster Control Plan relates to local or national disaster planning.

A Disaster Control Plan should set out the steps for *preventing disasters* (where this is in the museum's control) and *reacting to disasters* efficiently and speedily. Museum staff should be trained to deal with disasters. The museum should have disaster control equipment and supplies, and planned procedures. Such measures should be considered in relation to the museum's insurance and security policies.

Preventive measures to combat security and conservation problems are discussed elsewhere (see Units 55 and 67–8). Here we propose a series of steps to take in planning procedures and reacting to disasters.

THE DISASTER REACTION TEAM

A Disaster Reaction Team is made up of about six capable individuals, not necessarily all from the museum's staff, who are readily available in the event of a disaster. Many disasters occur when museums are closed and there are no staff on the premises. The team should therefore include people who have collections management and conservation skills with at least one person knowing the museum's collections. The team leader should have a good understanding of conservation requirements.

They should be briefed and trained on the layout of the museum building(s) and the location of emergency points, for example fire extinguishers, disaster boxes, telephones, alarm points and service control points. Each member should have ready access to a copy of the museum's Disaster Control Plan and this should be updated on a regular basis. The size of the museum will determine the number of Disaster Reaction Teams necessary.

DISASTER CONTROL EQUIPMENT

Basic equipment and supplies should be readily at hand in the event of a disaster. The museum should create disaster boxes containing protective clothing, emergency equipment, cleaning and packing equipment, storage containers and damage recording supplies. Disaster boxes should be clearly labelled, sited near high priority and irreplaceable collections, and not used for any other purpose at any time. A number of disaster boxes should be maintained off-site in a readily accessible location.

Remember that communication is one of the keys to effective disaster response and control. Telephone systems may well be put out of action in a disaster. Alternative channels of communication, for example mobile telephones, e-mail or couriers, will need to be available or on standby. Mobile telephones should be loaded with the telephone numbers of the Disaster Reaction Team.

SUPPORT SERVICES

The museum may need the support of other specialist or allied services, such as libraries or archive offices, in disaster planning and in the event of a disaster. Lists of organisations and individuals providing specialist services, including conservation services, should be kept together with emergency telephone numbers in the Disaster Control Plan and loaded on to the team's mobile telephones. Remember that suppliers of emergency equipment such as pumps, hoses or crates are likely to charge for services.

However, some large and multinational companies may be prepared to work with the museum in disaster planning and supply equipment or communications system at short notice as part of their service and responsibility to the local community. So, too, may emergency services such as glaziers, plumbers and builders. Insurance companies should be contacted as soon as possible after a disaster has occurred.

DISASTER PROCEDURES

If a disaster strikes a museum during working hours, the procedure for raising the alarm must include contact with the leader of the Disaster Reaction Team. Out of working hours, the relevant emergency services should be provided with full details of whom to contact. The museum should liaise closely with the emergency services on a regular basis to ensure that each is aware of the other's responsibilities.

The leader of the Disaster Reaction Team should ensure that the members of the team are gathered at an appropriate point, together with key museum staff responsible for the collections damaged or under threat. Services such as gas, water and electricity should be disconnected as and when appropriate.

DAMAGE ASSESSMENT

When the disaster area is safe and accessible, and not before, the extent of the damage should be investigated, and photographed where possible. Only when this investigation has been carried out carefully can a salvage plan be drawn up. Each member of the team should then be clearly briefed on his/her tasks, issued with protective clothing and set to work. Access to and movement within the disaster area should be controlled by the team leader. Secure areas should be designated for sorting, cleaning, labelling and packing damaged material.

Remember that security is of critical importance when normal security procedures may not be working properly.

REMOVAL OF OBJECTS

This is the most important part of the disaster reaction procedure. Speed is likely to be important, but care is essential. Objects must be removed, cleaned, packed and transported to areas of safety and conservation facilities. Early contact should be made with specialist conservation facilities to ensure that objects can be treated in the event of disasters.

The following points should be noted:

- items should be removed with the minimum of damage;
- items should be identified and a damage list drawn up;
- where possible, items should be photographed;
- where appropriate, items should be cleaned;
- items should be labelled, and packed as appropriate;
- all containers should be clearly marked;
- conservation assessment and remedial treatment should be carried out as appropriate (see Units 53, 63–4).

THE DISASTER AREA

The speed with which the disaster area can be returned to normal will depend on the nature of the damage. With flood or water damage from fire hoses (a common problem), the area will need to be dried out and ventilated. Care should be taken to inhibit mould growth with fungicides. RH levels should be regularly monitored.

▋ DISASTER PROCEDURES ASSESSMENT

Lastly, review the Disaster Control Plan. Did the Plan work well? Did the communications system work well? Did the team(s) carry out their tasks efficiently? Were all the disaster boxes properly equipped? What lessons were learnt for the future?

▋ STUDY EXAMPLE 65.1

A museums service responsible for twenty museums in its area established a series of disaster supply stockpiles in different locations. Each stockpile consisted of a series of bags of equipment and tools. (The numbers of items in each stockpile varied, depending on the extent of the likely risks.)

The resources included:

- A personal emergency bag, kept by each member of the disaster team.
Protective suit, safety helmet, head torch, safety torch, batteries.

- Bag 1 – Tool bag.
Hammers, pliers, saws, screwdrivers, extension lead.

- Bag 2 – Initial entry equipment.
Safety helmets, protective clothing, protective glasses, leather gloves, polythene sheeting, nylon ropes, first-aid kit (see Unit 97), respirators, safety masks, lifting straps.

- Bag 3 – Wet recovery materials.
Mops, plastic buckets, sponge cloths, blotting paper, dustpans, brushes, rubber gloves, water spray bottles, bandages, safety pins.

- Bag 4 – Recording and packing equipment.
Hand cleaner, lightweight vinyl gloves, plastic aprons, pencils, notepads, tie-on labels, string, clipboards, self-adhesive labels, stapler/staples, plastic bags, adhesive tape, scissors, rubber bands, paper towels, paper for packing.

- Loose items.
Folding tables, wrapping materials, polythene sheeting, waterproof clothing, salvage blankets, camera(s) and film.

These bags provide the basis for a disaster supply kit. Their contents, however, can be adapted to local circumstances and the availability of supplies.

Insurance

Related Units – 53–65, 67–8

Insurance in the museum concerns the following main areas:

- collections;
- buildings;
- building contents – furniture and fittings and equipment;
- staff and visitors.

These are examined in this Unit. Insurance is a complicated subject and because insurance requirements and approaches vary from one country to another specialist advice is required from reputable insurance brokers. In principle, insurance provides financial protection for property or people against specified contingencies such as loss, damage or injury. It involves the payment of regular premiums in return for a policy guaranteeing such protection. It does not prevent such contingencies, but compensates for them financially in whole or in part. Given the range of coverage – collections, buildings, building contents and people – insurance can also be expensive. It is therefore well worth comparing insurance products and prices from a number of companies to ensure best value for the museum.

COLLECTIONS

Insuring museum collections is complicated both by the very varied nature of museum collections and by the difficulty or impossibility of replacing rare or unique items. One approach is to break down the museum's collection into separate categories that can then be insured separately on an indemnity basis or on the basis of an agreed valuation. The museum may have a number of unspecified objects and some specified objects within these categories covered on an indemnity basis, and further objects covered individually at a value agreed with the insurers. This approach provides insurance cover for the museum collection as a whole. Rare or unique items in the collection can then be replaced with items of similar quality and significance if damage or disaster occurs.

Prices in the art and antiques marketplace, which is now global in its coverage, change on a continuous basis. Museums will therefore need to have regular valuations of items carried out in order to update their insurance cover for their collections.

Valuation of collections for insurance purposes can however be very expensive. Some companies working in the art and antiques markets will seek to charge fees based on a percentage of the value of the collections rather than on the professional time taken to undertake the valuation. Museums should use reputable commercial companies for valuation work and ensure that the basis of their charges is clearly understood. As with all external services, it is preferable to ask for quotations from several companies for valuation work.

It is important to ensure that items on loan from other museums or from private individuals are separately insured by the museum. Items on loan to the museum will need to be insured by the museum at a value agreed with the lender. Items on loan from the museum also need to be insured by the borrower. Remember that items in transit, for example as part of a touring exhibition or as loans from or to the museum, also need to be protected by adequate insurance cover for the transit period.

BUILDINGS

It is essential to have buildings insurance. Where the museum owns its own buildings, it is best to take out full rather than limited cover on an indemnity or reinstatement basis. This allows the museum to replace the building or part of the building following any disaster such as fire or flood.

Owners of buildings also need to insure against injury to the public caused by disrepair, e.g. from falling roof materials or uneven steps. The museum's governing body is normally liable for any injury to a member of the public caused in this way.

Where the museum leases or rents its buildings, the landlord will usually insure the building and recharge the museum as tenant. However, it is essential to examine the landlord's cover, especially where the museum is liable for repairs. The landlord may not be adequately insured for damage that the museum will then have to make good.

In the event of a disaster to its buildings (see Unit 65), the museum may have to suspend its day-to-day operations. In this case, where the museum is dependent on revenue income through admissions charges and its retail and catering operations, the consequences can be serious for the museum's cashflow. Staff costs will still need to be met and bills will still have to paid. Insurance against business interruption for a defined period of time will help to offset loss of income, although the premiums can be heavy.

BUILDING CONTENTS – FURNITURE AND FITTINGS AND EQUIPMENT

It is often surprising how much all of the contents of a museum can be worth when one comes to replace items after a disaster. Contents may include furniture and fittings, equipment such as computers, photocopiers, cameras and fieldwork equipment, reference books and journals, as well as retail and catering stock. Insurance cover should be taken out on an 'all risks' basis to compensate for loss or damage. A register of all items of furniture and equipment should be kept together with a record of their purchase value in case of the need to make a claim against the museum's insurance and a copy housed in a safe and secure place.

STAFF AND VISITORS

Museums as employers have a duty to ensure that their employees have a safe working environment. The museum as employer should provide appropriate insurance that protects the employee against injury or illness caused by any negligence on the part of the museum.

However, the definition of employee is complicated in law. The employer/employee relationship may differ, for example when someone is working for the museum only on a part-time or temporary basis. Volunteers may also pose particular insurance problems because they are not normally viewed as employees. It is essential to understand these issues and where necessary seek specialist advice, as insurance cover needs to be tailored to meet the needs of the museum and to protect its staff. Other forms of insurance for staff and volunteers that the museum may wish to consider include health and medical insurance schemes, and pensions and life insurance schemes.

Specialist museums, for example those with animals, moving vehicles or working machinery, will normally require separate insurance cover in addition to that discussed here. Different statutory liabilities will exist in different countries.

Museums also have a duty to ensure that their visitors and other members of the public have a safe internal environment. Museums should therefore take out appropriate third-party insurance cover against any injury to members of the public as general visitors to the museum or visiting in the course of their business. Where insurance does not exist, claims against the museum may be particularly punitive.

Unit

67

Collections security: physical and electronic

Related Units – Units 53–66, 68, 73

This Unit examines the approaches to physical and electronic security for museum collections. It should be read in conjunction with Unit 68, which looks at security systems and procedures in the museum.

PHYSICAL SECURITY

All museum collections, whether behind glass or on open display, are automatically at risk of theft or damage when the museum is open to the public. Ever-increasing market prices for museum items of all types means that theft has been increasing in museums worldwide as well as in the wider historic environment. Damage, whether intentional or accidental, through vandalism or fire, flood and other disasters (see Units 65–6), also needs to be protected against.

Remember that security systems and procedures are not simply in place to protect a museum's collections, they are also protecting its reputation – as a safe and reliable place to look after the public heritage.

Collections security depends on:

- effective protective measures;
- appropriate security procedures (see Unit 68); and
- good buildings security (see Unit 73).

In this Unit, some protective measures for collections are examined.

Display cases

Do not assume that a display case, whatever material it is made from, provides complete security – it does not! Two areas of weakness exist – the case glass and the frame, which can be broken/damaged by force; and the locking system that is often easy to overcome (see Unit 28). Museum managers should check display cases for weak points and they should be monitored regularly.

- Are the case locks visible and accessible to a would-be thief?
- How strong is the frame?
- Are wall cases securely attached to the wall?
- Can display cases be easily moved or shaken?
- Do joints provide entry points for screwdrivers or metal bars?
- Is the individual case alarmed?
- Is the case regularly checked by security staff?
- Are the case's contents regularly checked by curatorial staff?

Framed pictures

Pictures are vulnerable from theft and damage. Framed pictures should be fastened to walls or screens with mirror plates and screws. Screws should be strong and of suitable length, and the screwheads covered to obscure the type of screw used. Use different sorts of screwhead to increase security. Rod hanging systems are normally supplied with security screws or fastenings for height adjustment. Where required, portable alarm systems can be used for individual pictures, or pictures can be linked to the museum's alarm system.

Open displays

Where collections are on open display, discourage touching and handling by physical barriers, such as ropes or information panels on barriers and by putting items beyond arm's reach. Use psychological deterrents such as different floor coverings and textures for visitor routes, notices and requests in information leaflets. Never leave damage 'on display', for example graffiti on a display board, as it encourages repetition.

Some objects on open display may be provided specifically as touch exhibits. In this case, be clear in the information provided about what visitors may or may not do, especially if other exhibits on open display may not be touched.

ELECTRONIC SECURITY

Many small museums will not be able to afford electronic security. It is worth remembering that alarm systems in themselves do not *prevent* theft or *catch* thieves. They can be valuable components of your overall security system, which includes effective buildings security, physical security and security procedures. Alarms alert the museum's security staff and/or an alarm company's station.

Remember that a hand bell or a whistle can often be just as effective in alerting security staff to a security problem as expensive electronic equipment. Thieves and vandals will only be apprehended if the response time to the alarm is rapid, and the physical or buildings security helps to slow or halt their escape.

Wherever possible, alarm systems should be linked to an alarm company's station to ensure an immediate response, especially when the museum is closed. They should be installed by a reputable alarm company, and regularly checked and maintained. The control panel should be sited in a secure place in the museum, and only a limited number of people should have access to it.

Alarm systems must be maintained and the alarm company will normally carry this out for the museum on an agreed contractual basis.

Electronic detection systems

Electronic detection systems include among others:

- *magnetic contact* – if a magnetic contact, for example on a window, door or a display case is broken, the alarm is sounded.
- *wiring* – the alarm wire is embedded in a door or shutter, and is only triggered if the door/shutter is cut into.
- *vibration detectors* – these are set on doors, windows or display cases and activated by abnormal levels of vibration.
- *break-glass detectors* – these detect the frequency pattern of breaking glass, for example in windows and display cases, or roof lights.
- *passive infra-red sensors* – these sensors are designed to detect body-heat and provide an area such as a corridor or part of a gallery with an alarm screen.
- *activity detection sensors* – microwave or ultra-sonic sensors detect movement within a detection area. These can be used in conjunction with passive infra-red detectors to provide a cross-checking safeguard in case of a false alarm from one system.

- *smoke detectors* – sensors detect smoke, trigger alarms and if required activate water sprinkler or gas prevention systems.
- *closed circuit television (CCTV)* – CCTV is not a replacement for security staff. It must be watched continuously if a response is to be made to a security threat, and the watcher needs to be in immediate contact with security staff on the ground, for example through two-way radio. Some CCTV systems can be linked to passive infra-red sensors or activity detection sensors, and alert the watcher to possible threat and/or activate recording videotape.

The choice of alarm system will depend on the size of your museum, the level of risk and financial resources. Significant advances are being made in micro-electronics every year and systems need to be reappraised on a regular basis.

Collections security: systems and procedures

Unit 68

Related Units – Units 53–67, 73

This Unit examines security systems and procedures in the museum. It should be read in conjunction with Unit 67, which looks at the approaches to physical and electronic security for museum collections.

SECURITY STAFF

Security staff in the museum are an essential part of its security system. They deter criminal or anti-social behaviour in the museum and can provide a physical response to problems. Security staff should be properly trained, and regularly updated in security procedures and how to respond to emergencies. Where possible in small museums, there should be a minimum of two security staff on duty at any one time for personal safety. Security staff should have ready access to an emergency alarm system, for example an alarm button at the reception desk, two-way radio where appropriate, and an emergency telephone – landline or mobile. Emergency telephone numbers should be immediately at hand (see Units 65 and 67).

Security staff will have a range of duties among which should be:

- checking that doors and windows are locked and intact;
- regular, but random, patrolling of galleries and other public areas of the museum;

- checking displays and display cases on a daily basis;
- reporting damage or other problems, such as the need for replacement light-bulbs or the need for cleaning;
- being alert to possible problems with visitors such as rowdiness or suspicious behaviour.

In many small museums, museum staff often have to carry out other tasks as well as providing security cover, for example answering telephone enquiries or selling items in the museum shop.

The museum manager will have to give careful thought as to how the security and customer care and service aspects of the museum's work can be effectively balanced and carried out. The museum manager should also ensure that the security staff are fully under his/her management.

In too many museums, theft has been carried out by museum security staff who are often poorly paid and insufficiently trained and managed. On appointment, as far as the laws of the country allow, their personal records should be checked for any previous criminal activity.

Security staff should be regarded as key members of the museum's staff. In some countries, security staff also act as excellent guides to the museum's collections. Their interpretive and security duties, however, need to be carefully balanced to ensure their primary security responsibilities are not prejudiced.

SECURITY PROCEDURES

The museum should develop, as part of its procedure manual, clear security procedures that all staff should adhere to (see also Unit 67). The checklist includes a number of points to build into the procedure:

- *All* staff should sign in and out of the museum on entry and exit in a daily record book. This provides a checklist of people in the museum in case of fire or other emergency requiring evacuation. All staff should enter/exit from the museum only through official control points.
- Visitors to private areas of the museum should also sign in and out of the museum. They should be given security badges to wear and be accompanied by a member of staff. Anyone not wearing a badge can thus be challenged if seen in private areas.
- Key control is an essential part of the security procedure. No internal keys should leave the museum, and keys should be checked and present before the museum closes at the end of the day. One person should have responsibility for key control on a day-to-day basis, record them in a log book on issue and check them on return. Keys should be kept in a locked cabinet at all times and never left unattended, or lent to unauthorised persons. Keys should be provided only to those staff who need them and for no other reasons.
- Supervision of students and researchers is essential. Always ask researchers to write to the museum in advance to make an appointment and check the

credentials of a researcher before allowing access to collections. Make certain that the objects and their supporting documentation to be examined by the researcher are listed. This list should be signed by the researcher and member of staff supervising him/her at the outset of the period of study and the items checked off against the list at the end of the period of study. Never leave a researcher or visitor unsupervised, especially in an area where collections are accessible.

- Where contractors or delivery firms are entering the museum, stringent security precautions should also apply. The museum manager and security staff should be aware of their arrival and the reasons for their being in the museum. In many cases, contractors will be working in sensitive areas of the museum, internally and externally. Every care should be taken to ensure that security systems and procedures are not bypassed, that dangerous or inflammable materials are not left by contractors in vulnerable areas and that equipment, such as ladders, is not left unlocked and accessible.

- Responsibility for the alarm system, its maintenance schedule and testing should be assigned to an appropriate member of staff. The procedures for closing and locking the museum at the end of the day, setting the alarm system and opening the museum at the beginning of the day should be clearly defined, and the responsibility of designated staff. Museums can often be at their most vulnerable at opening and closing times.

- Adequate procedures for emergency evacuation in case of fire or other disasters should be in place and regularly tested. Staff should of course be trained in carrying out evacuation procedures efficiently.

It is the museum manager's and the security manager's responsibility to ensure that effective security procedures are in place, are monitored and updated where required, staff are adequately trained and risks are effectively managed and contained.

It is always better to be safe than sorry!

Section 4
The museum and its buildings

Museum buildings: form and function

Related Units – Units 13, 70–4

Throughout the world, museums are housed in an extraordinarily wide range of buildings. Buildings used by museums fall into two general categories – purpose-built and conversions. They include:

- historic, purpose-built museum buildings;
- contemporary, purpose-built museum buildings;
- important historic or contemporary buildings – originally used for domestic, public service/state, commercial, industrial, religious or military purposes – which have been converted wholly or in part for museum use; and
- redundant buildings of limited architectural significance.

The form that museums take at their establishment is conditioned by a number of linked factors:

- their cultural, social, economic, political, technological and architectural contexts;
- the locations that are available for the museum site and its building(s);
- the financial resources available; and
- the objectives set by the organisation developing the museum and its funding partners.

Many museums have been altered, adapted and extended through time as the different contexts within which they operate have themselves changed. As the history of museums shows, few museums are, or indeed should be, static. They should be established or managed in the knowledge that both their form and function are likely to change over time as values and attitudes, policies and professional practices change and evolve. It follows that museum architecture and design, both externally and internally, not only reflect changing museum needs and attitudes to collections management, user services and management, but can also act as a constraint when and where necessary change is required.

The form of a museum building whether converted or purpose-built should relate to its mission and objectives (see Units 80–1). The allocation and configuration of space and its treatment depend on a close understanding of the particular museum's aims and objectives, and on the priorities which the museum sets itself in the light of its policies and resources – public services, access and social inclusion, finances, staffing, collections management, etc. In essence, form should follow function.

There are three main considerations to bear in mind:

- the needs of the public using the museum and its visitor services and facilities;
- the needs of the collections available for the public; and
- the range of services supporting the museum and its collections – managerial, curatorial, administrative.

The simplified checklists here indicate the elements that might be included in discussing space allocation. The amount of space, the configuration of space and the requirements of that space for these different functions will differ from museum to museum. It is essential however that adequate space is given to priority functions; these are asterisked on the checklists.

Public space/services

- visitor entrance*
- reception*
- orientation*
- visitor information*
- cloakrooms
- assembly area
- rest areas*
- lavatories*
- catering facilities
- audio-visual theatre
- education room(s)*
- lecture theatre
- meeting rooms
- retail facilities*
- security office/desk*
- telephones/post boxes
- donations box

Public space/collections

- temporary exhibitions*
- displays*
- resource centre
- library
- documentation/information*
- archives/records
- study collections*
- collections management staff offices*

Supporting services

- management offices*
- administration/finance offices*
- duty staff offices
- security office and systems*
- collections storage*
- conservation laboratories
- technical workshop(s)*
- exhibitions storage*
- photographic studios
- design/display studios
- publications/shop stock stores*
- publications office
- information/PR/publicity office
- research/fieldwork*
- technician's stores*
- cleaning*
- staff rest room(s)*
- heating/air conditioning plant*
- garage(s)/parking areas
- delivery bay

A museum building should function cost-effectively and cost-efficiently, use environmentally sustainable materials and make a firm architectural statement about the museum and its values. Buildings should be sound and well maintained. They should be well sited in terms of public access and accessibility, for example near public transport. They should provide adequate space for existing requirements, and where possible for later expansion. The relationship and adjacency of one element to another needs very careful consideration if the building is to work efficiently for visitors and staff alike and the safekeeping and safeguarding of the museum's collections.

The museum's requirements for the display and storage of collections should be well understood and provided for. Every precaution needs to be taken to ensure that services such as gas, water, heating or air-conditioning plants do not run through or affect sensitive areas, such as storage areas, and put collections at risk.

A museum's surroundings will also have an important bearing on its functions. In many cases, the museum's range of activities and services may be extended into its surroundings such as open-air exhibition areas, gardens or car parks.

The form and operation of museum buildings and their surroundings will be affected by the planning and building regulations in different countries. Where museums are located in important historic buildings, museum managers must bear in mind their professional responsibilities towards the building as a historic artefact in its own right. Balancing building regulations with health and safety requirements, architects' and designers' 'solutions', public considerations and the needs of the collections is no easy task. Whatever the scale of development, a conversion of an existing building or the creation of a new building are both complex matters and require adequate time for planning and implementation.

The most successful museums are those that match their needs to the space(s) available. A rough rule of thumb for space allocation is reception/visitor facilities – 25 per cent; collections storage – 25 per cent; displays/exhibitions – 25 per cent; and support services – 25 per cent. In small- and medium-sized museums, it is more effective to use limited space for regularly changing exhibitions rather than 'permanent' displays. This approach makes use of the collections in a variety of different ways and does not take up space needed for other priority functions. It helps develop the museum's audiences by encouraging them to return to the museum on a regular basis.

As we have seen, museums are of course not only about exhibitions and displays, which is a common misconception in groups and individuals wishing to set up new museums. All museums are concerned with a wide range of interlocking functions, and the form of the museum building(s) must allow for an appropriate balance of functions.

Museum buildings: planning for access

Unit
70

Related Units – Units 8, 69, 75–6

How can museums make sure that everyone feels able, and is able, to make use of the services they offer? There are all sorts of reasons why people may not visit (they are sometimes called 'barriers to access'), and it is well worth while spending time trying to discover what those reasons are, and how they can be removed. Some of these barriers are physical – disabilities of various types – and some are social, cultural or psychological: we considered some of them in Unit 8.

Many museums find it valuable to list these barriers in an Access Audit (see Unit 8). This is a study – sometimes carried out by specialist consultants, sometimes by an Access Advisory Group – of the whole museum, to see what 'barriers to access', particularly physical ones, there are. These barriers are then identified in an Access Plan, which explains how the museum plans to overcome or minimise them. An Access Plan is a particularly valuable when thinking about buildings. Sometimes funding bodies require to see an Access Plan before they will give grants; it shows the museum is really trying to ensure that no-one is discriminated against.

The key to preparing an Access Audit and an Access Plan is *consultation*. Do not just guess what changes might be made to help people in wheelchairs or with poor eyesight enjoy the museum more: go and ask them. Every museum should have an Access Advisory Group comprising local people with various kinds of disability: mobility impairment, visual impairment, hearing impairment, learning difficulties, and so on. This group should meet regularly to advise the museum, and particularly to make sure the Access Plan is kept up to date and acted on.

Here is the Access Plan for one small museum – the Blankton Museum – housed in a historic building and with both local history displays and a working blacksmith's forge.

Possible barriers	*Suggested solutions*
Deciding to come – access begins with an individual, family or group finding out about the museum, and deciding to visit.	
Particular social groups may not see publicity or find it attractive.	Marketing strategy needs to target these groups.
People with disabilities may assume museum is inaccessible.	Ensure that all publicity includes access details.
Web site may be inaccessible to some.	Ensure museum's web site meets standards of Web Accessibility Initiative: www.w3.org/WAI.
Opening hours may be inconvenient.	Ensure opening hours meet visitor needs as far as possible, and regularly review them.
Cost may be off-putting.	Keep admission charges low; regularly review concession arrangements.
	Consider joint marketing with nearby attractions, to maximise cost-benefit of trip for visitors.
Families may assume museum is unsuitable for small children.	Ensure museum provides for young children, and that publicity makes the fact clear.
Getting there – convenient transport arrangements are key to ensuring access.	
Limited public transport may deter those without cars.	All publicity should give phone number for information on public transport.
No car or coach parking on site.	Arrange car parking nearby. Consider special arrangements for people with mobility difficulties. Arrange parking for coaches.

First impressions – visitors' receptiveness depends crucially on first impressions. The Blankton Museum is immediately attractive: an historic building in a cottage garden in a delightful village street.

Neglect is off-putting.	Maintain the garden and yard to highest standard.
Lack of confidence may inhibit potential visitors.	Maintain smart noticeboard, with opening hours and admission charge.
Fears for safety of young children may deter families.	Install self-closing gate to keep children away from traffic and create a safe environment.

Going in – a person becomes a visitor when she or he goes through the door.

When closed the front door may look forbidding and be stiff.	Hang or stand a clearly visible 'Way In' sign.
	Hang bell.
Wheelchair users will have particular needs.	Hang bell at convenient height.
	Ensure smooth passage.
	Design counter and displays at convenient height.
	Provide seating for accompanying people.
People with learning difficulties will have particular needs.	Train staff and volunteers to appreciate special requirements.
	Seek specialist advice on design of signage.
People with poor sight will have particular needs.	Train staff and volunteers to appreciate special requirements.
	Provide touch model and tactile plan of museum.
	Ensure signage is appropriate.
	Ensure colour schemes provide appropriate contrast.
	Consider Braille guide.
People with hearing difficulties will have particular needs.	Train staff and volunteers to appreciate special requirements.
	Provide loop system at counter.
	Consider including signing in videos.

Getting around – the museum comprises a small historic house, with uneven floors and awkward steps, together with a working blacksmith's forge. The museum's very attraction may itself be a barrier to people with mobility and sight difficulties.

Parts of the building cannot be rendered accessible to wheelchair users.	A video presentation in the entrance room, which will double as an introduction for all visitors, will show those parts of the building that are inaccessible.
The building includes numerous awkward floors and doorways, difficult for people with poor sight or who find walking difficult.	Install good lighting, especially at key points. Install hand-holds and rails at key points. Ensure all new colour schemes offer maximum floor/wall/furniture contrast. Site high seats with arms throughout museum and garden. Ensure smooth entry to forge; create small safe viewing area.
Drive and garden paths may be difficult for people with mobility problems.	Resurface drive with gravel on hard base. Consider garden paths: surface? kerbs? guide rails?

Understanding and enjoying what you see – though the size of the museum makes personal contact between staff/volunteers and visitors comparatively easy, visitors will still depend on displayed text panels for much of their understanding.

Different visitors will have different levels of interest.	Provide interpretation at different levels, e.g. extra information sheets for people with a specialist interest in local history, historic buildings and blacksmithing.
People with poor eyesight, or none, will find accessing some aspects of the museum difficult.	Use publicity to encourage blind visitors to book guided tours. Where possible, allow blind visitors into smithy when working. Design displays to maximise clarity and contrast. Allow visitors to touch exhibits wherever possible. Site plants that smell, close to paths.

Text that is difficult to see is not communicating.	Position text panels where they can be most easily seen, and use recommended typefaces, colours and sizes.
	Provide large-print versions of all labels.
People with learning difficulties may find text difficult.	Use diagrams and symbols wherever possible.
A forge may be difficult to understand if it is not working.	Site a replica forge as part of the museum displays.
	Include a video in the displays showing a forge working.
Deaf people may not be able to benefit from tours and events.	Consider providing signers at particular events, and publicise widely.

Feeling comfortable – in a museum, this will depend on a range of subtle factors.

Visitors can sometimes be inadvertently made to feel unwelcome.	Recruit volunteers for their liking of people, and encourage them to treat every visitor as a guest.
Rural museums tend to attract wealthier visitors.	Build links with schools and community groups from nearby poorer areas, and encourage them to visit.
A good experience is difficult without physical comfort.	Provide plenty of seating.
	Maintain good-quality café, with choices suitable to a wide range of tastes and ages.
	Keep toilets spotless.
The stock of the shop will send out subtle messages about who visitors are 'expected' to be.	Regularly review shop stock from this point of view.
Parents may be nervous of bringing young children.	Ensure publicity emphasises family.
	Provide games, etc. for children.
	Provide highchairs and suitable food in café.

The Access Plan, of course, only becomes useful when it is implemented. The Access Advisory Group must make sure that the museum really does do what the Access Plan promises. In particular, the museum should ensure that all staff and volunteers receive regular training to help them to understand and to meet the needs of people with disabilities.

Options analysis and feasibility assessment

Related Units – Units 69–70, 72–4

New building developments, for example new museums or new museum buildings, should go through two broad stages of assessment – options analysis and feasibility assessment. Major capital expenditure decisions made by the museum's governing body need to be defensible and robust, not least because they are likely to need to pass muster with external funding agencies. Options analysis helps to show that a range of options has been considered in terms of their costs and benefits and that a preferred option has been arrived at through detailed appraisal and evaluation.

Before considering options, it is critical to establish the aims and objectives of the project. The purpose of any new building development and the uses to which it will be put, whether it is a whole museum, an extension to an existing museum building or a new standalone ancillary building, such as a storage facility, need to be clearly defined and agreed. This work will form some of the first steps in developing an architectural design brief for the project. The results of the options analysis will also feed into the architectural design brief.

There is likely to be a number of ways that the project's aims and objectives can be met. It is also likely that there are different locations and sites on which a building can be constructed. All of these different options will have different capital costs and benefits and need to be compared and considered so that the museum achieves the best solution to its requirements.

OPTIONS ANALYSIS

In considering options, it is best to begin with a long list of options that is then narrowed down with rigour and transparency to a short list of, say, four to five options for more detailed review. The review process will lead ultimately to a preferred option for more detailed feasibility assessment.

The costs and benefits that must be accounted for in an options analysis will typically include:

- Capital expenditure for construction and fit-out.
- Residual value of capital assets at the end of the life of the building. It is likely that the residual value of a new museum building will be zero, as the building would be expected to serve the museum in perpetuity and therefore have no commercial resale value at the end of a predefined term.
- Other costs and benefits that can be valued in money terms. For example, costs might well be affected by the infrastructural requirements for developing each

of the sites identified for the building. Benefits might include capital receipts from the sale of other assets or cost savings, for example energy costs, through the transfer of existing functions to the new building. Partnership opportunities afforded by each option might help to reduce both capital and operational costs.

- Revenue costs and income streams over say, five- and ten-year terms.
- Quantified measures, or at least descriptions, of those costs and benefits that cannot be valued in money terms.

A baseline financial plan for a stable year of operation of the new building (usually year three) to show revenue costs and income streams will need to be developed. This should be extended into a ten-year cashflow projection with appropriate variables to account for changing patterns of demand, accrual rates and the need to reinvest in the museum at regular intervals. Projected cashflows that stretch beyond a ten-year period are impossible to forecast with any degree of accuracy. The financial plan for each option is likely to be broadly similar unless there is a marked difference between the options.

To aid in the costing of different schemes, a technical appraisal will be needed for each short-listed site, particularly with respect to any infrastructural requirements. Topographical and geological surveys are likely to be needed and there may be the need for decontamination and/or special building requirements, for example piling, for some options. A proposed site in a conservation area may impose a different and more expensive set of infrastructural requirements. These issues can have a major bearing on the spread of capital costs between the different short-listed options.

In advance of any architectural design solutions, it is important to note that build costs will be based primarily on the requirements set out in the initial architectural design brief and therefore similar for the short-listed options, unless there are radical differences between the options. A technical site appraisal will therefore be essential for quantifying the spread of potential capital costs across all options.

Distribution of costs and benefits should also be considered i.e. who will bear the burden? Who will reap the benefits? This is particularly important as different partnership opportunities in different locations for the building may help to create a greater spread in the results of the appraisal. For example, it is often the case that a new-build development will always cost roughly the same regardless of where it is located. Depending on what the facility is and does, there may be little significant variance in the revenue budget. In this case, the major difference between sites – in financial terms – is often made by any deal that can be struck with local partners in both capital and revenue terms. Potential partners may be able to make the site more attractive by bearing more of the capital costs and/or offering better terms in the long run.

Where possible assets should be valued in terms of their opportunity costs – i.e. the value of the asset building and/or land in its *best alternative use*. To a large extent, property values, market conditions and the planning and development context of the different locations examined will determine this. A notional rental stream based on current market prices is a valid assessment of opportunity cost, provided that commercial development is a realistic *alternative use* for the site. This is not always the case, however, and the interpretation of opportunity cost should be flexible. In some cases, what is genuinely the most 'valuable' alternative use of a site (in monetary terms) is to do nothing because the area is subject to some form of market failure and has no genuine commercial prospects.

All costs and benefits that can be valued need to be discounted at an appropriate rate to give a net present value (NPV) for each option. The calculation of NPV is contingent upon the development of a capital cost schedule and a ten-year financial plan for each of the short-listed sites.

OPTIONS ANALYSIS MATRIX

If *all* costs and benefits could be valued, then the outcome would theoretically be the selection of the option with the highest NPV. In practice, however, a range of criteria can not be valued in monetary terms and these can be as, if not more, important than straightforward income and expenditure items.

It is therefore necessary to analyse the results of the cost-benefit analysis together with an options analysis matrix. This will ensure a rounded interpretation of the results and the museum will be in a much better position to argue the case for the eventual preferred option.

An options analysis matrix is a *'weighted decision matrix'* used to measure all options against a set of weighted criteria. Some of these criteria will be more important than others and will need to be weighted accordingly. For example, capital cost feasibility could be considered a 'first hurdle' issue that must be properly addressed if the option is to be considered further. On a scale of 1 to 10, this would require a maximum weighting of 10. A hypothetical list for demonstration purposes is shown in Box 71.1.

All of the items listed in the evaluation criteria could be considered key issues for the appraisal. That they are weighted so differently is simply to give the results a wider spread. The weightings are not a reflection of their overall importance – since they are *all* important – but rather an indication of their *relative* importance.

Hence, the low weightings for 'fit with funding agencies' policy' and 'potential to attract matched funding'. Clearly, if it is to attract funding and sponsorship from the funding agencies, then the preferred option should advance – in some way – the main donors' objectives. However, the policy priorities of funding agencies and potential sponsors should not be the determining factor of the museum's strategy. By contrast, the development should not be *allowed* to proceed if is not in line with the museum's mission and objectives, and *cannot* proceed if it is infeasible in terms of capital cost. These items are therefore afforded the maximum possible weighting.

The short-listed options can then be scored out of ten against these weighted criteria and the results tabulated and ranked (see Box 71.2).

The results of an options analysis should summarise the following:

Box 71.1 Options analysis criteria

Analysis criteria	Possible weighting
1 Fit with the museum's mission	10
2 Capacity to meet the museum's immediate, intermediate and ultimate objectives with respect to public access, storage, conservation and staff accommodation	10
3 Capital cost feasibility	10
4 Sustainability	9
5 Potential to increase public access	7
6 Potential to improve the user experience	6
7 Efficient/effective use of the site and buildings	6
8 Fit with government policy	6
9 Market fit	3
10 Fit with funding agencies' policy	2
11 Potential to attract matched funding	1

- The project objectives.
- Long-list and short-list options (showing the rationale behind each option).
- Results of analyses (including cost-benefit analysis, options analysis matrix and commentary on methodology employed and criteria used).
- Implications for the way forward.

FEASIBILITY ASSESSMENT

Once a preferred option has been agreed, its feasibility needs to be assessed and tested in more detail than the options analysis has covered. While the options analysis will have provided a general assessment, more detail will be needed to ensure that the approach proposed is feasible and sustainable for the long term. Feasibility can be considered from two vantage points – technical feasibility and operational feasibility.

Answers to whether the project is feasible from a technical perspective will be addressed in the response to the design brief. The project architect should be tasked with assessing the technical feasibility of the preferred option. Depending on the site chosen, a wide range of technical and engineering assessment may be needed.

Answers to whether the project is feasible from an operational perspective will be addressed through further consideration of its day-to-day operation and continuing development of its business plan.

A useful tool for determining operational feasibility is shown in Box 71.3. The diagram is an iterative one with each element being assessed on more than one occasion as the project progresses. The different elements shown here are examined in greater detail in other Units.

Box 71.2 Options analysis matrix

Criteria	Weighting	Options						Total/rank
		Score out of 10	Option 1 Adaptation of building 1	Option 2 Adaptation of building 2	Option 3 Adaptation of building 3	Option 4 New building on site 1	Option 5 New building on site 2	Option 6 New building on site 3
Fit with the museum's mission	x 10							
Capacity to meet the museum's immediate, intermediate and ultimate objectives with respect to public access, storage, conservation and staff accommodation	x 10							
Capital cost feasibility	x10							
Sustainability	x 9							
Potential to increase public access	x 7							
Potential to improve the user experience	x 6							
Efficient/effective use of the site and buildings	x 6							
Fit with government policy	x 6							
Market fit	x 3							
Fit with funding agencies' policy	x 2							
Potential to attract matched funding	x 1							

Source: Locum Consulting

Box 71.3 Feasibility assessment

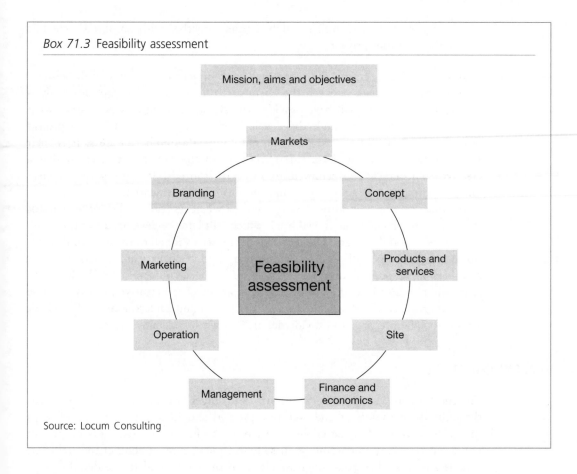

Source: Locum Consulting

Preparing briefs for architects

Related Units – Units 11–13, 18–21, 69–71

INGREDIENTS FOR SUCCESS

A successful new museum or building project is one that is based on mutual understanding and agreement between the client and architect. A good working relationship with the museum's architect(s) is therefore essential for success. The working relationship will depend on three main factors:

- a detailed explanation of the objectives and requirements of the museum;
- a clear understanding of respective roles and responsibilities;

• a comprehensive and well-researched brief, together with an agreed schedule for the building project.

It is essential to ensure that there are clear project objectives established and agreed from the outset between the client and the architect. The options analysis and feasibility process will have provided the client team with a clear idea of what they want to achieve through the development project, although as the project develops there may be a need to revisit thinking in a number of areas. It is their responsibility to communicate this effectively to the project architect so that a creative solution can be achieved to meet their needs. It follows that a clear understanding of each other's role and responsibility is essential.

In embarking on a building development, of whatever scale, sufficient time needs to be given to preparing an initial brief, which will later be developed as a full brief, for architects and designers. The detailed specifications for all of the museum's functional requirements will need to be drawn up by the client team. Briefs for other members of the project team, for example, researchers, conservators and educationalists will also be required. Working with an architect is a creative process, and one that requires clear briefing and detailed discussion and understanding. The client should thus be prepared to provide detailed answers to detailed questions.

PLANNING STAGES

The checklist in Box 72.1 identifies four broad stages of planning and development through which the client and architect proceed and illustrates the type of steps that will be taken. On the client's side, it is the first three stages of the project that are particularly important, as these reflect the client's briefing of the architect. This is a process that goes progressively from the conceptual to the detailed.

On the architect's side, it is the last three stages that are important. Here the architect's team develop their solutions to the brief provided by the client and then specify their requirements to the building contractor and a range of subcontractors who will carry out the building or building refurbishment through to completion.

The amount of time for each of the tasks outlined above will vary depending on circumstances such as planning requirements or the availability of materials. The order of the tasks may also vary. It is important, however, that the museum client is fully aware of the briefing and development schedule required for a museum development project, leaves adequate time for all of the tasks involved and complies with legislative and professional requirements. Time costs money, and it is essential that a building or development programme is carefully planned and adhered to. Deviations from the schedule, especially as the project progresses, will mean that additional costs are incurred.

PREPARING THE BRIEF

The first stage in preparing briefs for an architect (*project objectives*) is a clarification and explanation of the museum's mission, objectives and physical requirements.

Box 72.1 Planning and development stages

Client's team	*Architect's team*
Stage 1 Project objectives, informed by options analysis and feasibility assessment	
Mission and objectives defined	Selection process for architect
Market and concept for museum defined	Architect selected
Functional requirements for front of house and behind the scenes defined	Outline briefing, based on options analysis and feasibility assessment
Spatial requirements defined	
Locational requirements defined	
Capital and operating budget ceilings set	
Management/administration and timescale of programme defined	Preliminary response to brief
Stage 2 Development, informed by options analysis and feasibility assessment	
Preliminary assessment of site or building	Site assessment
Site or building selection/confirmation	Building assessment
Land or building purchase	Services assessment
Options for physical development	Space specifications
Technical needs defined	
Planning regulations	
Financial assessment	Preliminary cost assessment for preferred development option
	Feasibility assessment
Stage 3 Implementation	
Preferred development option confirmed	Outline design proposals
Detailed specifications drawn up	Planning applications
Detailed costings established	
Funding and fundraising programme	Sketch designs
Scheduling	Costings
Stage 4 Completion	
Agreement to proceed	Design development
Detailed timetable	Detailed specifications drawn up
	Working plans/drawings produced
	Tendering
	Contracts let for subcontractors
	Building work on site
	Fit out and completion
	Hand over/snagging/operation

This is the *outline brief* and will build on all of the work undertaken through the options analysis and feasibility study process. An outline brief deserves a great deal of attention and provides a valuable checklist for the architect's team in developing ideas and solutions. Everyone involved in the operation of the museum – including conservation and education staff – should be involved in providing ideas and suggestions as to how the museum can develop efficiently and effectively for the future. The outline brief should include sections on:

- *Function* – defining for example the type of museum and its organisation; the mission, aims and objectives of the museum; the range of its collections and the facilities that will be housed; the style and personality or brand of the museum (see Unit 71).
- *Collections* – explaining for example the range and type of the museum's collections; the significance of the collections; the spatial requirements for collections; display and storage needs; conservation and security needs; and relationships between collections areas, visitor areas, museum management areas and service areas (see Unit 69).
- *Users* – describing for example the types and anticipated numbers of museum users, including users with special needs; museum opening times and patterns of use; and visitor facilities, including reception and information areas, educational and study facilities, catering and retail areas, toilets, rest areas and seating (see Units 11–13, 18–21).
- *Museum staff* – identifying the type of accommodation for different staff, management, curatorial, conservation, education and administrative, and general staff facilities such as offices, meeting rooms, toilets and restrooms.
- *Displays and exhibitions* – describing the space and design requirements for displays and exhibitions; finishes to walls, ceilings, and floors; technical, mechanical and electrical services; signage; and conservation and security needs (see Units 29–33).
- *Space requirements* – specifying for example square and cubic metres for spaces; space hierarchies and priorities; the degree of flexibility in use and layout; zones, adjacencies and relationships; environmental controls and conservation needs; visitor flow patterns; security; and scope for later additions.
- *Services* – indicating for example the location of mechanical and electrical services and their relationship to other spaces; security systems; air-conditioning services; delivery and storage of supplies; loading areas; car parking; plant; and maintenance needs.
- *Location and site* – explaining for example servicing requirements; landscaping; planning permission; legal agreements; and expansion opportunities.
- *Scheduling* – defining the overall scheduling of the programme; phasing and payment schedule; appointment of specialists, consultants and subcontractors.

In producing the outline brief, the client will need to pay a considerable amount of attention to detail and also discuss with the architect's team what they expect to receive in terms of information. Much of this information may be readily available. However, there may well be a need, for example, to confirm policy in certain areas, carry out collections audits and research programmes or engage in field-collecting programmes in preparation for formal briefing. It is important therefore not to begin the formal briefing procedure until the necessary information has been or can be readily available, otherwise delays can ensue to everyone's frustration.

DEVELOPMENT

The second stage (*development*) includes the process of identifying existing buildings or sites for new buildings to meet the requirements of the client team, as laid down in the outline brief. The brief should be further developed at this stage and technical and space specifications more closely defined. The architect will be assessing the building or site through a series of separate specialist studies examining different factors such as geology, access, services, comparative cost data or structural quality.

Planning permission will have to be sought at this stage. The architect's team will present their findings and agreement will be sought on the preferred option for development.

IMPLEMENTATION

The third stage (*implementation*) will examine a range of proposals or solutions to the client's preferred option for development in the light of the outline briefing and the architect's information about the building or site. The client now needs to develop the outline brief in more detail as the proposals are progressively refined. The architect will then produce sketch designs to illustrate how particular requirements in the brief will be met and detail their cost implications.

COMPLETION

Once agreement has been reached on the way ahead for the fourth stage (*completion*) and a detailed schedule has been established, the architect will then further develop the design in consultation with the client. Detailed specifications and working drawings can then be produced. It is these that will form the basis for tendering and contracting builders and subcontractors to carry out the building or refurbishment programme.

Additional input, for example from display and exhibition designers or conservation experts, is essential at this stage to ensure that specifications and working drawings meet the museum's requirements. Adaptation at a later stage, for example to service ducting or wall finishes, lighting points or security features, can be expensive. It is essential to ensure that all details required by those operating the museum have been carefully and fully checked well in advance of the production of specification drawings. Once these have been finalised and the contracts let, it should not be necessary for the client to make any further alterations.

Where displays are being designed in parallel with the briefing and building programme, it is important that the designer is involved at an early stage in the programme. The designer's requirements as agreed with the client will form an important part of the overall briefing process for the architect.

Most countries will have professional associations of architects and they will employ standard procedures in working with clients of all types. The checklist given earlier should therefore be used as a general guide in conjunction with such procedures.

Museum buildings: physical security

Related Units – Units 67–8

Security is an essential component of museum management. Museum managers have a special responsibility to ensure that their buildings are secure, and that effective physical defences, security systems and procedures, and appropriate levels of staffing are in place during the day and night (see Units 67–8). Each museum will vary in terms of the level of protection it is able to provide. Different types of buildings will require different levels of protection related to their use. Different types of collections will require different forms of protection, depending on their significance or value.

All museums should review the physical security of their buildings in terms of the following checklist.

- *Have you and your team assessed the security risks?*
Museums should regularly assess security risks in terms of their location, buildings and surroundings. It is helpful to ask the following sort of questions:

- Is the museum in a busy or isolated area? Is there a record of crime in the area and what is the pattern of crime? Have other museums been targeted by criminals? If so, what is the nature of the threat(s)?
- What form does the building take? Are there too many windows, doors or skylights? Is the structure solidly built? Where are the weak points? Do they need to be strengthened? Can the doors be rammed by vehicles?
- Are the surroundings secure? Is there a fence or wall around the museum? What is its condition? Are gates securely locked? Does the perimeter need to be guarded?
- Is the museum lit externally at night? Are there buildings or trees nearby that might provide entry routes to criminals?

Survey your building as if you were a thief or a vandal. Think how you might gain entry, avoid security alarms and make your escape. Wherever possible, seek professional advice from police or security consultants who will know the levels of risk you face. Risk assessment should be a key consideration in the architect's brief for any new buildings or alterations to existing buildings. Security against theft or fire needs to be built into new developments from the outset. Changes later will mean increased costs.

- *Are the museum's surroundings secure?*

Review the museum's surroundings and check to see that you are not helping a criminal gain entry to the museum, for example, by having trees close to the building or climbing plants on external walls. If you have a wall or fence around the museum and its grounds, check its effectiveness against intrusion. Are all those gates actually needed and are they strong enough? Is the circuit strong enough and high enough to deter attackers? The perimeter is a front line of defence. Improve it if possible.

- *How secure are the museum buildings?*

The museum building itself is your next line of defence. Analyse its strengths and weaknesses. You may have a museum or a museum store based in a building that was not originally designed for the purpose. There may be conflict between security and safety, and architectural integrity. But the fewer openings in the building shell there are, and therefore potential entry points, the better your security.

If you have the option, light the exterior of the building and its surroundings. It serves as a useful deterrent, enhances security systems and promotes your museum at the same time.

- *Is the roof secure?*

The roof of a building can often be vulnerable to attack. Check that drainpipes and other building furniture do not provide easy access to the roof or upper floors. Trees, climbing plants, scaffolding for building repairs, adjoining buildings and unlocked ladders are all danger points.

Check the construction and physical strength of the roof. Will it deter attack? Or can it be strengthened by re-roofing or the addition of materials, externally or internally? Many roofs have doors and roof-lights built into them. These represent yet more weak points and require careful consideration. You may need to fit window grilles/bars, locks or alarms.

- *How strong are the walls?*

The strength of a wall will vary depending on the nature of its construction and its thickness. As part of your risk assessment, review the museum's walls and reinforce weak points, for example blocked-up windows or doors. The overall strength of a building should help to determine its use. In some countries, where earthquakes pose a threat, this is of particular importance.

- *Are your windows weak points?*

Two main considerations should be borne in mind – the nature of window glazing and making windows secure. Windows are weak points in your defences. Use glass that is appropriate and check its resistance qualities with manufacturers and security advisers. Protect windows with bar or mesh grilles, security bars, lockable shutters, steel sheet panels and locks, as appropriate. Remember that upper floor windows are also vulnerable from attack from above, for example from the roof, or from below.

• *Are doors secure?*
Like windows, doors are always vulnerable points on your circuit. Check the strength and standard of the door itself, and also the strength of its frame. Consider its location in terms of the building. Doors vary in design as do their methods of fastening. Exterior and interior doors will vary in strength and type of manufacture. It is important to ensure that door hinges and frames, together with their locking systems, are strong enough to resist attack.

• *Are your locks the key to security?*
There is a very wide variety of locking systems available for doors and windows, and professional advice should be sought on the most appropriate for your needs. External doors should be fitted with two locks at one-third and two-third heights, preferably the mortice-lock type that meets accepted security standards. It is important to recognise the strengths and weaknesses of different types of locks and bolts, and fasteners. Key systems and key procedures are an essential part of your defences (see Unit 68). Cheap door locks and fastenings are no insurance policy.

To summarise, physical security should be the result of detailed and regular security assessment. Wherever possible, seek professional advice on security and risk limitation. Remember that physical security by itself is only part of the museum's overall security. Physical security must be supported by effective alarm systems and staff procedures (see Units 67–8).

Prevention and protection should be your watchwords.

Museum buildings: management and maintenance

Unit 74

Related Unit – Unit 73

Museums not only have to look after their collections, but they also have to manage and maintain the buildings in which they are housed. Museum buildings vary in size, form and construction from one country to another. Their surroundings also vary with many museums set in gardens or on sites associated with the theme of their collections such as industrial or maritime museums. Whatever type of building(s) your museum is housed in and whatever its surroundings, there are four basic requirements for their management and maintenance. Museum managers should:

- have a detailed knowledge of their museum buildings(s) and their site and surroundings and have a full and up-to-date set of building and site plans;
- assess the museum's maintenance needs on a regular basis, with external assistance if required;
- develop a schedule of maintenance work to meet these needs;
- determine the costs of the maintenance work and budget for the work to be carried out.

It is helpful to build up a series of files about the management and maintenance needs of the museum building(s). For example, these might include the following:

- details of building construction;
- floor plans and internal layout;
- location and construction methods of doors and windows;
- plumbing systems;
- electrical systems;
- heating/air-conditioning systems;
- leases and insurance policies;
- information about electricians, joiners, glaziers, etc.,
- information about previous maintenance costs for comparative purposes.

Maintenance needs have to be determined through inspection procedures. Inspections inside and outside the building have to be carried out on a regular basis if they are to rectify problems that have occurred or prevent problems arising. It may be necessary to bring in specialists, such as architects and surveyors, roofers or electricians, to help carry out inspection procedures.

Maintenance needs vary widely. They will arise on a regular basis such as cleaning, painting, and clearing drains and gutters, or on an irregular basis such as mending storm damage to roofs, reglazing broken windows or resurfacing paths. The museum should draw up a written maintenance schedule identifying timescales for regular inspection. Timescales will vary with different needs. Where necessary these requirements, for example costs of redecoration, can be included in the museum's financial and forward planning.

Rather like conservation that can be thought of in preventive and remedial terms, inspection and maintenance schedules are useful in preventing problems developing and avoiding expensive repairs through further serious deterioration. For example, leaking roofs, if ignored for any length of time, can create damage that may cost a substantial amount to put right and may also adversely affect museum collections in store or on display.

Maintenance is not only necessary to identify problems and prevent problems escalating, it is also important in maintaining a pleasant and safe environment for museum staff and visitors. The museum may have legal responsibilities with which it has to comply in this latter respect. While this Unit focuses on the management and maintenance of buildings and their surroundings, it is also important to note the need for regular maintenance and servicing schedules to be drawn up for equipment (for example computers, photocopiers, typewriters, power tools), furnishings and vehicles as well as for displays and exhibitions.

Regular maintenance will help to ensure the efficient and sustainable operation of the museum and in the long term will help to save money. Well-maintained museum buildings and their surroundings reflect efficient management. Buildings and the sites in which they are set are after all some of the museum's most important assets.

This checklist provides an indication of some regular maintenance needs that might be put into a maintenance schedule.

EXTERNAL

- Picking up litter.
- Cleaning windows.
- Unblocking gutters and drainpipes.
- Unblocking drains.
- Refreshing paintwork on doors and windows.
- Cleaning stonework.
- Mending roofs.
- Rust-proofing roof furniture, for example weather vanes.
- Mending fences and walls.
- Resurfacing paths and roadways.
- Tidying and replanting garden areas.
- Cleaning off graffiti.
- Replacing light bulbs in external lighting.

INTERNAL

- Cleaning windows.
- Replacing light bulbs.
- Cleaning paint work on walls, ceilings and woodwork.
- Checking heating/air-conditioning systems.
- Cleaning displays and exhibitions.
- Picking up litter.
- Servicing toilets.
- Emptying wastepaper baskets.
- Cleaning floors.

Monitoring how well the maintenance schedule is implemented is an important management task.

Orientation

Related Units – Units 13, 35, 70

Orientation means showing people where they are and where they can go. If visitors to museums are to get the most out of their visit, they need to know both what they are going to see (intellectual orientation) and where things are (physical orientation).

PHYSICAL ORIENTATION

Every visitor – except perhaps in the largest museums – should be welcomed personally. In some museums, especially where visitors speak many different languages, it may be possible only to say 'good morning, welcome to the Smalltown Museum'. But the visitor's arrival is an opportunity to give some information as well. For example:

> Good morning; welcome to Smalltown Museum. Is this your first visit? Would you like to know what there is to see? If you go that way, you will find the archaeology galleries – you may have heard of our Smalltown Bronze Hoard. The other way are the natural history galleries, and we've got a special exhibition of local paintings this month. If you want to see everything, it would take you probably two hours, so you might like to choose.
>
> There's a cloakroom to leave coats in over there, and a restaurant if you need a cup of tea. We close at 5 o'clock. Please ask if you need anything. I hope you enjoy your visit.

It is a good idea to give every visitor a leaflet containing a plan of the museum, and perhaps pictures of some of the principal exhibits. This is particularly important in a museum that charges for admission; visitors must get something for their money that they can take away. This leaflet could perhaps contain a voucher for use in the shop, which would encourage visitors to buy something. It might include information on the museum's events and activities programme (see Unit 17), and information about other services and opportunities for engagement with the museum.

The entrance area should contain a plan of the museum, but remember that not all visitors will be able to understand plans. An alternative might be a 'bird's-eye view' drawing or painting of the galleries, or a model. Even better is a model that can also be touched and understood by blind people.

There should be a well-designed and carefully planned system of signs throughout the museum. The toilets, restaurant and exit (including emergency exits) should be well signposted!

Above all, there should be people to answer visitors' questions. All staff should be able to answer the ten most common questions (do you know what they are?) in the language spoken by the majority of visitors. Someone in the entrance hall should be able to answer the fifty most common questions: that may be the ticket-seller, the custodian or someone at a special information desk. A manual detailing common questions and appropriate answers is a useful way of ensuring consistency between staff and continuity when the museum employs new staff. It can be updated on a regular basis and used as part of the museum's training and induction programmes (see Unit 97).

INTELLECTUAL ORIENTATION

Explaining to visitors what there is to see is an important – but often neglected – part of the museum's service to visitors. Intellectual orientation is, of course, closely related to physical orientation and to the museum's programme of interpretation (see Unit 22). The following are some of the techniques.

Before the visit

The museum's web site and publicity should both be carefully considered: do they truthfully show the potential visitor what there is to see, and describe the services the museum can offer? Ideally both will be designed in the same style as the museum's displays.

The welcome

The welcome described earlier in the Unit gives the visitor a first idea of what there is to see, and an opportunity to ask questions. The welcome should be in the main languages of the museum's visitors.

The leaflet

The visitor's leaflet described earlier gives a little more information.

Guides

Where the museum employs guides, or where guides from outside are permitted to work in the museum, intellectual orientation will be easy. A good guide can readily explain what there is to see and why the visitor might find it interesting. He or she can give as much or as little information as the visitor seems to want, and can adapt it to the visitor's interests and background. But it is crucially important that the guide actually knows a lot about the museum and its displays, as well as being a good teacher; training is essential (see Unit 26).

Orientation Gallery

Some museums have experimented with Orientation Galleries. An Orientation Gallery tries to tell the visitor what he or she is going to see, and also to suggest how to look at it – what aspects to look at and what question to ask. For example, an exhibition of Coptic icons could be looked at from different points of view: How were they made? Who were the saints depicted? How were they used by worshippers? How did the artistic style change over the centuries? An Orientation Gallery could encourage the visitor to look at the exhibition from one or other points of view. By changing the Orientation Gallery, it is to some extent possible to change the visitor's experience of the displays.

Study gallery

In some museums, computerised information is made available in special information or study galleries. Here the visitor can explore the collection on interactive computer screens and either support or plan a visit. While such systems are unlikely to be within reach of many small museums, the principle can be developed using study materials of different types linked to illustrated catalogues and indexes of the collections provided in traditional formats. Such resource or study centres are a valuable opportunity to invite visitors to add to the museum's information resource and thus encourage greater participation in the museum's work.

Exit orientation

Providing information for people at the end of their visit can also be seen as orientation in some ways. Visitors should be thanked for their visit, and invited to come again and to bring their friends. Did they enjoy their visit? What could have made it better? Would they like to join the 'Friends of the Museum'? Would they like to make a donation? Is there any other way the museum can help them to follow up their visit, for example through the museum web site or its events and activities programme? Small museums, where the staff may have time to talk to visitors individually at the exit, have a great advantage.

Unit
76

Atmosphere, pace and flow

Related Units – Units 13, 75

In this Unit, we consider how visitors use the museum, and what museum managers, curators and designers can do to make their experience more enjoyable and inspiring.

ATMOSPHERE

Atmosphere or ambience is the most difficult of all aspects of a museum to define, but in many ways it is the most important aspect of all. Why do you like some museums much more than others? Is it just the quality of their exhibits and the standards of their displays? Very often it is neither; some museums just seem to have a special atmosphere that makes them more memorable.

A few of the things that contribute to a special atmosphere can be identified. The first is a personal welcome. *Every* visitor in every museum – except perhaps the very largest – should be greeted personally with a smile and a 'welcome'.

The most welcoming museums are like the most welcoming houses; they may not be rich, but they are clean and neat, and give the visitor the impression that someone cares about them very much.

One way of helping to create a good atmosphere is to use some of the furnishings and decorations traditional in your country. For example, mosques and houses in the Middle East often have floors covered with rugs that help make them feel much more welcoming than museums with cold hard floors. In cold countries, an open fire or traditional stove will instantly make a room seem welcoming – though there may be strong conservation reasons against them! In many countries the display of flowers or plants is customary in both private houses, shops and offices; they too make a museum seem more homely.

Sound is also an important aspect of atmosphere. The sound of a fountain or of quiet music may help enormously.

PACING

A typical feature film consists of a series of different *moods* and *pace*. A slow conversation will be followed by a furious fight between hero and villain. A tense, quiet sequence will be followed by a noisy battle. There will be constant changes of mood: long sequences with sad music as the camera pans across the landscape, changing to love scenes, or short sequences of jokes and comedy, even dance routines. In all these ways the film director keeps our interest by varying the pace of the film and by changing its moods. In a similar way the museum designer keeps the visitor's interest by varying the pace of the museum.

Where a guide shows visitors around the museum, design is less important because the guide can vary the pace of the tour and can respond to the visitors' needs. Every good guide knows how to spot when their visitors are getting tired or bored. He or she might tell an amusing story, ask the visitors questions, speed up or slow down, draw attention to an unusual object or change his or her voice. Like a good teacher, a good guide knows how to keep the interest of his or her group. But for visitors who are looking around a museum on their own, the displays themselves must awaken and keep the visitor's interest.

One important way the museum can prevent its visitors getting bored is by varying the appearance and 'feel' of the different rooms or different parts of the museum. Ceiling heights, floor surfaces, brightness or darkness, colour schemes, 'hardness' or 'softness' of the furnishings can all be varied to suit the exhibits and theme, and moving from one to another will keep the visitors alert!

The types of display should ideally be varied, too. Thus a visitor who moves from a gallery of paintings to an archaeological display to a science gallery with plenty of 'hands-on exhibits', will be invited to take a new interest each time. Some displays, too, might be inspirational, some didactic, some just fun.

Another way of keeping boredom or tiredness at bay is by providing plenty of 'escape hatches'. Even the most interested visitor needs a break from time to time. When there is somewhere to go to for a few minutes rest that is quite different in atmosphere from the museum gallery, it may allow the visitors to return refreshed to the displays. Catalogues and other books might be provided. If possible this rest or study area should be close to all of the galleries. In many ways the traditional museum laid out around a courtyard or central hall is best.

Every museum should have a place to eat – a café or restaurant, or at the very least somewhere in the museum where the visitors can get tea or coffee, or simply a drink of water. And there should be plenty of seats and rest areas everywhere.

FLOW

How do visitors actually use displays? How do they move around them, and how long do they spend in which areas? 'Flow' – movement around the museum – refers to the way visitors flow through and around the museum displays; how long they spend in the various rooms; which direction they go in; and which displays they choose to look at first. In planning a new display or exhibition, it is crucially important to plan very carefully for the movement pattern or flow, based on your

---

Box 76.1 Museum fatigue

'Museum feet' is the nickname for *museum fatigue*, the special sort of tiredness that museum visitors can suffer from. What causes it?

- Learning on your feet – only in museums are people expected to do this.
- Disorientation – not knowing where you are or what you are looking at.
- Looking, but not using other senses of touch, hearing or smell, for a long period.
- Looking for long periods at similar but different things.
- Lack of contrast, sameness of surroundings.
- Crowds of people.
- Excessive heat.

Minimising fatigue on the part of your visitors is a challenge to be met by the museum.

knowledge of the target audience, their characteristics, and forecast of the numbers likely to visit at various times. It is worthwhile observing how your visitors move around the museum. Plot movement by different types of visitors on a plan of the museum. You may be surprised how many visitors bypass a particular display or object! Their movement pattern can help in evaluating the success or failure of an exhibition or display.

Box 76.2 Gallery space

To work out how much space will be needed in a new gallery or exhibition ask the following questions, and then allow roughly 5m² space per person:

- How many people are in the museum at the busiest time?
- How many extra are likely to be attracted to a new display?
- How many of them are likely to be in the gallery at any one time?

Remember about 80 per cent of the gallery space may be used for circulation and about 20 per cent for the displays themselves.

Section 5
The museum and its management

Legal status and management structures

Related Units – Units 78–83, 90

Every museum worker should understand the legal basis on which his or her museum operates. The laws of different countries vary so greatly that it is often difficult to know how their different museums are established. Within countries, too, the legal basis on which different museums are established varies greatly. Of three museums that seem to the visitor very similar in size and type, one may be set up by a special decree of the state authorities, one may be run by a government department as part of their general activities, while the third may be run by a Board of Trustees operating under laws that govern voluntary associations.

Do these differences matter? They do matter because they affect what the museum is allowed to do, and especially because they affect the options open to the museum when it is considering how it will develop in the future. For example, a museum run by a Board of Trustees may not be able to develop a close relationship with the local Schools Service, while a museum run by a government department may not be free to run a museum shop.

It is not only its legal basis that determines the character of a museum, but the actual management structure. It may seem, for example, that the director runs the museum, but his or her ability to take decisions may be very severely constrained. The director may, for example, be responsible to a senior bureaucrat who has no time to attend to the museum, but without whose approval no decision can be made.

Finally, the character of the museum will be determined by the actual people who are in control. A Board of Trustees who treat the museum as a private club, and have no interest in the public, may run the museum. Or a politician may have set it up, whose successor has no interest in it. Or there may be someone in a key position in the wider organisation whose support may permit the museum a period of lively growth.

There is no doubt, though, that in the best system there are two levels of management: the governing body, which decides on the policy of the museum, and the director and his or her staff, who both advise the governing body and who put its policy into practice.

The governing body may itself be responsible to a central or local government agency, to a university council, to a military authority or to a commercial company. Or it may be an independent trust. Every museum, though, should have a governing body responsible for deciding the overall policy of the museum.

The ways in which the governing body will decide the museum's policy, especially through its forward plan, are described in Units 78–83.

The first responsibility of the museum's director is to advise the governing body on the museum's policy. First, he or she must ensure that the members of the governing body know the museum and its work well. They should visit the museum regularly, and the director should take every opportunity to keep them in touch with the wider world of museums both nationally and internationally. When new members are appointed to the governing body the museum should try to provide at least a one-day training session, to help them to learn their new responsibilities, and to introduce them to the museum and its work. A number of museums have devised a manual for the members of their governing body that explains the mission and objectives of the museum, its policies and the role and responsibilities of the governing body.

The second responsibility of the museum's director is to implement the governing body's policy. Museums vary greatly in the amount of responsibility the director is given: what matters most is that everyone concerned is clear who is responsible for what. That is the fundamental purpose of the museum's management planning, which is described in Units 80–1.

Key word

Governing body – the formal body of men and women responsible for deciding the overall policy of the museum and ensuring that it is carried out by the director and his/her staff.

Box 77.1 Structures

Everyone associated with a museum should be able to answer these basic questions about the power structure behind the museum:

- What is the legal basis on which the museum operates?
- What is the chain of command leading to the museum director?
- At what level are key policy decisions taken?
- Who are the people involved, what is their background and how effective are they?

Unit
78

Partnerships

Related Units – Units 79–81

In many countries, all museums – or nearly all – belong to a State Antiquities Service of some type, and gain strength from being part of a large organisation able to share staff and other resources. In other countries, museums have grown up one by one, and attract fierce loyalty from their stakeholders and supporters who value their independence above everything.

Can museums gain both the strength that comes from alliance with other museums and other organisations, and the flexibility and appeal that independence brings? This Unit looks at some of the opportunities for partnership that museums may investigate.

PARTNERSHIP BETWEEN MUSEUMS

The museums profession worldwide is small, friendly and helpful. Few museums could operate without the informal help of colleagues in other museums, and there is a constant exchange of informal advice and help going on without the need for formal structures (see Unit 79).

Sometimes, though, even nearby museums do not know each other well, especially perhaps when some are big and others small, or where they cover different subjects. However different their museums, though, it is valuable for museum staff to meet regularly and exchange news and ideas. Museum directors should always allow staff the time to meet colleagues from other museums, and encourage them to do so. This should be seen as part of their training and professional development (see Unit 96).

Often, more formal partnerships are valuable: they allow sharing of resources – and saving of costs – on a larger scale. All sorts of resources can be shared, for example:

- Staff training. This is one of the easiest areas to share, and a good way of starting where there is no history of partnership working.
- Equipment.
- Management resources. Much more difficult for independent museums to share are management resources, for example personnel administration, or bookkeeping and accountancy.
- Collections. Increasingly, museums are agreeing to share collecting. Sometimes this simply means museums agreeing to make sure that their collecting policies mesh together rather than conflict (see Unit 42). Sometimes it involves two or more museums working together on a fieldwork project, sharing the responsibilities and the resulting collections of objects and information. Increasingly, larger museums are joining together to buy an expensive work of art, and each exhibiting it for part of the year.

In many countries, there are voluntary associations of museums that exist to encourage partnership; sometimes this role is played by a national museums association, or by the national committee of ICOM (see Unit 100). Museum directors should always make sure their museum plays an active role in these.

PARTNERSHIP WITH LOCAL GOVERNMENT

More and more museums are involved in some kind of partnership with local or regional government, as government recognises the value that museums can bring to society, and as (in many countries) cultural agencies are set up as independent bodies, no longer directly run by government.

Few museums can manage without any sort of public subsidy, and this often comes from local or regional government. While such support is always welcome, the danger, of course, is that it may result in government imposing its priorities on the museum. Rather than rely on a simple subsidy or grant, it is often better for both sides to agree a contract that sets out exactly what the museum will deliver over the contract period, in return for what money. These public-sector contracts are sometimes called Service Level Agreements.

PARTNERSHIP WITH OTHER ORGANISATIONS

There is almost no limit to the variety of other organisations with which a museum may forge a partnership. They include:

- tourism organisations and agencies;
- universities;
- theatre groups;
- schools;
- archaeological organisations;
- National Parks and wildlife reserves;
- sports clubs;
- community groups;
- hospitals and old peoples' homes;
- religious organisations;

and many others.

PARTNERSHIP WITH THE PRIVATE SECTOR

Partnership with private companies or wealthy individuals is often seen as a part of fundraising (see Unit 86–7), but it may have a much more positive purpose than that. Museums, for example, can create really valuable partnerships with local businesses, offering opportunities for staff events, corporate celebrations, joint exhibitions and so on. Hotels and restaurants can work with museums on joint marketing and on joint promotions, for example including a meal, overnight accommodation and a museum event.

When working with the private sector it is helpful to ask oneself '*why* do we want to partner?'. The answer is often 'to build up the museum's critical mass: to make it more attractive to visitors'. Partners may include other attractions (such as a local zoo or boating lake or theatre), services in support (such as cafés, shops or garages), or infrastructure (for example, railways or car parks).

It is of course crucial not to get carried away with enthusiasm. The museum must ask of every proposal: is this activity central to our mission, or does it clearly support our mission? And what are the real costs going to be, including all the staff time likely to be taken up?

STUDY EXAMPLE 78.1

A museum with a good mineral collection wanted to put on an exhibition about crystals and their contemporary uses. As part of the exhibition's associated events and activities programme, the museum approached a ballet company and a local group of people with physical disabilities. The ballet company devised a dance on the theme of crystals, and taught the local group how to develop dances based on the theme of crystal growth, using their wheelchairs. The result was not only a series of very beautiful, original and attractive performances that completely absorbed all involved, but also enormous publicity for the exhibition, which attracted unprecedented audiences including many people who had never visited the museum before.

Unit
79

Networking

Related Units – Units 4, 78

New technology – above all e-mail and the Internet – has allowed the development of much closer partnerships between groups of museums. These are sometimes known as networks, and the co-operation and partnership between them is known as networking. Of course, networking is possible using old-fashioned communications too!

Networks may be between museums geographically quite close to each other, but they may be between museums in different parts of the world: for example museums with similar and complementary collections. The new network technologies know no geographical restriction. Similarly, networks may be between museums of a similar size, but they may also be between one or two very big museums and a group of small museums.

▌WHAT BENEFITS CAN MUSEUMS GAIN FROM BEING PART OF A NETWORK?

- *Continuing professional development.* The greater resources and wider experience offered by a network can greatly benefit staff; more ambitious joint training and professional development programmes are possible and there are valuable opportunities for exchange of staff.
- *Sharing research information.* The Internet supports the creation of shared data-bases, e-mail and lists and allows researchers to share text and images instantly, while mobile phones (cellphones) mean they can be in constant touch.
- *Managing joint projects and programmes.* Joint exhibitions, publications and public programmes become very much easier when museums are accustomed to working together, and can share the management, staff and other resources they require.
- *Sharing experience and expertise.* Networks overcome the isolation felt by many workers in small museums, and working with colleagues encourages greater productivity.
- *Sharing new ways of working and creating opportunities for involvement in product and service development.* Museums are often reluctant to introduce new ways of working, but when they can see their success elsewhere in the network, museums are more willing to share the experiment.
- *Achieving economies of scale and cost.* This is often the main motive for networking. Shared staff, premises and equipment are all possible when the network is a fairly local one; even when the museums are far apart, the costs of – say – exhibition production can be significantly reduced by sharing resources.
- *Attracting financial support.* Funding agencies and sponsors are often more willing to support a flourishing group of museums rather than an individual museum.
- *Helping with benchmarking and comparative studies.* Sharing management information, for example on cost per visitor or other measures of efficiency, allows each museum in the network to judge its performance against others'.
- *Gathering market data.* Small museums can seldom devote much time to carrying out market research; when the task is shared, gathering the data on which an effective marketing programme can be based is much easier.
- *Supporting collections documentation.* Joint management of collections is one of the greatest benefits that networking can bring. It may perhaps start with an agreement over who collects what, but it can lead on to shared public catalogues and other benefits.
- *Developing new forms of access.* Networks make new forms of public access possible, particularly through pooling resources in developing a really effective presence on the Internet.

It is wise to develop a network slowly and carefully, especially where the museums have a proud tradition of independence. The key to success is mutual trust between the key people involved, and experience suggests that a good way to start is through shared staff training. This gives opportunities for people to meet and get to know each other, and for staff to begin to learn to work in similar ways. The many existing museum groups, for example the ICOM national and international committees (see Unit 100) are an excellent basis on which to build new networks.

Policy development and management planning

Unit

80

Related Units – Units 77, 81–3

POLICY AND PLANNING

Planning is an essential aspect of museum management. Every museum should have a clearly written and agreed management or forward plan. The plan is an expression of how the museum's policies agreed formally by its governing body will be put into action over a defined period of time. A forward plan essentially describes the museum's mission, its strategic objectives and its programme of action, explains how its resources will be used to implement the programme and defines the steps that will be used to monitor progress and evaluate the impact of the museum's work (see Unit 81).

The forward plan must derive from policies that have been agreed by the museum's governing body. Museum managers therefore have to work with their governing bodies first to establish a policy framework within which they can develop their management planning and carry out the museum's work. Policy development requires a great deal of time and consideration. It needs reference to existing professional codes of ethics, conduct and standards and comparison with other museums. Policy development should cover all aspects of the museum's activities in the broadest sense and set out what the museum wants to achieve. The museum's management plan then explains how the museum will achieve its policy goals.

The museum's policies must follow in the first instance from the museum's formal constitution that identifies its legal status, not-for-profit nature, and mission and strategic objectives. The constitution should be drawn up in accordance with the appropriate national laws relating to museums, the cultural and natural heritage and not-for-profit institutions.

The governing body should publish a clear statement of:

• the museum's mission, policies and objectives;
• the role and composition of the governing body itself.

It should confirm that it recognises its professional obligations to:

- its collections, in terms of their safeguarding and safekeeping;
- its buildings, in terms of their care and maintenance;
- its staff, in terms of their well-being and professional development; and to
- its users, in terms of their education and safety.

Reference should also be made to the governing body's recognition of existing professional codes of conduct and standards at national and/or international level (see Unit 6).

POLICY DEVELOPMENT

Policy development should cover the following key areas of the museum's operation:

- the purpose of the museum – many museums define their role through a 'mission statement', a succinct expression of their primary purpose (see Unit 81);
- collecting and disposal of collections – with due reference to professional and legal requirements;
- care and security of collections;
- collections research and fieldwork;
- communications – including all forms of communication with the public, exhibitions, displays, enquiries, educational services, web site and marketing;
- access and accessibility;
- finance and accounting procedures and sustainability;
- staffing, and staff training and professional development;
- housing the museum – buildings care, insurance and maintenance;
- conformity with relevant national and international laws.

Developing a general policy statement or a number of linked statements, covering these areas, helps to clarify objectives and provides a single point of reference for the governing body and the museum's staff. It shows that the governing body is aware of its responsibilities for policy development and its maintenance. A general policy statement of this type should be formally reviewed every three to five years. The museum should, however, also maintain a policy manual so that in the intervening period any new policy decisions by the governing body can be duly recorded and used to update the formal statement later.

The policy statement can then be used as a basis from which a set of strategic objectives can be drawn. These are simple working statements of the museum's policies, and encompass the definition of a museum as an 'institution which collects, documents, preserves, exhibits, and interprets material evidence and associated information for the public benefit' (see Unit 2).

█ MISSION AND OBJECTIVES

Here is a mission statement and set of strategic objectives for a local government museum as an example:

- The purpose of the museum is to provide a sustainable range of high-quality services for the benefit of the collections in our care and for the education and enjoyment of all our users.

The strategic objectives listed here are together designed to meet this mission and fulfil the policy requirements of the governing body:

- to provide a high standard of care and management for the museum's collections in order to ensure their long-term safeguarding and safekeeping;
- to develop new collections and associated information within an agreed collecting policy in order to reflect the cultural and natural history and heritage of the museum's area;
- to undertake and commission research on collections in order to ensure that up-to-date and accurate information is available for use by museum staff and the museum's users;
- to undertake and commission scientific recording programmes in order to support the work of the museum;
- to provide identification and enquiry services relating to items held by the public;
- to provide displays and exhibitions interpreting the museum's collections of a recognised standard of excellence for the education and enjoyment of the museum's users;
- to provide educational services to formal education groups in order to maximise the educational potential of the museum's collections;
- to organise informal learning opportunities through events and activities programmes in order to encourage public interest in and engagement with the museum;
- to ensure that the museum is accessible to its visitors and users, in physical, intellectual, cultural and social terms;
- to market the museum effectively to the public in order to maintain existing audiences and to develop new audiences for the museum;
- to provide high-quality retail and catering services for the public in order to enhance their enjoyment of the museum;
- to provide opportunities for all staff to engage in training and professional development programmes;
- to generate funding support from a plurality of sources to assist in the development of the museum's work; and
- to ensure that the museum at all times provides for efficiency and effectiveness in its financial management.

Translating these requirements into an action plan across an agreed time period is the subject of Unit 81.

Key word

Forward plan – a written management plan to guide the future development of the museum. A 'forward plan' is an expression of how the museum's policies will be put into action over a defined period of time.

Unit

81

Developing a forward plan

Related Units – Units 80, 82–3

The process of writing a 'forward' or 'management' plan for your museum will provide valuable insights into the ways in which the museum can carry out its overall objectives. However large or small your museum is, the preparation of a plan is something that supports all aspects of the museum's work and every member of staff, professional or volunteer, as well as the governing body.

The creation of a forward plan is a method of bringing all those working for the museum together with a common purpose and provides a framework for a programme of action to drive the museum forward. As we have seen in Unit 80, a forward plan must derive from the museum's mission and policies. The plan will describe:

- the mission of the museum;
- a synopsis of its historical development;
- its current context;
- its policies and the strategic objectives derived from them;
- its programme(s) of action to meet those objectives;
- its resources and their use;
- and the methods by which it will monitor progress and evaluate the impact of its work.

Forward planning can help to:

- assess the strengths and weaknesses of the museum in an objective way;
- identify those areas of your museum's operation that require improved management or increased resources;
- pinpoint areas of new development and innovation that require new resources or expertise;
- provide a mechanism that allows staff and others to see in what directions the museum is moving;
- improve the quality of decision-making by means of performance indicators and management information systems;

- provide the basis of a case-for-support to funding bodies;
- demonstrate to funding bodies and patrons of all types the professionalism of the museum and its management.

The purpose of forward planning is thus to provide the museum and its staff with a sense of purpose, a sense of direction and a sense of achievement.

PRODUCING A FORWARD PLAN

The steps to take in producing a forward plan can be simply described as:

- assessment and appraisal;
- discussion and drafting;
- agreement and implementation;
- evaluation and updating.

Within these steps, the museum should consider the points shown in the check-list:

Collections management

- collecting and disposals policy;
- collections documentation;
- collections storage;
- collections security;
- preventive conservation measures;
- remedial conservation services;
- research programmes;
- information management.

User and visitor services

- market research and analysis;
- access and accessibility;
- displays;
- temporary exhibitions;
- education services;
- informal learning services;
- events and activities programmes;
- on-line and off-site services;
- retail and catering services;
- publications;
- marketing;

- public relations;
- user facilities – cloakrooms, toilets.

Management

- staffing structures;
- Friends/volunteers;
- training and professional development programmes;
- health and safety;
- security;
- communications systems;
- buildings – space allocation and use;
- buildings – internal and external condition;
- buildings – maintenance programme;
- finances – capital;
- finances – operating;
- finances – income generation;
- finances – fundraising;
- standards and performance indicators/measurement.

Assessment and appraisal

The first step is the *assessment and appraisal* of your current position (see Unit 71 for feasibility assessment). This needs to be carried out in a systematic way to ensure that all aspects of the museum have been reviewed. In management terms, all aspects of the museum are interdependent, and the review process will illustrate how change and development in one area will impact on another.

Some questions might be:

- Is the museum's constitution and legal status appropriate?
- What policies is the museum operating under at present?
- Do they cover all necessary areas of the museum's work?
- What are its mission and stated objectives?
- When were these last considered and do they need modification or updating?
- What markets is the museum operating in?
- What range of market research has been undertaken and do you have an up-to-date understanding of who is visiting the museum and who is not?
- What standards of collections management are being pursued?
- Are there backlogs with documentation or collections storage?
- What range of services for the museum's users is being provided?
- Are there barriers to public access?
- Is the museum's web site being managed effectively and is it up to date?
- Is the museum's current staffing or staffing structure adequate?
- What is the security of collections/buildings/staff like?

- What condition are its building(s) in?
- What sources of finance does the museum have?
- How is it monitoring and measuring progress?
- What standards of comparison are being used for all its operations?

All of these questions follow on from the checklist earlier and in many cases reflect guidance in other Units. You will have many more. Questions like these should be used to generate discussion among the museum's management and staff, instigate comparative research with other museums and allied facilities and help management and staff look objectively at the questions *Where are we now? How have we got here? And what are we here to do?*

Discussion and drafting

The second step is *discussion and drafting*. The key questions posed here are *where do we want to get to* and *how are we going to get there?* As we have seen, it follows that the process of assessment and appraisal provides a draft plan that covers the following points:

- purpose or 'mission' and objectives (see Unit 80);
- historical development – a brief perspective on the historical development of the museum to date;
- contemporary context – an examination of the market and competitor context within which the museum is operating (see Unit 9);
- a series of *strategic objectives* and *programme areas* based on the checklist above (see Unit 80);
- a series of *tasks* to be carried out within these programme areas designed to meet the strategic *objectives*;
- a *timescale* against which these objectives and tasks need to be carried out, for example a one- to three-year period. Some aspects of the museum's work may of course need a longer timescale;
- and an allocation of existing resources and an identification of additional resources required to carry through everything that needs to be done.

The tasks then have to be allocated to staff to carry out on a team or individual basis. These have to be built into their personal work programmes. A set of *performance indicators* (see Units 82–3) helps to monitor progress on these tasks and show how successfully they are being met.

Agreement and implementation

The third step is to reach *agreement* over the draft plan proposals with staff and then present the finalised draft to the museum's governing body for scrutiny and their formal agreement. The plan can then be circulated in a final version, a résumé prepared for publication and fundraising purposes, and regularly consulted by managers and staff in their work planning and day-to-day work. Remember to build in sufficient flexibility to allow for change and those unsuspected developments!

Evaluation and updating

The fourth and final step is *evaluation and updating*. The key questions posed here are *have we achieved what we planned to achieve and if not, why not?* It is the task of management to monitor progress and evaluate the impact and success of the action programme and the individual tasks within it (see Units 82–3). Regular reviews and reports of progress need to take place for both staff and the museum's governing body. The plan also needs to be revised and 'rolled forward' on an annual basis to maintain currency and to mesh with the preparation of the coming year's operational and capital budget estimates.

In this way, the museum is always working within the framework of a forward plan and can always demonstrate what it has to do. The plan should go hand in hand with the museum's annual report providing a convenient written and illustrated summary of the museum's achievement against its mission and strategic objectives.

The museum should use its forward plan to plan for success and its annual report to demonstrate success.

Box 81.1 'SWOT analysis'

One useful method of assessing and appraising the position of the museum is by SWOT analysis. SWOT stands for Strengths, Weaknesses, Opportunities and Threats. Try analysing each of the points covered in the checklist by this method, or analyse the museum as a whole using this approach and list the findings as bullet points in the matrix. By involving staff as well as outside observers, you can develop valuable understanding of what needs to be done in the museum through steps two to four of your forward planning.

Strengths	*Weaknesses*
•	•
•	•
•	•
•	•
•	•
Opportunities	*Threats*
•	•
•	•
•	•
•	•
•	•

Box 81.2 Annual reports

An annual report is a valuable way of demonstrating how well the museum has achieved the planning objectives and tasks it set itself over the previous year. An annual report can be structured in a variety of ways and can be produced in a variety of different styles. Available resources for production will condition length and design style (illustrated, typeset, etc.). Its distribution costs will depend on size and weight. You may also want to upload it onto the museum's web site to achieve wider distribution. Whatever style of production you choose, target the annual report at all those whose support the museum is concerned to maintain or attract. It can be a valuable tool in helping the museum to build its reputation, and has a year's 'shelf life' (see Unit 10). It is also an important tool in charting the history of the museum year on year.

Unit

82

Performance measurement in museums

Related Units – Units 80–1, 83, 85, 94

The measurement of performance in museums is an important management function. Museum managers should monitor the achievements of their museum in terms of the museum's mission, objectives and tasks set out in their forward planning (see Unit 81). A system of *performance measurement* can be developed to help managers assess and communicate how well the museum is meeting its objectives over time. Performance measurement can help to lead to greater accountability and efficiency, and an improved sense of corporate purpose and success.

Museum managers are accountable for the effective and sustainable use of the resources for which they are responsible, whether these are people, collections, equipment, buildings, money or time. Museum managers are also responsible for how well the museum performs. How then can museum managers working with their staff develop a system of mutually acceptable and meaningful performance measures to assist in their work?

Performance measurement can be related to the museum itself as an organisation; to the personal performance of members of staff (see Unit 94); and to the financial efficiency of the museum (see Unit 85). Performance can be measured in *qualitative* and *quantitative* terms.

Qualitative performance tends to be more difficult to measure than *quantitative performance*. Where possible, qualitative performance should be measured against agreed standards, whether these are set internally by the museum, or devised by external bodies. Performance can thus be measured as the attainment of a specified standard.

A museum may reach a defined standard, for example in terms of the quality of care or storage for its archaeological collections. A member of staff may be able to demonstrate a level of competence within an overall standard in terms of documenting an archaeological collection. Another example might be a museum or member of staff winning an award in a national or regional competition, because they have achieved a particular standard set by the competition.

Quantitative performance can be measured in different ways at different levels of complexity. Simple performance indicators might be represented through the measurement of numbers, for example numbers of objects conserved in one month, one year, etc. More complex indicators might be based on comparisons or percentages, for example what percentage of the items in the museum collection are waiting for conservation treatment? The measurement of input and output provides a method of determining efficiency or value for money. For example, how many hours of staff time – and therefore cost to the museum – have been invested in the accession and documentation of a new item for the collection? Is this the normal amount of time required for this procedure? Can this be improved for the future?

While qualitative measurement against standards can often provide an immediate picture of performance, the benefit of quantitative measurement will only be effectively realised through the analysis of trends in terms of year-on-year comparisons of performance in the museum.

PERFORMANCE MEASURES

Museums should develop a range of performance measures or indicators in a number of key areas of their work so that the work of the museum as a whole can be monitored. The key performance indicators chosen will vary from one museum to another, depending on circumstances and priorities. The number of performance indicators used needs to be manageable in terms of staff time. Managers need to be aware that there is a cost implication for every indicator employed in terms of staff time spent on monitoring performance.

Performance indicators used in performance measurement are only a means towards an end. They should be used to complement the professional judgement and experience of the museum manager, and support the museum's management information system. The principal focus of museum management should be on its mission, not on the performance system.

Performance measurement should be focused on the three main areas of a museum's work – collections management, user services and museum management or operation. Each area can be broken down into a number of sub-sections. For example, collections management may include acquisitions, disposals, preventive conservation, storage, remedial conservation, research, documentation and collections security (see Unit 80).

These areas will all relate to objectives and tasks in the museum's forward plan. Within these sub-sections, museums should define a series of performance indicators to help the museum measure its performance against its planning objectives (see Unit 80–1). Some examples are given here:

Collections management – documentation

Performance measurement

- Numbers of items documented.
- Numbers of items in collection not documented.
- Percentage of collections documented.
- Percentage of collections not documented.
- Change in percentage documented on an annual basis over three years.
- Cost of documentation per item.
- Quality of documentation against agreed documentation standard.
- Hours of work/staff cost spent on each new object accessioned.
- Use of documentation by staff and/or members of the public.
- Percentage of records available to the public.

User services – education

Performance measurement

- Number of school class visits to the museum.
- Number of schoolchildren visiting the museum.
- Use of the museum's Schools Loan Service.
- Percentage of schools in the museum's catchment area serviced.
- Production of education packs.
- Quality of design of education packs.
- Number of downloads of educational material from the museum's web site.
- Cost per child of museum visit.

By measuring and analysing performance against objectives and tasks in a systematic way and on a regular basis, museum managers and their staff can monitor performance over periods of time within their forward planning. Many aspects of performance need to be measured over defined periods of time, and trends identified and understood. Performance measurement helps museum managers take informed decisions, builds team spirit in the workforce, and forms an important part of the museum's management information system.

Performance measurement also provides information of value for governing bodies and for funding agencies, as well as for the public presentation and publication of the museum's work. Measuring performance on a regular basis therefore provides much of the information needed to present the museum's achievements to both internal and external audiences.

Evaluation

Related Units – Units 4, 34, 80–2, 84, 94–5

Closely aligned with performance assessment at institutional and personal level (see Units 82 and 94), evaluation for museums is of increasing importance in many countries. Critically, it examines what benefits flow from a museum and its work (see Unit 4) and seeks to present these in quantitative and qualitative terms to support arguments for investment.

Bodies responsible for museums at all levels increasingly recognise that their economic impact and cultural value – especially in terms of economic, physical and social regeneration – need to be presented in new ways to show how communities benefit from their work in the short, medium and long term. Museums' management planning needs to include sets of performance indicators to illustrate the wide range of benefits they provide (see Units 80–2).

As we have noted in Unit 4, there is increasing expectation for museums to work individually and in partnership as catalysts for sustainable development in the areas that they cover. Central and local government for example, as agents of economic and social development, spend money on museums assuming that there are benefits from their work and critically, benefits aligned to their core objectives.

Museums therefore require robust statements reporting the economic, social, cultural and environmental impacts and benefits that they provide and explaining the methodologies used for evaluating those impacts and benefits. Arguments for investment need to be evidence-based in order to convince funding agencies and stakeholders to support museums.

EVALUATING IMPACT AND BENEFITS

The impact of museums and their work thus needs to be considered in sustainability terms and be evidence-based. As we note in Unit 71, impact may be examined in advance of a new development (appraisal) or in operation (evaluation). The description of impact may be in quantitative terms e.g. numbers of jobs created or sustained in the local economy, or in qualitative terms e.g. enhanced civic pride.

Evaluation as a discipline makes the museum consider the outcomes of its work. Evaluating impact helps the museum to learn lessons and inform future decisions.

It can underpin publicity and advocacy, and where a museum is part of a larger organisation or partnership, it can add value to those with whom it is working.

Impacts can be positive or negative; short term or long term; one-off or ongoing; increasing or decreasing; or be cyclical or random. A museum can impact on many different types of organisation and on many different types of social groups. Positive impacts might be where a museum is able to generate new employment both on-site and off-site within the local economy through attracting more visitors or where a new museum development helps in regeneration terms to increase property values in the wider destination in which it is set. Negative impact might be where a new museum development displaces the audiences from existing museums by increasing competition between them or helps to increase property values in a destination out of reach of local markets.

Different methodologies have been developed to measure different forms of impact and benefit (see Unit 71). It is worth seeking specialist advice from economic planning experts when considering impact evaluation. Evidence-based arguments to demonstrate how investment in your museum will provide economic and cultural benefits that are aligned with the funding agency's own objectives are a powerful way of unlocking support for the museum.

Unit
84

Project management

Related Units – Units 71–2

Project management is the application of knowledge, skills, tools and techniques to projects of different types in the museum. While projects will inevitably differ in scale and type, there are a number of steps that are common to most projects in museums.

The role of the project manager is a very important one. The project manager requires a high standard of planning, organisational, monitoring and communication skills, and an understanding of the implications of the project for the museum's resources, finance, administration and quality assurance. An appropriate investment of time in the planning and monitoring of any project will serve to ease the stress of the project team in its implementation.

There are some general principles of good practice in project management that are worth emphasising. The project manager should:

- develop a project plan that includes the objectives of the project, the tasks to be carried out, the people to carry them out, the timescale and programme for the project, and the resources required;
- ensure that the members of the project team have clearly defined roles and responsibilities and that these are confirmed in writing;

- ensure that the methodology, schedule and outputs of the project are agreed and understood;
- break the project into smaller pieces and agree who is responsible for delivering these pieces;
- not promise what cannot be delivered within the project plan;
- monitor progress with the project team on a regular basis;
- communicate progress with museum management as well as the project team on a regular basis;
- keep museum management informed at all times and be absolutely sure to point out the resource and financial implications of any changes to the project plan that you may suggest;
- ask the museum 'project steering group', if there is one, to appoint a single point of contact for ease of communication;
- set realistic deadlines for team members to keep moving at a steady pace;
- identify the key processes for your project and focus attention on them.

If you start falling behind, reprioritise your task list and delegate less important work to those who are capable of handling it. If you meet problems, talk to museum management and ask them for any support required. Do not stick your head in the sand and hope that problems will go away!

THE PROJECT MANAGEMENT PROCESS

Project management can be broken into four distinct phases:

1 project inception;
2 project planning;
3 project monitoring;
4 project completion/closure.

These four stages are described in more detail in the following paragraphs.

Phase 1 – project inception

It is important to get things off to a good start. The project manager should:

- Make sure that the brief for the project has been agreed with museum management.
- Arrange an inception meeting for the project team to go through or develop the project plan and make sure that everyone understands their role and responsibilities.
- Establish details of contacts, milestones in the project plan and deadlines. A project 'database' is an extremely useful project management tool, so it is worth spending time assembling core information at the start of a project and then

adding to it as the project proceeds. It is also a useful record of a project that may be helpful for further projects.

• Circulate a project contact list to the team. This is particularly useful when the team includes contractors as well as staff.

Phase 2 – project planning

Project planning is absolutely crucial to successful project management. Time spent here is really worthwhile and should not be overlooked. For museums that have access to computers, computer software is now available to help in project planning and monitoring. The majority of the project planning should take place at the inception meeting, which the project manager should organise and chair.

Box 84.1 provides an agenda for a project inception meeting. It is particularly important to get all the team members to establish and agree the amount of time to be allocated to the project, especially where the project is additional to their normal workloads. Wider resource implications (i.e. other demands on time, additional financial implications) should also be considered. At the end of the meeting, information regarding changes to the project or changes to milestones and deadlines should be fed into the project plan.

Phase 3 – project monitoring

In all projects, communication is the key to success: communication with stakeholders, communication with museum management and communication with the project team. Museum managers will be reassured and respond more positively if they receive regular updates on how the project is progressing. It is good practice to let the museum manager or 'project steering group' know about work that is being done and to let them know if the project is still on target for meeting its deadlines.

Well-organised filing (paper and/or electronic copies) can save an enormous amount of time for the project manager and the project team members.

The project manager should:

• monitor the progress of the job against the project plan;
• monitor the delivery and quality of the project outputs;
• monitor the progress of the job against the project budget;
• reallocate team resources where necessary, while re-forecasting the financial outcome of the project;
• highlight potential problems at an early stage, particularly with regard to overrun of staff or contractor time.

Project managers should encourage team members to be closely aware of the proposed allocation of time for their involvement on the project and let them know of any potential difficulties.

All projects require deadlines and it is critical that all efforts are made to try to meet them. Shifting deadlines will inevitably place extra costs on a job. If deadlines do have to change, be sure to update the project plan and alert the team as a whole to the change.

Phase 4 – project completion/closure

Completing any project brings a great sense of relief, but there are still a few things to be done to 'close' the project:

- Check with the museum finance manager that all invoicing is in order and that all external contractors have submitted their final invoices.
- Conduct a 'de-briefing' meeting with the project team to discuss lessons learnt and their experience of the project as a whole.
- Ensure that the project records and papers are archived for future reference.
- Liaise with the museum's communications manager regarding how the completed project is to be used in public relations and marketing terms, for example through press releases, launches, etc.
- Think how best to capture what the museum has learnt from the project process for the future.

Project management can sometimes seem like a chore. However, experience suggests that good project management certainly helps to ease the stress of carrying out a museum project for all those involved and is fundamental to the project's success.

Box 84.1 Inception meeting – agenda

Project name:
Project manager:
Attendees:
Date of meeting:

1 Background to project.
2 The brief for the project.
3 The project manager's role.
4 Key stakeholders – internal (for example, the museum governing body) and external (for example, funding agencies).
5 Roles, responsibilities and tasks of team members.
6 Project plan, tasks and milestones.
7 Time allocations and deadlines.
8 Next steps and meetings.
9 Any further business.

Financial management

Related Units – Units 81–2, 86–7

One of the fundamental responsibilities of the governing body and the museum manager is to ensure that the museum has robust financial management systems in place. Effective and efficient financial management is a key aspect of sustainability (see Unit 5).

The money that a museum needs to carry out its operation can be described under two headings – *operating* and *capital*.

OPERATING BUDGETS

An *operating budget* is concerned with the day-to-day finances of the museum. It defines the relationship between *operating income* and *expenditure*. For a maintained museum, its operating income is the money that it receives from its parent funding body, for example state or city government and what it earns through other sources, for example through retailing or catering activities or through external grants. For an independent museum without a parent funding body, its operating income will depend on money earned through, for example, admission charges and retailing and catering activities, together with any grants or donations it raises through its fundraising programme. Operating expenditure is the money that a museum pays for staffing costs, collections management requirements, marketing, energy costs, etc. (see the example budget on p. 260). The balance between income and expenditure represents profit and loss.

The museum's governing body is accountable for the museum's financial management. The museum manager is responsible for ensuring that the museum's finances are soundly managed on a day-to-day basis and deficits do not occur.

Where required, museum managers should seek external professional advice from qualified accountants who will help to draw up guidance and procedures for managing finances. For museums with computerised financial systems, there is a range of software available that can help in financial management at all levels, for example staff payroll, retail and catering activities, and taxation. Financial advisers will also provide help over record-keeping and taxation. Laws on finance and tax vary from country to country and the museum may be required under law to submit regular financial returns. It is therefore of critical importance for internal and external purposes that scrupulous records are kept of the day-to-day earnings (income) and outgoings (expenditure) of the museum.

Within the museum, financial matters should be controlled by one individual who reports to the governing body or a finance committee of the governing body on a regular basis. The governing body should ensure that monitoring procedures are established so that monthly statements of actual expenditure are provided against the estimated expenditure of the museum. This helps managers and staff with day-to-day responsibility for income/expenditure to know precisely how well the museum's finances are doing. If necessary, action can be taken to reduce expenditure if income is not as anticipated, or to generate more earnings.

The museum should also draw up a *cashflow projection* for the coming year. This will show on a monthly or weekly basis how income and expenditure are expected to fluctuate during the year. The projection will include *fixed costs* such as salaries or energy costs, as well as *variable costs* such as equipment costs. A clear understanding of the pattern of your cashflow is important for effective financial planning. Many museums are dependent on seasonal fluctuations in visitors and therefore income from admission charges and related retail and catering sales. Bills are often paid at set times of the year. Such anticipated fluctuations need to be taken into account when planning forecasts of income and expenditure.

In summary, seek professional advice where required. Ensure that income and expenditure projections are drawn up in the light of your and others' experience. Monitor progress on a monthly or weekly basis and ensure close financial controls are kept over cash-handling and expenditure. Your annual report should include an audited statement of the museum's finances for the year. Report regularly to the governing body; all of its members are ultimately accountable for ensuring the museum is in robust financial health.

CAPITAL BUDGETS

Capital is money that is used for purchases or developments, such as new buildings, equipment or major refurbishment programmes. It does not appear in the operating budget because it is additional or 'one-off' expenditure to the day-to-day finances of the museum.

However, capital expenditure may have major implications for operating budgets. For example, a new museum development may require significant amounts of capital secured from endowment funds, appeals, government grants, or borrowing to cover building costs. When the building work is completed and the building comes into use, there will then be recurrent costs such as interest charges, heating, lighting, staffing and furnishing that have to be covered in your revenue budget and may be additional to the current expenditure. Capital programmes therefore should only be entered into with these new operating costs firmly established and understood.

Capital funds may be sourced through a variety of means. They may be provided through the parent body of a maintained museum, awarded by grant-giving agencies or secured through a fundraising programme from a variety of sources, large and small. They may be derived from the sale of assets, such as land or buildings. They may be borrowed from a financial institution on the basis of a financial agreement that requires the loan to be repaid over a period of time. Whatever method or combination of methods the museum chooses for raising capital funds, fundraising need to be very carefully managed, and strict controls and monitoring should be put in place in advance. Professional advice and careful forward planning will provide significant benefits (see Unit 87).

A museum's reputation and success in meeting its mission and objectives will depend on how well its operational and capital finances are managed. An efficient and sustainable museum operation is dependent on efficient and sustainable financial management. Without effective financial management, the museum's responsibilities will not be met.

Operating budget checklist

This checklist provides suggestions for the type of headings for income and expenditure to be used in a budget. One heading may include a number of line items within it. The exact number of headings and line items used by a museum will depend on its circumstances.

Operating expenditure	*Operating income*
Museum management	
Staff salaries and on-costs, e.g. insurance, pensions	Admission charges to museum
Staff travel and subsistence expenses	Museum shop, including web site retail sales
Building maintenance	Museum catering
	Merchandising
Energy costs – water, electricity, fuel	Events and activities programme, e.g. informal learning programmes, museum guided tours, conferences and seminars, temporary exhibitions, concerts
Insurances	Facilities hire by external bodies
Cleaning	Services, e.g. advice and consultancy, conservation services for other museums, touring exhibitions
Security	Donations
Telephone/fax	Bequests
Postage/stationery	Grants from grant-giving bodies
Office equipment, includes computer network	Sponsorship from private-sector companies (may include financial sponsorship, but also gifts in kind)
Depreciation on equipment	Membership subscriptions, e.g. Friends
	Membership events
Specialist services such as auditors, accountants	Loans, e.g. from financial institutions

Operating expenditure	*Operating income*

Collections management
Staff salaries and on-costs, e.g. insurance, pensions
Staff training and professional development
Travel and subsistence expenses
Conservation – materials
Conservation – equipment and maintenance
Documentation – materials
Documentation – equipment and maintenance
IT systems
Storage – materials
Storage – equipment and maintenance
Disaster kits
Insurance
Collections security
Purchase funds for collections

Visitor and user services
Staff salaries and on-costs, e.g. insurance, pensions
Staff training and professional development
Travel and subsistence
Displays
Exhibitions
Exhibitions transport and storage
Equipment and maintenance
Shop stock
Catering supplies
Publications for resale
Other publications, e.g. annual report
Marketing, includes advertising, direct mailing, leaflet distribution
Web site and maintenance
Education service supplies
Events and activities programme supplies

Unit

86

New sources of income

Related Units – Units 85, 87

Museums and money go together. Museums need assured funding to undertake their day-to-day work as well as additional funds to carry out one-off projects (see Unit 85). Identifying sources of operational income as well as capital funds is thus an ongoing challenge for museums of all types. In general terms, it is considered more difficult to generate operational income or additional operational income than to raise capital funds for museums. This is because one-off projects may require significant amounts of funding at one time, but they do not require the sort of continuous funding that the museum's operation requires. If the museum wishes to increase the level of its activities, for example through new staffing or new programmes, it will generally require additional operational funding for the purpose unless it can reprioritise its existing funds. Museum managers will therefore need to consider how to identify and secure additional income.

Sources of income for the museum's operation were illustrated in Unit 85. In this Unit, further comment on each of these sources is given.

ADMISSION CHARGES TO MUSEUMS

For those museums that charge for admission, as well as for other services, a pricing policy is required. This may need to take account of wider pricing policies, for example where the museum is part of a local government department that charges for a range of other leisure or cultural services, or be developed specifically for the museum. Setting an admission charge needs to be informed by a number of factors:

- what the museum has charged historically;
- what admission prices other museums and heritage facilities are charging;
- what the likely rate of inflation will be for the coming year;
- what target audiences the museum is seeking to attract;
- what discounts the museum will provide, for example, for old people, for children, for family groups, for educational groups, for unemployed people or for special promotions; and
- what income the museum needs to generate to meet its operational costs.

Admission charges need to be set at the time the museum's budget is being revised for the succeeding year. This also allows the new charges to be included in marketing materials such as publicity leaflets that will need to be distributed in advance of the museum's financial year.

The level of admission charges will depend on a museum's individual circumstances, but should be set so as to provide value for money for the visitor and to encourage repeat and regular visitation.

MUSEUM SHOPS INCLUDING WEB SITE RETAIL SALES

Museum shops provide an important source of additional revenue income for the museum. Unit 19 describes the management of museum shops and this Unit provides further comment on shop finances. The museum shop must make a profit if it is to contribute effectively to the museum's income, and as with admission charges the shop's pricing policy is important. Pricing of stock needs to be informed by a number of factors:

- what the museum's shop has charged historically;
- what percentage mark-up on the wholesale prices of stock the shop will charge;
- what shops in other museums and heritage facilities and more generally are charging for their goods;
- what target audiences the museum is seeking to provide services to;
- what the associated overheads are;
- what discounts the museum will provide;
- what level of sales the museum shop needs to make to meet its operational costs and provide a profit.

Good financial management of the museum's retail operation, on-site and on-line, is essential if the museum is to maximise the profits from retail sales whether the operation is franchised or run in-house.

In considering what items to purchase for resale, it is critical to ensure that you do not tie up capital in stock that is difficult or slow to sell. A close understanding of the nature of the museum's visitors and users and their needs is the key to success.

MERCHANDISING

Licensing other organisations to produce sales items based on your museum's collections can provide a valuable source of additional retail income (see Unit 19). It is worthwhile undertaking a *merchandising audit* of the museum's collections as a first step to developing contractual relationships with manufacturers and distributors. This will help to identify which items or groups of items in the collections might be suitable for merchandising and licensing purposes. There is a wide range of possibilities from replicas through to the application of design motifs drawn from objects in the museum's collections to products of different type, for example bed linen, clothing, jewellery or even wrapping paper. Drawing up the contractual and financial arrangements between the museum and the licensee requires professional legal advice. Museums should be careful to ensure that adequate research is given to this subject in advance of their involvement with commercial companies.

MUSEUM CATERING

Catering facilities in museums provide an important source of additional revenue income for the museum. Unit 20 describes the management of catering facilities and this Unit provides further comment on their finances. The museum's catering operation must make a profit if it is to contribute effectively to the museum's income. As with admission charges and retail operations, pricing policy is important. Pricing needs to be informed by a number of factors:

- what the museum café or restaurant has charged historically;
- what percentage mark-up on wholesale prices the café or restaurant will charge;
- what catering outlets in other museums and heritage facilities more generally are charging;
- what the associated overheads are;
- what target audiences the museum is seeking to provide food and drink to;
- what level of sales the museum's catering facilities need to make to meet their operational costs and provide a profit.

Good financial management of the museum's catering operation is essential if the museum is to maximise the profits from sales, whether the facilities are franchised or run in-house.

EVENTS AND ACTIVITIES PROGRAMMES

A rich events and activities programme, e.g. informal learning programmes, museum guided tours, conferences and seminars, temporary exhibitions and concerts, provides multiple opportunities to generate income for the museum (see Unit 17). While different events and activities will have different pricing levels associated with them, the events and activities programme as a whole should be designed to make a profit for the museum. A mix of events, on-site and off-site, which address different audience types is a powerful way not only of earning money for the museum but also for developing new audiences.

Each event should be considered in financial terms and a financial plan drawn up for it, identifying both the related expenditure and the potential income. Income may be generated from the event itself or from products developed with it, for example exhibition or conference publications. Policy decisions as to what pricing levels to charge and what overheads to cost against the event, e.g. staff costs, energy costs, will need to be taken. It should be possible to reduce the costs of some categories of event by running them on more than one occasion.

FACILITIES HIRE BY EXTERNAL BODIES

Providing facilities for hire by external organisations is discussed in Unit 21. While hiring facilities in the museum to outside bodies may provide a valuable income stream, for example for corporate events, filming, or conferences, it is important to understand the full cost implications that such events carry. These include additional staffing or security requirements and costs, special insurance cover, depreciation costs or general wear and tear, and energy costs. The museum may wish to develop a policy that allows certain organisations to be subsidised. However, in general, museum managers should ensure that the museum does not suffer any financial loss from facilities hire and that the full costs of making facilities available should be recovered.

SERVICES

Museums represent considerable sources of expertise and experience. In some cases, it may be possible to develop these so that services can be supplied to other organisations outside the museum. For example, regional museums may provide some of their conservators' time to support the conservation needs of other museums in their regions or develop exhibitions that then tour to other museums. Smaller museums may also have particular expertise that they can make available to other museums through, for example, consultancy services. At the same time, museums may decide to provide some of their services to other types of organisation or individuals. There is a wide range of opportunity. Museum services may be provided on-site, off-site or on-line.

Where a museum is providing such services, it will need to establish an appropriate pricing policy, taking into consideration the different clients, for example cultural, educational or commercial, that it may wish to serve. As with all service provision the full cost of the service needs to be established, before a level for fees, expenses and materials is set. The purpose of service provision is to make a profit for the museum.

DONATIONS

Many museums benefit from donations of money and donations in-kind. For the museum visitor who has enjoyed his or her visit to the museum, a donations box located near the museum exit provides an opportunity for them to contribute to the work of the museum. Donations boxes should be securely designed and clearly labelled with an explanation of how visitors' donations will be put to use in the museum's work.

Donations may also be made through appeals for funds for specific projects, or through gifts prompted by different reasons, perhaps a previous visit, a concern to support a good cause or as a recognition of the value of the museum's work. Donors should be thanked promptly. If the donation is towards a specific project, the donor should be kept in touch with its progress. If the donation is a more general gift, then the museum should explain what aspect of its work it will put the donation towards. Unless there are specific requests not to publicise the gift, donors should also be thanked publicly for their contribution to the museum. This helps to promote the idea of giving to the museum in the public mind.

Donations in-kind can be a very valuable form of support. They may take many forms, but are often provided by companies who will make one or more of their products available to the museum. The museum should take care that there are no ethical difficulties associated with accepting such gifts (see Unit 6).

BEQUESTS

Bequests are a form of donation in money or in-kind. A bequest may have been left to the museum without the museum's prior knowledge or it may have been discussed with the museum director previously. In fundraising terms, eliciting bequests is a highly sensitive area and needs to be handled with great care and tact. Any conditions associated with a bequest also need to be considered carefully in advance of the museum's acceptance. Museums embarking on a fundraising programme or the development of a particular aspect of their collection might meet with local solicitors to discuss how to draw their clients' attention to the programme and suggest the possibility of a bequest on the museum's behalf.

GRANTS FROM GRANT-GIVING BODIES

Grants from grant-giving bodies may be towards the museum's operational costs or for one-off projects. In approaching a grant-giving body for funding support, it is essential that the museum carries out its research in advance. There is a primary need to understand the nature of the grant-giving body's aims and objectives, its grant programmes, the form of application that it requires applicants to make, and the timescales to which it works. The museum will need to make a case-for-support for funding, and guidance is given on its contents in Unit 87.

SPONSORSHIP FROM PRIVATE-SECTOR COMPANIES

Sponsorship from private-sector companies is most usually given for one-off projects rather than towards operational costs. As with grant-giving bodies, it is essential that the museum undertakes its research on potential sponsors in advance of approaching them for their support. The museum will need to understand the work of potential sponsors, their aims and objectives, the type of sponsorship they might provide, and the nature and timing of applications. The museum will need to make a case-for-support for sponsorship, and guidance is given on its contents in Unit 87.

MEMBERSHIP SUBSCRIPTIONS

Friends' organisations provide a valuable body of support for the museum. Through their programmes, they can provide an important and regular source of funding for the museum's work. In general, Friends' organisations are more likely to support one-off projects of various types, for example the purchase of new items for the collections or the conservation of objects. Their financial support can be a very helpful source of local funding to match grants from grant-giving bodies.

A Friends' organisation is in place primarily to support the museum financially; the museum is not there to support the Friends. It follows that while the museum should be represented formally at Friends' meetings and events, it should not spend its own funding providing services to its Friends' group. Subscriptions to the Friends' group should therefore be set at an appropriate level that enables it to cover all its own costs, for example postage and stationery, telephone calls, secretarial support, computer database, dedicated space within the museum and the costs of events.

MEMBERSHIP EVENTS

Friends' organisations will wish to hold events and activities within their annual programme. Indeed, the social value of events and activities is an important reason for people to join Friends' organisations in the first instance. While the costs of some of these might be covered by the annual subscription for members, others will have an additional charge. Events and activities are an important part of the Friends' overall fundraising efforts and different events may generate significant amounts of net profit. Where the Friends' organisation wishes to make use of the museum's facilities for an event, the museum should consider the request in the light of its policy towards facilities hire by external organisations (see Unit 21). Members of the governing body and museum staff should make every effort to attend events organised by their Friends as a matter of courtesy and as a mark of thanks for their fundraising efforts on behalf of the museum.

LOANS

Loans from external financial bodies can provide an additional area of income for the museum. However, as with all loans, these need to be entered into with due care and attention to the details of the loan arrangement. Wherever a loan is being contemplated, for example towards a major capital project, the museum needs to be certain to factor the costs of loan repayments into its cashflow forecasting (see Unit 85).

Unit
87

Fundraising

Related Units – Units 84–6

Museums raise funds for many different types of projects, for example building programmes, temporary exhibitions, special events, publications, fieldwork and research programmes. The need for fundraising varies from museum to museum. Generally speaking, museums seek to raise funds for projects of one sort or another that they would not otherwise be able to fund from their normal revenue budget. Funds may be raised from public- or private-sector sources – international bodies, central or local government agencies, charitable trusts or foundations, commercial companies or individual patrons.

SOME BASIC QUESTIONS

In fundraising, the first basic question to ask is *what are we fundraising for?* The answer to this question will largely determine what sources of funding you should approach.

For example, if the museum is seeking funding for a special temporary exhibition, then commercial sponsorship may be the answer. If the museum is seeking to extend a building or provide new facilities for the disabled, then a government agency or a charitable trust that will fund capital projects is likely to be the source. If the museum needs equipment, then a gift in-kind rather than in cash may be obtainable from a private-sector source. If the museum is seeking special skills, then a secondment or a recently retired professional person may be available at reduced or nil cost.

The second question to ask is *who will be carrying out the fundraising?* Fundraising has its own techniques and rules. It is never easy. It should be carried out by somebody capable of carefully researching possible sources of funds, producing a well-constructed and well-written 'case-for-support', persuasively arguing the case for the museum and keeping accurate records. Once funding has been secured, they have to ensure among other things that all the necessary follow-up is carried out, the conditions of funding are met, the relevant people are thanked, progress reports on the project are provided and appropriate acknowledgement is given to the funding body.

Above all else, the fundraiser – whether a museum employee or a professional consultant on contract to the museum – needs tact, persistence, optimism and energy. It is best for somebody with the right skills and professionalism to raise funds rather than to get the museum manager, who will have plenty of other things to do, to add this responsibility to their workload. This does not mean that the museum manager will have no role to play in fundraising. There may for example be a need to agree the draft case-for-support, sign letters or agreements drafted by the fundraiser, and meet and thank representatives of the funding body formally for their support.

The third question is *what sort of return will the funding body want for their investment or support?* In the case of government agencies or charitable trusts, requirements will vary, but accounting officers will expect to see formal receipts, audited accounts and evidence that their money has been spent well and wisely. Your case-for-support will need to include what other sources of funding are being used to support the project. Raising funds is a competitive process, and the strength of your case-for-support will be important (see p. 270).

A good project will always attract financial support if fundraising is handled with tact, professionalism and care. The fundraiser does not necessarily need glossy brochures and expensively designed information packs to beat the competition. You must consider your needs and objectives carefully before you type a letter, pick up the telephone or send off a case-for-support. Inadequate research, preparation and carry-through can waste a lot of people a lot of time and money!

FUNDRAISING THROUGH COMMERCIAL SPONSORSHIP

In many ways, fundraising is more complex with commercial sponsors. Commercial companies are looking for specific returns from sponsorship and sponsorship is a business relationship between the museum and the sponsor. The museum should enter the relationship knowing the basis on which an agreement with the sponsor will be struck. The museum has to decide what it can offer the sponsor in terms of publicity, acknowledgements and services, for example letting the museum's galleries be used for corporate entertainment.

Companies look for the following in sponsorship deals:

- projects that will appeal to their customers and target markets;
- the opportunity to mix sponsorship with their other activities;
- value for their money: the value of the benefits package from the museum must reflect the investment from the sponsor;
- publicity potential and media coverage;
- opportunities and high-quality facilities to provide entertainment and hospitality for clients;
- professionalism on the part of the museum;
- a detailed description of what is and what is not included in the sponsorship agreement;
- a list of responsibilities for action on the part of the museum and the sponsor;
- a timescale and schedule for meetings;
- an evaluation of the project and its sponsorship.

Hence the need for the case-for-support to set the scene, make the sponsorship proposal, identify and list the benefits for the museum and the sponsor, and demonstrate the track record of previously sponsored projects. Writing up projects that have been sponsored into case study material for later use with cases-for-support can be particularly helpful in demonstrating success. Press coverage, video, photographs and testimonials are all helpful.

If a museum is involved or going to be involved with commercial sponsorship, it is essential to look after your sponsors. Maintain contact throughout a sponsorship deal, and afterwards. Successful fundraising in the commercial sector is about retaining sponsors and increasing their investment.

The museum should however be realistic. It is pointless asking sponsors for sums of money that are unrealistic. Museums have to recognise that commercial sponsorship is a two-way process. More and more companies now base sponsorship deals on a contractual basis to ensure that the museum delivers the benefits that the company is 'buying'. Marketing and public relations departments have to justify what they are sponsoring to their governing boards; they are looking for value for money.

THE CASE-FOR-SUPPORT

In structuring a case-for-support for a project, bear in mind that the recipient may know little or nothing about your project. It is therefore up to you to present the case-for-support in a form that enables them to understand the project and its rationale, and to see how their contribution will help to secure the success of the project. Many funding bodies will have set application forms to complete or will ask for particular information in a particular format. Others will simply ask you to make your own application and argue your case in line with their stated policies and interests. They may ask you to limit your proposal to a few sides of paper or to provide a highly detailed breakdown of all of the different elements of the project.

An example of the contents of a case-for-support for a new museum building project is provided in Boxes 87.1 and 87.2. It is based on the application procedures of a major grant-giving heritage agency. It is in two parts – a project description (Box 87.1) and a set of supporting appendices (Box 87.2). Not all applications for funding will of course be as detailed as this example, but the general principles are the same for whatever scale of application. It can be adapted to suit the needs of different scales of projects.

Box 87.1 The case-for-support – development project description

Introduction to the document
- Executive summary
- Introduction to the application for funding
- About this document
- Terminology used in this document
- The museum and its setting
- Brief history of the museum
- The museum – mission, objectives, policies and plans

The development project
- The need for the development project
- Visitor service elements to be included in the development project
- Collections to be included in the development project
- Relationship between the development project and the rest of the museum

The market
- General market context
- Strategic market review
- Market research
- Market analysis
- Marketing strategy

Box 87.1 continued

The visitor experience
- Interpretative approaches to be used
- Intellectual and cultural access to the new facilities
- Visitor areas
- Products and services for the visitor
- Programming
- Virtual access

The benefits of the development project
- The significance of the museum's collections
- Conservation benefits for the collections
- Access benefits provided by the project
- Learning benefits provided by the project
- Cultural heritage benefits
- Other public benefits
- Public support for the development project

The development project
- Design development
- Proposed design
- Options analysis
- Feasibility assessment
- Agreements with planning authorities
- Capital costs and funding
- Architectural and building quality
- Eligible costs from the funding body
- Request for funds from the funding body
- Funding and fundraising strategy for the development project
- Capital cashflow (including impact on the museum's revenue budget)

Development project delivery
- Previous management of major projects by the museum
- Management strategy and staffing for the development project
- Procurement approaches
- Transitional planning
- Project programme and timetable
- Development project risk management

The operational case
- Operational plan for the new development
- Staffing for the new development
- Operational costs of the new facilities
- Revenues generated from the new facilities
- Ten-year cashflow projection
- Sensitivity analysis
- Operational evaluation
- Operational risk management

Source: UK Heritage Lottery Fund

Box 87.2 The case-for-support – development project appendices

- Constitution of the museum
- Last three years' financial accounts for the museum
- The museum's strategies, policies and plans including (but not limited to):

  - Learning policy
  - Learning strategy
  - Collections management policy and plan
  - Statement of significance of the museum's collections
  - Access policy and plan
  - Charging or pricing policy
  - Energy and environmental policies
  - information and communications technology policy and strategy
  - Audience Development Plan
  - Other policy documentation, e.g. the museum's policy manual

- Authorisation to submit funding application
- Proof of ownership of the museum site
- Proof of ownership of the museum's collections
- Proof of ownership of other assets
- Market research report(s)
- Marketing strategy and plan (including market analysis)
- Virtual access strategy
- Statements of support for the museum's development project
- Report of public consultation process
- Options analysis
- Feasibility study
- Project briefs (architectural, exhibition and storage, externals and infrastructure, etc.)
- Architectural design report (building, site infrastructure, landscape, etc.)
- Exhibition design report (fit-out, storage, etc.)
- The museum's property strategy
- Planning agreements
- Capital cost plan
- Capital funding strategy
- Operational management and financial plan
- Monitoring and evaluation plan (covering aims, actions and measures of success)
- Transitional plan (relocation of staff, collections, etc.)
- Project team CVs
- Procurement strategy
- Project training plan
- Development project risk management plan

Source: UK Heritage Lottery Fund

The project description provides an introduction to the case-for-support, a description of the development project, its market context, the nature of the experience for the visitor, the benefits of the project, the design of the project, its delivery, and its operation once completed. The supporting appendices provide a range of more detailed information on which the project description is based. The case-for-support can be tailored to meet the needs of different funding agencies. Together, the two parts of the case-for-support provide readers with a clear understanding of the development project and its rationale and give them confidence in the museum's management of the development project.

Management of change

Related Units – Units 80–1, 89–90, 93–6

All museum directors are faced with implementing change in their museums. Change may be small-scale and affect a relatively small number of people or it may be large-scale and affect everyone connected with the museum – governors, staff, stakeholders and audiences. The spectrum of change is a wide one and change, whether physical, organisational or operational, carries with it many management challenges.

Generally speaking, people do not respond well to change. It can be unsettling, especially where systems and procedures have been in place for some time or where change is implemented without effective communication or consultation with those people who will be principally affected (see Unit 89).

Museum directors and managers who are managing change at whatever scale first need to be clear about why change is required. They need to be able to demonstrate both to their governing body, which is ultimately responsible for the well-being of the museum and to their staff, who will be responsible for implementing change, that change and its implications will be carefully considered in line with the museum's mission and strategic objectives and with its forward planning (see Units 80–1).

Depending on the nature and scale of change and the solution proposed, it is often helpful to undertake an options analysis to explore the different ways in which the museum's strategic and planning objectives can be best met to achieve cost-effectiveness and cost-efficiency (see Units 71 and 84). This enables:

- different options for change to be examined objectively;
- comparisons to be drawn with good practice elsewhere;
- external specialist assessments to be undertaken as appropriate;

- discussions to be held with all those involved with the change process and its impact;
- decisions to be made on a considered and objective basis;
- and then the final decisions communicated and explained to those involved.

CULTURAL CHANGE

More complicated for museum directors is the process of managing cultural change within a museum organisation, especially where the culture has been conservative rather than innovative. Many museum directors will be appointed to a museum where change is required to develop the quality of the museum and its work. The need for change may have been already recognised internally and/or externally. Indeed, the appointment may have been made by the governing body with this in mind, or the director may himself or herself recognise that cultural change is required from a professional perspective.

While personal qualities of leadership undoubtedly have an important part to play in implementing change, so too does clarity of vision and professional under-standing. We have emphasised throughout *Museum Basics* that successful museums of whatever scale and type require a clear vision and a well-considered mission statement supported by strategic objectives (see Units 80–1). Form should always follow function. Unless those responsible for leading the museum know and agree where they want to go and what they can realistically achieve, they are unlikely to command the support of their staff or their stakeholders.

Working with the museum's managers and staff and stakeholders to define that vision and mission is an essential first step in cultural change. Testing the emer-gent ideas about the museum externally with the museum's audiences may also be important. Consultation and involvement, participation and engagement are watchwords of effective cultural change in museums. It is the responsibility of the museum's director and senior managers to make sure that they harness the experi-ence and expertise of the whole museum team in considering vision and mission. While there will always be a need to impose a timetable for change to take place, and the ultimate decisions will rest with the governing body, an appropriate amount of time needs to be given to internal and external consultation to ensure that all perspectives have been taken into account.

The process of developing a new vision and mission, and a new forward plan for a museum needs to be seen as part of a professional development programme for staff. It provides multiple learning opportunities. Exposing the museum's staff to other ways of thinking and working through for example study visits to other museums or allied institutions, a set of seminars or workshops led by external professional facilitators, external reports and presentations on different aspects of the museum's work, e.g. market analysis and research, conservation assessments or interpretation, or simply guided reading, helps to generate new thinking to feed into the forward planning process and makes cultural change easier to implement.

At the same time, it is important to demonstrate how proposed changes – whether these are organisational (for example, new staff posts, staff structure and line management), operational (for example, communication systems, administrative systems and procedures) or physical (for example, new displays or exhibitions, new support services or new offices) – will provide benefits, internally and externally, over the existing position (see Units 4 and 83). Being able to demonstrate what benefits for staff and visitors will flow from proposed changes helps people understand why change is important and necessary.

Ultimately, of course, change in the museum may be regarded as for the better or for the worse, depending on your perspective. The change process however will be a lot less painful for all concerned if it is well considered and well managed and recognises that the success of the museum will be dependent on the interest and enthusiasm of the museum's staff in meeting its objectives.

Unit
89

Internal communications

Related Units – Units 10, 81

A museum should develop a communications strategy so that *external* communications with its public can be managed effectively (see Unit 10). It is equally important for the museum to have good *internal* communications procedures so that governing bodies, management and staff are kept informed of the progress and achievements of the museum. Information flow through the organisation needs to happen in a variety of ways. Some of the communications procedures that museums use are examined here.

All individuals within the museum should have access to the information they need to carry out their jobs effectively, maintain and develop interest in their work, see how their work is contributing to meeting the museum's objectives and understand more generally its achievements. No one person can or should know everything! All people working in and for the museum should be served by its communications procedures that should ensure an appropriate direction and level of information flow.

GOVERNING BODIES

What do members of the governing body of the museum need to know and how do they gain access to relevant information? In the first instance, governors have a responsibility to ensure that the museum is operating within the policy framework that they have formally agreed and is working to meet its defined objectives. The museum's forward plan is the management mechanism that translates the museum's policy and objectives into a plan of action (see Units 77, 80–1). Governors need to know and agree both how their policy and objectives are being carried out and receive regular reports on progress within the different programme areas of the plan.

Governors will also have to respond to new requirements, new opportunities and new difficulties that appear from time to time and have an effect on the overall performance of the museum. They therefore need to meet regularly, between four and twelve times per year as appropriate, to receive written and oral reports on progress and external developments that may impact on the museum. Governors of small museums may need to meet more regularly than those with professional staffing.

These progress reports come from the museum manager and other senior management staff or from external advisers such as auditors or consultants. They allow governors to monitor progress against the objectives and tasks within the forward plan and take further policy decisions as required. Where more specific attention needs to be paid to particular areas of the museum's work, the governing body may wish to establish committees from its membership or advisory panels of external advisers. Committee or panel meetings will also need to be serviced by management staff. Their timing should relate to the schedule of governors' meetings to which they will report.

All formal meetings of governors or committees and advisory panels should be minuted in writing, typed up with copies sent to all members and agreed as a correct record at the subsequent meeting. The steps necessary to implement any new decisions should be described in an action checklist or memorandum for implementation and sent to all relevant staff, with a timetable for the action to be taken and subsequently reported on. In these ways, governors who are ultimately responsible for the well-being of the museum can be kept fully informed of progress and take decisions within their agreed policy and forward planning.

MANAGERS

Museum managers at all levels from the director to line managers have to ensure that progress within the museum's forward plan is communicated to staff. They also have to ensure that staff inform them of their progress in the workplace. Managers have a responsibility to explain those issues that affect people's work and that affect people working. Staff do not necessarily have to agree in order to co-operate with a management decision, but they must understand why and how it has been made.

No matter how large or small the workforce, formal systems need to be established for efficient information flow. In small museums especially, where communications may be relatively informal, it is easy to think that someone knows something. The opposite may all too easily be the case if they have not been informed within a communications procedure that ensures their inclusion!

Museum managers have to ensure that their staff receive accurate and correct information, and take every step to discourage and correct, if necessary, rumour and distortion. Reporting mechanisms need to be established so that information, and critically ideas and suggestions from staff at all levels can be fed into the communications system. Managers need to consider carefully how most effectively to communicate with their staff and what communications mechanisms they should use for what purpose.

BRIEFING MUSEUM TEAMS

One method of communicating with the museum's workforce is through 'team briefing'. The workforce is divided into teams who are then briefed on the museum's work by their team leader. Team leaders are themselves briefed as a team and their responsibility is then to 'cascade' their briefing through the organisation.

Briefing can be structured in four sections:

- progress and forward planning – progress made against planning objectives since the last briefing and work planning for the month ahead. This information can be written down and circulated in advance of the meetings;
- policy – new policy decisions taken or initiatives under development;
- people – new appointments, people leaving the museum or qualifications gained by individuals;
- points for action – specific action points, reminders of dates/events, 'housekeeping' points.

Team briefing may take between half an hour and an hour on an appropriate timescale. This may be weekly, fortnightly or monthly depending on the needs of the museum. Questions and clarification of points should be sought and answered, later if necessary, following reference to senior management. This ensures that essential core information is transmitted quickly and accurately through the organisation.

Such a briefing procedure needs to be informed by progress reports from each member or unit of staff to their line managers on a regular basis to mesh with the team briefing cycle.

OTHER FORMS OF COMMUNICATION

There is a wide range of other forms of formal and informal communication within the museum – some will be more or less appropriate depending on local circumstances. This checklist provides some guidance:

- news or information bulletins in written format circulated on an internal post system to designated staff;
- e-mails – the use of electronic mailing systems needs to be carefully managed if they are to be used effectively. High dependency or overuse can mean that other more effective forms of communication, for example interpersonal discussion, may be overlooked;

- current awareness circulars, including copies of press coverage of the museum's activities;
- noticeboards (physical and virtual) – but make certain these are the responsibility of a designated individual to manage and ensure that all notices are signed to identify their source and therefore status;
- museum manager's newsletter (physical and virtual) – which may reflect on overall progress and communicate decisions made by the governing body;
- employees' and governors' handbooks or information packs. It is essential to keep these updated, but they are invaluable for reference purposes and ensure consistency of communication;
- project presentations to staff by project leaders;
- annual reports on the museum's work in different areas for employees;
- staff meetings – any meeting for staff needs to be well organised and well managed if it is to be effective.

STAFF

All staff have an important part to play in information and communications procedures. It is essential that all staff are encouraged to recognise, record and transmit information that will be of value to colleagues or the museum as a whole. A museum that is well informed and can communicate effectively internally will be a more efficient and successful organisation. It is therefore vital for all staff to communicate effectively with each other at all times and to participate fully in the museum's communications procedures.

Unit
90

Staff structures

Related Units – Units 91–6

Every museum has staff, even the smallest independent museum is run by one person. As soon as two people are involved, even if they only meet at weekends, the museum has a staff 'structure'. The staff structure describes the relationship between the people who work for the museum: who can tell whom what to do, who does what part of the work, and who needs to give information to whom.

Normally one person is in charge and must learn to manage, to delegate and to inform, while the others must learn to advise, to report and to carry out instructions. Even if the museum is run by a co-operative in which everyone is equal, there is still a need to have formal arrangements for decision-taking, the division of the work and the exchange of information (see Unit 89).

A great deal of thought should be given to the best staff structure in a new museum: an old museum, too, will benefit from a fresh look at its staff structure every few years (see Units 80–2). See Boxes 90.1 and 90.2 for examples of old-fashioned and new staff structures.

The staff the museum needs, and their relationships, should reflect the nature and purpose of the museum. If it is a university museum, teaching and research may have a high priority and early appointments may be a lecturer and a researcher. If it is an educational museum, an education specialist may be one of the first people appointed. A small community museum deciding to concentrate on lively temporary exhibitions may decide that a designer/interpreter is the most important post.

In the same way, as the museum grows, the staff structure should reflect the priorities of the museum. The staff structure should also reflect the work that actually needs to be done in the museum. The museum managers should measure the work that needs to be done and ensure that it is clearly someone's responsibility. Otherwise vital work will go undone, or else more and more jobs will end up being done by one or two overworked people.

Areas of responsibility often forgotten in museums include administration, documentation, fieldwork and building maintenance. A well-thought-out staff structure will help the museum maintain its policies and achieve its objectives.

However, there is no perfect structure for the staff of a museum and the governing body will need to develop a structure that meets its needs and allows for flexibility to develop for the future.

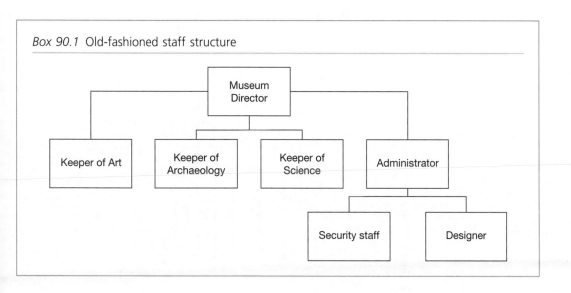

Box 90.1 Old-fashioned staff structure

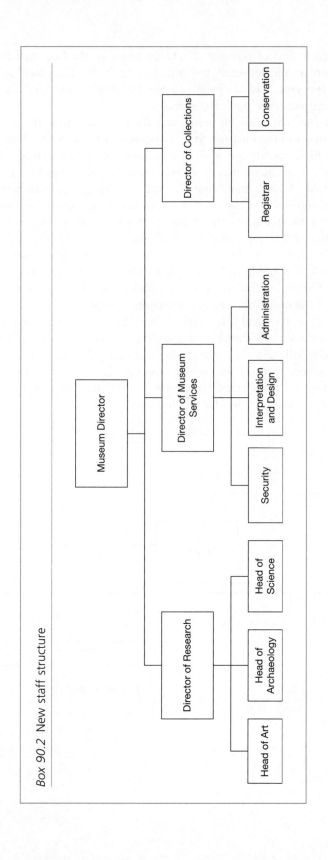

Box 90.2 New staff structure

Unit
91

Volunteers in museums

Related Units – Units 66, 92–7

Few museums could manage without the help of any volunteers at all, though the way in which volunteers are involved varies greatly from museum to museum and from country to country.

Many people argue that the key to getting the best out of volunteer help lies in treating volunteers as formally as you treat paid members of staff. Expect the same level of commitment from them, and accord them the same degree of respect. Others, though, suggest that many volunteers work for museums precisely because they can come and go as they like, and are *not* treated formally, as if they were staff. They do it just because they enjoy it. Every museum must decide its own policy, but it is worth noting how many other organisations, in for example child care, treat their volunteers very formally.

DEFINING THE JOB

Just as with the appointment of paid staff, the first step must be to define the job that needs to be done. It may indeed be worth going through the same procedures as for a paid job, and drawing up a job description and even a person specification (see Unit 94).

RECRUITING VOLUNTEERS

Ways of recruiting will vary from country to country, but a museum's volunteers will be a valuable link with the community it serves. It is important, therefore, to try to make sure that the volunteers reflect the community, and do not come from just one group. Rather than rely simply on word-of-mouth to recruit volunteers, it is often worth advertising formally, or writing to organisations that might include potential volunteers.

SELECTING VOLUNTEERS

If the formal approach seems appropriate, people applying to work as volunteers at the museum can be asked to apply formally and be interviewed and selected just as if they were applying for paid work. If acceptance as a volunteer is seen to be a privilege, it will be valued the more. They should be asked to promise to be available for a minimum number of hours each week or each month.

THE ATTITUDE OF THE STAFF

There are two reasons why paid staff sometimes object to a museum using volunteers. The first is that they fear that volunteers will replace them, and will end up doing their jobs for free. The second is that they will be expected to spend a lot of time training and supervising volunteers, who will prove more of a hindrance than a help.

The first worry will need to be handled very tactfully and sympathetically by museum management, who should make quite sure that volunteers are used only in a supporting and complementary role and never to replace paid staff. In some museums, it may be necessary to negotiate the use of volunteers with the trade unions concerned.

The second worry will be lessened if staff see that the volunteers are willing to commit a substantial amount of time for a long period – that their commitment is serious.

INSURANCE

It is important to make sure that the museum's insurance policies cover volunteers (see Unit 66).

A VOLUNTEERS' ORGANISATION

If the museum has more than a few volunteers, it is probably worth forming a formal organisation, perhaps itself run by a volunteer.

TRAINING VOLUNTEERS

The training of volunteers is as important as the training of professional staff. Every museum with more than one or two regular volunteers should have a formal training programme for them. The volunteer body should be trained by a volunteer trainer.

This will have four elements:

- *On-the-job training.* Informal training will be the most important element, whether the volunteer is acting as a guide for visitors, sorting pottery, helping to build displays or fulfilling any other role.
- *Lectures.* Formal lectures and gallery tours are essential, and should if possible be arranged especially for the volunteers, so that they feel special. They can cover all aspects of the work of the museum: their purpose is to make the volunteers' work richer by helping them to understand more of its context.
- *Discussion sessions.* Discussion sessions are especially important in the training of guides, but all volunteers will benefit from a regular opportunity to discuss different aspects of their work with each other and with museum staff.

- *Trips to other museums.* Where possible, it is helpful for volunteers to see the standards being met in other museums. Arranging study visits is a good way to support the training programme and can be seen as a significant benefit for the volunteer body.

BENEFITS FOR VOLUNTEERS

If we expect volunteers freely to give their time to the museum, and to accept the discipline of regular work, we must make sure that they receive real rewards.

The first reward that every volunteer is seeking is the assurance that he or she is doing something valuable, which is of real benefit to society. It is therefore important that volunteers are properly thanked: the museum director should make a regular habit of speaking to volunteers, of paying tribute to their work and of introducing visiting dignitaries to them.

Many people volunteer because it gives them an opportunity to get to know like-minded people. The museum should ensure that there is a programme of social activities for them that will help to weld them into a team and that will help them identify with the museum. Volunteers could be given free admission to the museum and its events and exhibitions. Everyone likes to be allowed 'behind the scenes', and to be allowed to go where others cannot. Volunteers should be given a regular opportunity to see all aspects of the museum's work and to talk to museum staff about their work. Some museums will find it helpful to give special titles – and perhaps badges or other insignia – to volunteers who have worked at the museum for a long time.

WORK DISCIPLINE

In a small museum where there are only two or three volunteers who are almost personal friends of the staff, arrangements will be comparatively informal, but in a larger museum volunteers must be willing to accept the same work discipline as the paid staff. That means, for example, that they must carry out the instructions of whoever is in charge of them, and must arrive for work on time.

The museum must carry out its side of the bargain, and must ensure that the volunteers understand to whom they are responsible and what their conditions of service are. It is worth considering providing them with a 'volunteers' handbook' like the 'staff handbook' given to paid staff (see Unit 98). Occasionally, it will be necessary for the museum to tell a volunteer that his or her help is no longer needed. This is always an extremely difficult situation, and a resentful volunteer who feels he or she has been unfairly 'sacked' can cause the museum a great deal of harm. There is no simple answer, though a formal relationship with the museum, and perhaps an agreed time-limit on the 'job', will help to make the parting more mutually satisfactory.

For the most part, though, volunteers bring to the museum not only their time and their skills, but a fresh enthusiasm and links with the wider community that are invaluable to its mission.

Finally, it is worth remembering that volunteers are often the people who actually run museums. Throughout the world museums are set up and run by groups of volunteers or single enthusiasts, while the governing bodies of the world's greatest museums are composed largely of volunteers.

<table>
<tr><td>Unit</td></tr>
<tr><td>92</td></tr>
</table>

Recruiting museum staff

Related Units – Units 90–1, 93–6

In many countries, museums cannot recruit whom they want to join their staff. They may be obliged to take as curators the people sent by the government to work in the museum. They may be obliged to accept as security staff people rejected as unfit by the police. They may be obliged to accept as assistant curators people transferred from another part of the State Antiquities Service.

Fortunately, many museums *can* choose their staff. The staff are the most important aspect of any museum. Without good, well-trained staff it is impossible to create a good museum. Recruiting staff is therefore one of the most important things that the museum director does.

This Unit outlines the steps the director must go through in recruiting staff for any position in the museum – from deputy director to ticket-seller.

THE JOB DESCRIPTION

There should be a job description written for every job in the museum. When a job falls vacant, it should always be reviewed. Is this an opportunity to change the job, perhaps to change the whole structure of the museum, or a part of it? Or has the job changed slightly, so that the old job description is now out of date? A security guard's job may have become more to do with welcoming visitors or with interpretation, and less with security. A curator's job may have become more to do with archaeological fieldwork and less with care of collections.

The good museum manager should be continually reviewing the jobs of his/her staff, and making sure that they contribute most effectively to the purpose of the museum. A new appointment is an extra opportunity to make changes.

THE PERSON SPECIFICATION

Having written the job description, the next step is to write a person specification to match it. Where the former describes what the jobholder is expected to *do*, the latter describes what sort of person he or she is expected to *be*.

What qualities and what skills are you looking for in the jobholder? Set them down on paper, and it will be easier to assess applicants for the post. Make sure that the qualities you decide on really are appropriate to the job, and not merely the result of your own prejudices!

ADVERTISEMENT

The usual way of attracting applications for museum jobs is by advertising the job in the newspapers or in a professional journal. It is important to think carefully about both where to advertise (which are the newspapers most likely to be read by good applicants?) and about the contents of the advertisement.

The advertisement should include:

- The name of the museum.
- A brief, accurate but attractive-sounding description of the job.
- The pay offered, with any other benefits.
- Where the job will be based.
- The hours worked, and other conditions.
- A brief description of the sort of person you are looking for, and the qualifications you require or would like the applicants to have.
- Where further details of the job can be obtained.
- Information on *how* to apply (by letter, or on an application form?), *where* to apply and *when* to apply.

Be very careful to make sure that the advertisement obeys the law, for example any laws forbidding discrimination on grounds of sex, age or race. The aim of the advertisement is to attract a sufficiently large pool of applicants from which to select.

FURTHER DETAILS

Information should be ready to send to enquirers. This information will probably include a description of the museum, a description of the work of the section in which the job is based, a copy of the job description itself and an application form. A great deal of care should be put into preparing these 'further details': efficient, well-presented and helpful information will encourage the best people to want to work in your museum.

For the same reason, it is crucial to reply promptly and courteously to all enquirers and all applicants, even if they are likely to be quite unsuitable for the job.

SHORT-LISTING

The process known as 'short-listing' or 'screening' selects the best six or so applicants for further investigation.

The best way to do this is to use the person specification as a checklist, and tick off for each candidate those essential and desirable characteristics, experience and qualifications they seem to have. It is helpful to have three people carry out this process, and then to compare results.

Check, if you feel it is necessary, that the applicant has told the truth about his or her experience by writing to or telephoning the referees whose names are given. Did she really pass these exams? Was he really promoted to that post? Why did she leave that job so soon?

Write promptly to those applicants you have rejected, and thank them for their interest.

SELECTION

The interview is the traditional way of assessing and selecting people for jobs. It will probably always continue to be used, but research shows that it is a very bad way of choosing someone for a job. A good performance at an interview does not guarantee good performance in the job.

The effectiveness of the interview can be improved, though, and everyone who has to interview applicants for jobs should take every opportunity to acquire training. You may wish to have preliminary or secondary interviews to discuss candidates in greater detail.

A much more successful selection technique is the work sample. This simply means giving the applicants a sample of the work they will be doing in the job, and assessing how well they do it. If you are appointing a typist or a bricklayer, devising a sample will be easy, but it should be possible for any job, even a very varied one such as a curator in a small museum.

Other selection techniques increasingly used in large organisations involve various types of psychological testing. These are very effective, but they should only be carried out by experts.

MAKING THE DECISION

The aim now is to choose the best candidate for the job – *not* the candidate you liked most! You now have a good deal of information about all the candidates – from their application forms, from their referees' comments, from the notes you took at their interviews and from the work samples and any other tests they may have been given.

Now look again at the person specification, and give each aspect a weighting out of ten. Then give the candidates marks out of ten for each aspect. Multiply the weighting for each aspect by each candidate's mark for that aspect. Then add up each candidate's now-weighted marks. This is as objective as possible a method of finding the best person for the job, but no method is perfect: we are dealing with human beings!

Conditions of service

Related Units – Units 94–6

Museum staff will work better and more happily if they know precisely what is expected of them, and on what conditions they are employed.

Different countries vary greatly in the laws that govern employment. Different museums vary greatly, too, in the working conditions and practices of their staff. In this Unit, therefore, we can only mention some of the points that every museum employer should consider.

▌ PUT IT DOWN ON PAPER

Every employee should be given a document setting out the conditions of service under which he or she is employed, and his or her rights. In some cases this will be a formal legal contract; in others a less formal set of notes for the guidance of employee and employer. In either case a great deal of trouble should be taken in drawing up the document, which will normally be given to the employee before or immediately on starting work. It could include the following points:

- The names of the employer and the employee.
- The employee's job title.
- The date on which the job will start.
- The date on which the job will end, if it is for a fixed term.
- Normal working hours and any other rules about working hours, such as overtime payment or time-off instead of overtime payment.
- The rate of pay.
- Holidays, including public holidays, and rates of holiday pay.
- Rules of sickness or injury absence, and sick pay.
- Rules of maternity and paternity absence.
- Pension arrangements.
- Notice to be given, on either side, to end the contract.
- Rights to belong to and be represented by a trade union.
- Arrangements for meals, e.g. staff canteen or lower rates in the museum café.
- Rules of dress or uniform.
- Grievance procedure; if the employee has a grievance, who should he or she discuss it with first, and who afterwards, if not satisfied?
- Disciplinary procedure: a good employer has a formal disciplinary procedure that is set out in every employee's contract or Conditions of Service document.

Box 93.1 The staff handbook

An excellent idea for any museum with more than a very few staff is the staff handbook. A staff handbook is an excellent way of backing up their staff training.

The handbook should be designed for the individual needs of the museum, but the sort of things that might be included are:

Background information about the museum
- History of the museum.
- Statement of the museum's purpose and objectives.
- List of staff and their responsibilities.

General advice and information on working at the museum
- Working hours.
- Rules on punctuality, uniform, dress and behaviour.
- Security arrangements and responsibilities.
- Health and safety arrangements and responsibilities.
- Disciplinary and grievance procedures.
- Summary of conditions of service.
- Sickness arrangements.
- Staff privileges and discounts.
- Team briefing timetable.

Guidance on helping visitors
- Answers to the ten most common questions visitors ask.
- Notes on location of toilets, café, cloakroom, etc.
- What to do in the event of fire.
- What to do in the event of theft.
- What to do with lost children.
- First-aid arrangements.

A loose-leaf handbook allows the easy addition of new information, new rules, details of exhibitions and events, and different sections appropriate to different members of staff.

Performance standards for the individual

Related Units – Units 82, 95–6

All staff working in the museum environment need to be able to measure their personal performance against defined standards. Without standards, staff and management cannot judge their performance objectively as they do not know how well they are working. Standards can be developed and agreed internally by the museum's management team working in conjunction with their staff, or the museum can adopt standards that have been developed externally. These will have been drawn up by relevant professional bodies that establish standards for the different types of work undertaken in museums.

A standard is a means both to define and measure performance. It is thus important both for the employer and the employee. By measuring an individual's performance against a set of objective standards, it is possible to determine how effectively the individual is meeting the requirements of their post. If their performance does not meet the requisite level, then appropriate training may be required. The outcome will be better job satisfaction for the individual, improved efficiency and effectiveness for the museum and the individual, better service for the public, and enhanced career opportunities for the individual. If a member of staff still cannot meet a requisite level of performance, other steps may need to be taken to relocate them.

Standards also provide an opportunity for the employer to clarify precisely what has to be done in a particular job, what skills and qualifications are required on the part of staff and how the tasks should be carried out. They thus help in job definition and in recruitment.

Performance standards should be set at a level that the individual can or has been trained to achieve. It is pointless establishing performance standards that are too difficult to reach, are beyond the level of the competence of staff or so difficult to achieve as to create anxiety and worry on the part of the individual. Where possible, they should be agreed in conjunction with the individual so that they can feel 'a sense of ownership' of the performance standards to which they are working. Where a museum is establishing its own sets of standards for staff posts, reference should be made to other museums and the standards that they are using for comparative purposes.

The relationship between performance standards for the individual and performance measurement for the museum is a close one (see Unit 82).

For example, one of the strategic objectives of the museum might be *to provide high-quality learning services to the formal education sector in order to maximise the learning potential of the museum's collections*. In this case, the member or members of staff who will have responsibility for ensuring that the objective is met, will need precise descriptions of what they must do. By analysing the tasks to be carried out to meet that objective, standards of performance can then be set and staff know what it is they have to do and what is expected of them.

For an education specialist, these might include for example:

- Teacher training

Standard: Ensuring that six in-service training days are organised each year for schoolteachers in schools located in a specified area.

- Museum teaching

Standard: Providing five museum lessons per week from month 3 to month 7 for schoolchildren from schools located in a specified area.

- Information provision

Standard: Developing four information packs on key syllabus topics in years 1–3.

- Administration

Standard: Responding to enquiries from schoolteachers within five working days, and so on.

Time available and other constraints, such as resources and specialist staff will determine the number of standards developed under each of these four main headings.

Each museum would of course approach this strategic objective in a different way, depending on their resources. However, the museum would be able to demonstrate:

- how that strategic objective had been broken down into component tasks;
- what tasks needed to be achieved in what timescale;
- how, given staffing and other resources, staff would meet those tasks;
- what measurable standard of performance they would be working to. In each of the standards set above, there are quantified measures.

Further qualitative refinements can be made. For example, standards can be developed for each in-service training day to ensure that training is carried out in a consistent and systematic way; or standards can be set for each information pack to provide quality assurance. In the examples given earlier, it is clearly not enough simply to require a set number of in-service training days for teachers to be held. They each have to be of a quality that is acceptable to the museum and those taking part. Performance measurement and appraisal should therefore also take on a qualitative dimension by examining the outputs and outcomes of the activity.

It is the task of museum management to agree standards of performance for each staff post, to monitor performance on a regular basis against those standards and to provide support and training to help staff meet the standards.

Job appraisal and measuring performance

Unit **95**

Related Units – Units 82, 93–4, 96

REPORTING ON PROGRESS

A key responsibility of museum managers is to ensure that the museum's forward plan is implemented successfully. The success of the museum is dependent upon the success of the museum's staff in meeting the objectives and tasks set down in the forward plan, through their routine day-to-day work and any additional projects to which they have been assigned. Managers have therefore to assess on a regular basis how staff are carrying out their duties or meeting specific project targets. As we have noted in Unit 94, this process is made substantially easier if specific performance standards for routine tasks have already been established.

The ways in which performance assessment is carried out will vary from museum to museum depending on a number of factors, for example the nature of the work undertaken and staffing levels. In some cases, performance assessment may be on a daily basis with verbal reporting from staff to their managers; in others, written progress reports from staff to their managers might be made weekly or monthly. In addition to written reports, group or individual meetings may take place to discuss progress where specific projects are being developed or carried through.

Managers should essentially be continuously tracking progress against forward planning requirements and monitoring the success of members of staff in carrying out their duties to the required standard. Regular progress reports should be written, preferably typed, and filed for later reference. Managers, however, should note any points of concern over an individual's performance in writing and discuss these at an appropriate time. All museums should devise their own reporting procedures and use them consistently (see Unit 94).

REPORTING ON PERFORMANCE

A formal job appraisal or performance review should be carried out for all members of staff at least annually. Shorter time periods may be required, for example three months or six months, depending on circumstances. The appraisal should be conducted by the member of staff's line manager, and should examine achievement (or failure) over the year, explore any areas of difficulty or complication, seek genuine feedback on the manager/employee relationship, identify training and development needs, and provide appropriate training and help to meet these needs.

In advance of the appraisal, the individual member of staff should be provided with a structured checklist of questions to record any significant points or concerns for later discussion. The line manager should then undertake an interview on the basis of the completed checklist with the member of staff. The interview should be minuted and written up and this record should be agreed and signed by both the line manager and member of staff, and passed to senior management for consideration. Any action points or improvements, changes to performance standards in the light of experience, or training provision should be implemented as appropriate.

The individual performance standards that were discussed in Unit 94 were all quantitative. In measuring an individual's performance, however, qualitative standards should also be used or developed for assessment purposes. These are more difficult to develop, but should be used in job appraisal and formal performance reviews. For example, the museum's learning services manager may be asked *to organise and run six in-service training courses for schoolteachers each year*. This is a quantitative standard. An associated qualitative standard might be *to ensure that each teacher attending the courses was satisfied with the arrangements, found the course content relevant to their work and planned to attend future training events organised by the museum*. A questionnaire for each participant could be used to determine how well the courses had met these expectations. The results could then be used in turn to help assess the performance of the learning services manager in meeting that standard.

In job appraisal therefore, line managers should seek to comment on the quality as well as the quantity of work carried out and to assess the range and quality of achievements that have taken place during the review period.

The key benefits of job appraisal are that a member of staff gains improved job satisfaction through knowing that their work in terms of quantity and quality has been duly recognised, acknowledged and valued by the museum. Any weaknesses can be identified and overcome through training or readjustment of work programmes. Managers are able to report to senior management and their governing bodies on the effectiveness and efficiency of their staff in terms of their performance within the forward planning framework.

Staff training and professional development

Related Units – Units 94–5

It is necessary for museum governing bodies to 'recognise the need for, and value of, a properly qualified and trained staff, and offer adequate opportunities for further training and retraining in order to maintain an adequate and effective workforce' (ICOM, *Code of Ethics for Museums*).

Developing the museum's staff through in-service training programmes is an important responsibility of all those managing museums or in management positions in museums. The benefits of training and professional development, in whatever form they take, will impact on the museum's users, the museum's staff and the museum's collections. The success of your museum depends very largely on the quality of staff in all aspects of the museum's work, on their skills and abilities, knowledge and understanding.

The museum director should ensure that an up-to-date training policy and training programme exists for all staff. Individuals working for the museum will have experience or qualifications of different types. But, as we have seen in Unit 94, it is the responsibility of managers to identify when and where in-service training is needed to complement existing skills through regular performance appraisal of the museum's staff. Every effort should be made to meet training needs through whatever forms of provision are available and, of course, affordable.

Because so many different skills are required in museum work, and so many different disciplines and professions are represented, it is not surprising that a correspondingly wide range of training provision is required. Gaining access to training in different areas of museum work varies greatly from one country to another and museum training cannot always be provided locally.

There are different types and levels of training. Some training programmes can lead to vocational training qualifications. Some training programmes are not qualifications-based and are provided on a more informal basis, such as ICOM workshops. Some are residential programmes, some are provided through distance-learning methods, some can be sourced through the Internet and some are built up in-house through local resources.

Wherever possible, the use and organisation of training courses should be based on training and educational institutions with recognised standards, appropriate curricula and a good reputation in museum education and training. It is well worthwhile discussing training provision with professional museum associations, colleagues and staff in other museums, as well as seeking advice and information through national documentation centres where these exist.

In-house training programmes devised by the museum might include a mix of guided reading, visits to other museums, web searches, discussion groups, seminars, project work, and dedicated study and reading time. Distance-learning programmes are becoming more widely available on an international basis and through the Internet, and some of these are qualifications-based. Information on training programmes and materials is available through national, international and specialist journals and periodicals, including *ICOM News* and ICTOP's training bulletin, and web sites (see Unit 100). Training resources acquired by the museum – publications, videos, information sheets, films, audio-tapes – should be kept up to date.

Where the availability of training provision is limited and resources are scarce, it is important to spend hard-earned money wisely. Seek advice on developing a selected range of up-to-date textbooks, training resources and journals in key subject areas such as collections management, user services and museum management. Develop your own information manuals through acquiring information sheets, photocopies and notes in those areas of museum work relevant to you. Use the Internet as an additional source of information to build up training materials.

As a rule of thumb, museums should allocate at least 2 per cent of their annual operating budgets for training. Training should be designed to help people become more flexible, adaptable and versatile in their work. Training should be related to people's needs either in their current posts or for their career development. Career guidance should thus be provided to all staff, as appropriate. Training provides increased job interest and commitment, as well as giving staff more incentives to achieve their personal objectives. Qualifications provide recognition and credit for skills and knowledge gained through training programmes.

Training is essentially about learning, and learning from other's experience and knowledge through different media. Gaining access to that experience and knowledge can only prove beneficial. Keeping yourself and your staff up to date through training and professional development is essential if your museum is to achieve its full potential.

Health and safety

Unit

97

Related Units – Units 80, 98

Every museum has a responsibility to protect the health and safety of its employees, volunteers and visitors, as well as of the public generally (see Units 6 and 66).

Because so many different activities take place in museums there is a great variety of potential hazards. How can the museum reduce the risk of danger to people?

▋ THE SAFETY REPRESENTATIVE

The first and most important step must be to make one person responsible for maintaining health and safety in the museum. This safety representative should ideally be someone who is trusted by everyone – staff and volunteers. Even in a museum with only two or three staff, one person should be the safety representative.

The safety representative should be the person who sees all the official literature about safety. He or she must have authority to go anywhere in the museum without special permission, and must be allowed time from their job to fulfil their safety representative responsibilities. They will need training, and should take advantage of any regular training that is available.

The safety representative should – except in a very small museum – probably not be also responsible for fire prevention (see Unit 65), because he/she may end up spending all available time on fire precautions at the expense of other dangers.

The work of the safety representative involves:

- Regular inspection of every part of the museum. This is the health and safety review (see Box 97.2), the aim of which is to identify potential risks.
- Examining the cause of every accident and making sure that as far as possible the cause is removed for the future.
- Providing information on health and safety to everyone working in the museum, and organising regular training for staff and volunteers, for example on how to lift things safely, on dangerous chemicals, or on first aid.
- Liaison with the health authorities and other official bodies concerned with safety.
- Ensuring that health and safety are taken into account during the planning of new exhibitions and special events. Extra care is needed when anything unusual is happening in the museum, such as the construction of new exhibitions or public events.
- Making sure that everyone knows what to do in the event of an accident.

THE SAFETY REVIEW

'Safety Review' is the name given to regular inspection of all parts of the museum, to try to identify potential safety risks and health problems. It should be carried out regularly by the safety representative who should not only look for, but should also talk informally to other members of staff and encourage them to notice potential hazards. The safety representative should keep a book in which to record every Safety Review, and note every danger found and what was done to eliminate it.

The Safety Review will be looking at five different sorts of things:

- *Safe practices.* Are the ways in which people do things the safest ones?
- *Authorised people.* Are the right people doing things? For example, is everyone using a circular saw trained and authorised to do so?
- *Equipment and clothing.* Is all the necessary equipment available and in use? Are guards in place on cutting machinery? Is electrical gear safe? Is everyone wearing proper safety clothing?
- *Notices and warnings.* Are all the necessary warning signs and notices in place? Do staff read them?
- *Staff awareness.* What potentially dangerous things have happened? Are staff safety-conscious? What training is needed?

THE SAFETY COMMITTEE

In some larger museums, it will be helpful to set up a Safety Committee. This will consist of representatives of management and of workers, of all parts of the museum's staff. Health and safety is in *everyone's* interest. The Safety Committee should meet

Box 97.1 The Safety Review

Every safety representative will make their own list of things to check during the regular Safety Review.

Subject	Points to check
Persons to be protected	
Employees	How many, which work places, what duties, how much travel, special risks.
Non-employees	How many volunteers, visitors on premises, contractors on premises, persons passing premises, special risks.
Users of products	Customers of shops and cafés, recipients of loans, reproductions, etc.
Identification and control of dangers	
Premises	Emergency evacuation, fire precautions, first aid, electrical safety, lifts, access to roofs, toilets and messrooms, housekeeping.
Articles and substances	Poisons, fire hazards, gas cylinder, pesticides, laboratory materials, collection materials.
Operations and processes	Workshop and laboratory activities, construction of displays, glass handling, electrical work, movement of objects, use of synthetic materials, model making, gardening, forestry, farming, excavation fieldwork, café, sales, warehousing.
Environment	Heating, ventilation, lighting, noise, vibration, dust, fumes, radiation, cleaning, plant maintenance.
Jobs and work methods	Staff qualifications, training, supervision, working hours, workloads. Has training plan been implemented?
Work systems	Staff responsibilities, standing orders, regulations, timetabling, monitoring, working conditions.
Products and waste	Disposal of workshop or laboratory waste, taxidermy post-mortem materials, sewage, items sold or lent.
Monitoring and revision	
Safety inspections	Regular inspection of all premises. Checking of duties at all management levels. Are systems for introducing new equipment, substance processes effective? First aid, welfare and emergency procedures adequate.
Accident, near miss and health records	Are accidents being reported and investigated? To whom are they notified? Are health records monitored? To whom are they notified?
Safety representatives and workforce consultation	Which trade unions represent the workforce? Who represents non-unionists? Are workforce aware of consultation procedure. Is it effective?
Formal audit and review	Senior management reviews. Changes to safety policy.

regularly and should receive a regular report from the safety representative. Everyone working in the museum should know about its work and should be encouraged to make suggestions for improvements.

THE ACCIDENT BOOK

Whether or not it is required by law (as it is in some countries), every museum should have an accident book in which are written down not merely serious accidents, but small incidents and things that happen which might have harmed people.

FIRST-AID ARRANGEMENTS

However careful we are, accidents will happen, so it is important to make sure that first-aid arrangements are adequate for visitors and staff. Planning in advance will ensure that in the case of accidents people know what to do.

Every workplace should have at least one person always present who is trained in first aid, a 'first aider'. Usually that will mean that two or three members of staff must be sent to regular refresher training courses – if more are trained, so much the better.

The first aiders will ensure that the first-aid box (see Box 97.3) is properly maintained and kept in the appointed place. The first aiders will ensure that everyone knows how to call an ambulance or doctor in the event of more serious accidents.

Box 97.2 Hazards and dangers

There is a huge number of potential hazards in museums. These are just a few of the sorts of dangers for which all museum staff and volunteers should be constantly on the lookout:

- lifting too heavy items;
- carrying objects wrongly;
- dangerous chemicals in laboratory or workshop;
- unguarded machine tools;
- dangerous wiring;
- sharp tools in workshop and studio;
- old and dangerous insecticides in reserve collections;
- legionnaires disease bacilli in humidification and air-conditioning equipment;
- lack of cleanliness in kitchen or staffroom;
- steps and uneven floor levels;
- cluttered stores, offices, etc.;
- arsenic in old mounted specimens.

Box 97.3 The first-aid box

In some countries, there is a legal requirement to provide a first-aid box, and what should be in it is laid down by law. For example, the following are required in Britain:

- A general guidance card on first aid.
- Twenty individually wrapped sterile adhesive dressings (assorted sizes) appropriate for the work environment.
- Two sterile eye pads, with attachments.
- Six individually wrapped triangular bandages.
- Six safety pins.
- Six medium-sized individually wrapped unmedicated wound dressings (approx. 10cm × 8cm).
- Two large sterile ditto (approx. 13cm × 9cm).
- Three extra large ditto (approx. 28cm × 17.5cm).

Where mains tap water is not readily available for eye irrigation, sterile water or sterile normal saline solution (0.9 per cent) in sealed disposable containers should be provided.

Box 97.4 The first-aid room

Every larger museum should have a separate first-aid room, used for nothing else. Smaller museums should provide one, too, if at all possible, and should certainly have somewhere to take people – staff or visitors – who are taken ill. The first-aid room should contain:

- sink and running hot and cold water;
- drinking water and disposable cups;
- paper towels;
- smooth-topped working surfaces;
- first-aid box;
- chair;
- couch with waterproof cover, pillow and blankets;
- soap;
- clean protective garments;
- refuse container with disposable plastic bags;
- record book;
- bowl.

It should be the responsibility of the first aiders to maintain the first-aid room.

In many countries there are laws prescribing arrangements for first aid and for other aspects of health and safety. It is the job of the museum director to make sure that those laws are known and observed.

INSURANCE

The museum director must ensure that the museum is fully covered by insurance against any risks to members of the public or staff or volunteers. In many countries this is a legal requirement (see Unit 66).

Unit

98

Administrative procedures

Related Units – Units 89–97, 99

Just as in any other organisation, so in museums: efficient administration is almost more important than anything else. Efficiency consists of:

- systems that achieve their aims with the least trouble and least paperwork;
- people understanding the systems and knowing who should do what;
- people doing their part of the work promptly and accurately;
- people doing their part of the work intelligently, making sure that the aims of the museum, and not the administrative systems themselves, are being served.

None of these things can be taught or described in a book. But there are some pieces of advice that may be helpful.

There are two main areas with which administration is concerned: finance and personnel. Units 85 and 90–7 describe some of these aspects. In many museums, the administrative procedures will be laid down by others, with little possibility for the museum director to make changes. What he or she can do, though, is to ensure that the procedures are regularly reviewed, and that a report is prepared assessing their strengths and weaknesses, and recommending improvements. Such a review is best done not by the person in charge of administration, but by someone from outside the museum staff altogether, working closely with the *junior* staff of the museum – they are the people who know all the problems! Such an outside review is valuable even in a very small museum.

Administrative procedures tend to grow up haphazardly over the years, with only long-serving members of staff understanding them, and many procedures continuing long after they have ceased to be useful. One way to avoid this creeping bureaucracy is to ensure that all procedures are set down in an administrative handbook (see Box 98.1). Copies of the handbook should be given to every senior member of staff, and some sections of it will be included in the handbooks given to all staff and volunteers (see Unit 93).

Regular briefings of some sort are essential for all staff (see Unit 89). An important element of these staff briefings must be to assess whether the administrative

---

Box 98.1 The administrative handbook

A handbook, available to all staff and containing an outline of all the procedures used in the museum, is a very helpful way of ensuring that everyone knows the procedures, and that they are kept up to date. In a small museum, the administrative handbook may be combined with the staff handbook (see Units 89 and 93). Their contents will certainly overlap.

What goes into the handbook will vary greatly from museum to museum, but the following will be found in most:

Financial administration
- Accounting procedures
- Petty cash
- Staff travel arrangements

Office procedures
- Filing
- Correspondence
- Answering the telephone
- Answering e-mails

Materials administration
- Purchasing procedures
- Control of stores
- Fuel and light

Personnel administration
- Recruiting policies and procedures
- Induction
- Leave arrangements
- Sickness arrangements
- Grievance procedure
- Disciplinary procedure
- Briefing/reporting procedures
- Training arrangements

Health and safety
- Health and safety arrangements (see Unit 97)

procedures are working to support the museum's aims, and to assess whether museum staff are fulfilling their responsibilities. It is all too easy for bad feeling to develop between administrative staff, who accuse their colleagues of laziness and inefficiency (for example not completing time-sheets accurately or not recording expenditure properly), and curatorial and other staff who come to believe the administrators create unnecessary procedures just to keep themselves in jobs. Such bad feeling can seriously damage the work of the museum; a regular opportunity to discuss difficulties will help to prevent its growth.

Computers in the museum

Unit 99

Related Units – Units 49, 98

For many museums, computers are familiar everyday tools, without which it is hard to imagine how the museum could work. For other museums, the nearest computer may be in a distant town, and the idea of the museum actually having one just a dream.

In museums that have used them for years, computers have transformed most working practices. Among the areas computers have helped museums to improve are:

DOCUMENTATION

- Greatly improve and extend their documentation, particularly the speed and efficiency of retrieving information.
- Make information about the collections readily available to enquirers and – through the Internet – to the general public.
- Include pictures of each object in its documentation.

COLLECTIONS MANAGEMENT

- Using hand-held computers, barcodes, etc., greatly speed up and simplify the management of collections in store.
- Simplify condition audits and security audits.
- Make possible remote measurement and control of temperature and humidity conditions.
- Improve security through remote sensing systems.
- Simplify and speed up conservation records.

DISPLAYS

- Make possible a vast new range of exhibition techniques, ranging from audio-visuals to computer interactives.
- Simplify and widen the scope of the production of graphics.
- Make more efficient the management of large projects.

MARKETING AND PUBLIC SERVICES

- Allow the museum to maintain a lively, up-to-date web site that both promotes the museum and extends its services.
- Allow better management of sales and ticketing.

MANAGEMENT AND ADMINISTRATION

- Greatly speed up letter-writing and report-writing, and improve their visual presentation.
- Improve and speed up financial management and book-keeping, and produce better financial reports for management.
- Improve and speed up retrieval of records.

RESEARCH

- Open up, through the Internet, access to a vast range of information.
- Allow co-operation in research between museums and other researchers based far apart.
- Allow the use of digital media, cameras and sound and video recorders.

NETWORKING

- Hugely simplify, through e-mail, communication with other museums and other organisations, greatly extending the museum's potential partners.

INTRODUCING COMPUTERS INTO THE MUSEUM

If computers can offer all this, surely every museum should acquire computers as soon as possible? In reality, it is not as simple as that. Naturally, keen young members of staff want computers: they want to be 'modern'. But a museum considering computerisation should think very carefully indeed, and should ask:

- What exactly is it that we want the computer to do?
- Can we afford not just the computer, but the programs, the printer, and other peripherals and materials?
- A five-year-old computer is very old. Can we afford to replace it (or them) every three years or so?
- Do we have access to expert advice on what computer hardware and what software and programs best meet our needs?
- What other organisations do we need to share information with? Can we acquire programs that are easily compatible?
- Who exactly is going to use it? How will their working time be re-allocated?
- How will they be trained? When they leave, can we be sure of recruiting replacements with the necessary computer skills?
- Computers and their programs keep going wrong. When that happens, how long will we have to wait for an expert to come and solve the problem?
- Should we continue with our paper-based systems until we are really confident?

In developing countries especially, a small museum will need to consider these issues carefully before deciding on introducing computers to the museum. A needs analysis study may be a helpful preliminary step. But remember to get objective advice from a computer expert rather than advice from sales staff who are more likely to promote their own systems over others.

Section 6
Supporting resources

Unit 100

Sources of information and support

Related Units – Units 79, 101

Museum staff use a wide range of information sources in their work. Some of these are listed here. They include:

- information about the theory and practice of museum work;
- information about other museums and their work;
- information about the museum's collections;
- information about other museums' collections, for purposes of object identification and comparative research (see Units 41–50);
- information about the museum's markets (see Unit 9);
- information about organisations and individuals able to support or work with the museum;
- information about suppliers of services and goods.

▌ INFORMATION INSIDE THE MUSEUM

Information for museum staff may be available within the museum or from outside sources. Whatever balance of information materials you develop in-house, they should reflect the priority needs of the museum and its staff. Some information can be assembled systematically within the museum at limited cost, for example by compiling files relating to suppliers of services and goods for different aspects of the museum's operation or by assembling information via downloads from web sites. Other types of information may require regular financial outlay, for example through subscriptions to significant professional publications.

The museum should establish clear policies for the development and management of its reference library or information centre. In building up and managing a reference library, careful thought should be given to the most effective deployment of limited financial resources and staff time. Maintaining the currency of information in a museum reference library is an important consideration. Keeping your reference library up to date and properly documented means that staff can be kept up to date in turn.

Different kinds of information require different collection methods. For example, in identifying objects, much information can be obtained about different classes of objects from illustrated examples in specialist journals or other publications. But this may also need to be complemented by museum staff visiting other museums and examining and recording comparative material in their collections, for example through digital photography and detailed notes. Recording and managing this information for future use should be carried out in a systematic way.

INFORMATION OUTSIDE THE MUSEUM

What sources of information outside the museum are available to you? Other museums can provide assistance in many ways, for example through advice over management issues or procedures, help with identifications and research, assistance with marketing intelligence, the loan of publications or the provision of information about suppliers or manufacturers of products. Using information that is readily available in this way helps to avoid 'reinventing the wheel' and makes use of expertise and experience that may not be otherwise available in your museum. Building up networks of information at local, regional, national and international level plays an important part in all museum work. Every effort should be made to stay in touch with colleagues in other museums. Electronic mail systems are now a powerful mechanism in this respect.

Second, museological information centres or centres for museum studies can be of enormous assistance in finding the most reliable information or sources of information you may need. Wherever museums have access to such centres, they should make the most of them. Much information is also now carried in virtual information centres on web sites.

Third, library networks are also a valuable source of support. The nature of library services varies from one country to another. Wherever possible, use existing libraries to source information rather than going to the expense of duplicating reference material that may not be needed regularly. Many libraries operate inter-library loan systems and access through these systems to material too expensive to buy may be a useful way of obtaining the publications that you want.

Where budgets are limited, it is always better to devote resources to buying standard museum reference works and publications rather than acquiring material that is of interest but will only be used very occasionally. Take advice from museum studies centres or information centres on which publications to acquire. Remember also that joint purchase or subscriptions through groups of museums, specialist groups of curators or other museum workers may be an effective way of using limited resources. Specifying books required on a 'books wanted' list may also result in donations of publications to the museum's reference library from other museum workers, Friends of the museum or visitors.

A very wide range of publications about museum work is now available internationally. Most museum organisations or associations will provide guidance on availability. Publishers will always provide information about their publication lists on request or you can download these from their web sites. Publishers may also be prepared to provide review copies of publications, if the museum or a group of museums has a regular publication that can carry reviews.

Finally, wherever possible, participate in training programmes and conferences. They provide a wealth of information and help to build up useful contacts and networks (see Unit 79). Training programmes and conferences allow for the free interchange of ideas and experience. Learning from others is the most valuable source of information there is available.

CHECKLIST OF INFORMATION SOURCES

External

- other museums;
- museum studies centres;
- documentation centres;
- reference libraries;
- professional journals;
- reference books;
- web sites;
- museum associations;
- professional colleagues;
- training programmes and conferences.

Internal

- museum reference library;
- information files on other museum collections;
- village files (see Unit 46);
- information files on suppliers and manufacturers;
- examples of other museums' marketing materials;
- publishers' lists.

STUDY EXAMPLE 100.1

The manager of a small museum with a limited budget developed a series of 'topic files'. The files covered issues such as conservation, design, display cases, education, and provided a ready source of information when the need arose. Copies of articles, suppliers' information, fact sheets from museum associations, references to publications, contact names and addresses were all included. Whenever a member of the museum's staff needed information, the topic files were a useful first source of information. A system of this type needs to be kept up to date in a rigorous way if it is to be useful.

The manager had made the best use of available budgets to build up information that was regularly needed.

Resources on the Internet

Related Units – Units 99–100

The Internet provides a rich and rapidly growing resource of information for museums. Museums will find the Internet useful in supporting all aspects of their work on a day-to-day basis and in supporting training and professional development programmes.

However, the Internet is not a substitute for a good working library or information centre in the museum. While it provides a wide range of material, it does not cover all aspects of museum work and much information published in conventional form, for example textbooks, journal articles, or collections information, is not available through the Internet. It should be considered therefore as one information resource among a set of resources, complementing other forms of publication and information.

Information on the Internet that is of relevance for museums is growing all the time. Types of resource include:

- Individual museum web sites and gateway sites that provide links to a number of museum web sites (see Unit 37). Apart from general information about the museum for visitors and special pages such as virtual exhibitions, individual museum web sites often carry management information such as forward plans with their key performance indicators or annual reports that can be useful for comparative purposes.
- Professional museum associations at international, national, regional and local level. These sites carry a rich resource of material for museum work and include the important web site of ICOM, which alongside its own materials, provides a number of links to other sites at international and national level. Most national museum associations have web sites, which are an important resource for keeping up to date with the wider museums world and for professional information.
- Specialist museum organisations or associations, often membership-based, which provide information on their specialist areas of activity for members as well as other visitors.
- Museum networks that link museums with similar interests or museums working on joint projects.
- Museum studies and other related departments of universities, which can carry significant amounts of useful information and guidance for students and practitioners. Increasingly, web-based training programmes are being provided by museum studies departments and these are a valuable resource for professional development.
- National and local government departments and government agencies with responsibility for museums and the wider cultural sector, which provide a huge range of material and statistics relating to governmental policy about museums,

reports on museums and other cultural institutions, and advisory notes on different aspects of museum work and the wider contexts in which they operate.

- Information resources for museum workers, for example advisory notes, articles, information sheets, standards. These may be derived from the web sites of professional museum organisations, university departments or from government agencies responsible for museums.
- Information about different types of equipment from suppliers.
- Information about services from suppliers, such as conservators, architects, designers or management consultants as well as suppliers specialising in web site design and site evaluation methodology and other forms of information and communications technology.

Providing a definitive list of resources within this Unit is not possible because of the speed of change in the virtual world. However, the web site of the International Council of Museums (ICOM) at www.icom.museum/ is an excellent first port of call for those exploring the Internet for professional purposes and provides a number of useful links to museum organisations worldwide, including its own international and national committees.

Glossary

We provide here a list of terms appearing in the text with comments on their usage. These have been selected on the basis that they may be unfamiliar terms to readers in some countries. In most cases, they are introduced and defined within the most appropriate Unit in greater detail, sometimes as 'key words', and the Unit reference is also given here.

Access Plan   A document that sets out what the barriers are that prevent people gaining the maximum benefit from the museum, and how they can be avoided or removed (see Unit 70).

Animatronics   Models of people or animals that move mechanically (see Unit 24).

Attractor   A place or facility to which tourist visitors are attracted.

Brief   Written instructions for architect or designer, describing what is wanted. Sometimes known as *Functional Brief* (because it describes how the museum or gallery must function) or (in US English) *Functional Program.*

Carers   People who look after children on a voluntary or professional basis. For adults, the preferred term is personal assistant (see Unit 17).

Case-for-support   A written statement of need used for fundraising purposes (see Unit 87).

Conservator   A specialist in the scientific care and treatment of museum objects and specimens. Conservators have a postgraduate training in a specialist field, for example archaeological objects, natural history specimens, ceramics, oil paintings or works of art on paper. Some conservators also have craft skills, for example in cabinet-making. Conservators are also able to advise on the best arrangements for caring for collections, and carry out treatment of objects that reverses or slows down their deterioration. For this, they require a well-equipped laboratory. *Conservator* in this museum sense should not be confused with other uses of the term in English: for an architect who cares for historic buildings, and for a biologist who cares for the natural environment.

Dehumidifier   An item of equipment electrically operated designed to decrease the level of relative humidity where environmental conditions are too damp (see Unit 57).

Desk research   Information gathered from published and non-published sources (see Unit 9).

Destination   A location at macro or micro level that attracts visitors.

Diffuser panel A panel of translucent plastic or other similar material used to diffuse or spread light from a light source. Diffuser panels are often used in display cases to obtain a more even light for display purposes (see Unit 27).

Diorama A three-dimensional presentation technique consisting of scenes based on models in the foreground and painted backgrounds or surrounds (see Unit 24).

Director The senior member of staff with overall responsibility for the museum's day-to-day operation, who reports to the museum's governing body.

Disaster Control Plan A written plan that sets out the steps a museum should take in preventing and reacting to disasters of all types (see Unit 65).

Display The means by which museums present and interpret objects to their visitors, usually involving design, text and graphics. In the United States and Canada the equivalent term is exhibit.

Exhibit The term used in the United States and Canada for the means by which museums present and interpret objects to their visitors, usually involving design, text and graphics. In British English, the equivalent term is display, while 'exhibit' means the object displayed.

Exhibition A temporary or short-term museum presentation.

Formative evaluation The techniques associated with testing the effectiveness of displays and exhibitions in process of production (see Unit 34).

Forward plan A written management plan setting out the museum's functional and planning objectives to be met over a defined period of time (see Unit 81).

Friends' groups/Friends' organisations or membership programmes An organised group of people who support the museum and its work generally through fundraising and advocacy activities of different types (see Unit 39).

Front-end evaluation The techniques associated with the testing of ideas and proposals for displays and exhibitions before production begins (see Unit 34).

Governing body/Governors Those people with overall responsibility in law for conducting the policy and affairs of the museum, and to whom the museum staff are accountable (see Unit 77).

Heritage centre A visitor facility providing interpretative displays on the cultural and/or natural history of a place or area. 'Heritage centres' that hold collections are functionally museums, although they may be called heritage centres for marketing reasons (see Unit 3).

Humidifier An item of equipment electrically operated designed to increase the level of relative humidity where environmental conditions are too dry (see Unit 57).

Hygrometer An item of equipment used to measure relative humidity (see Unit 57).

Interpretation Explaining an object, place or landscape and its significance (see Unit 22).

Lux A unit of illumination measured by a light meter (see Unit 56).

Market The overall social and economic context within which a museum operates (see Unit 9).

Market analysis Analysis carried out on the structure and composition of the market (see Unit 9).

Marketing   The techniques associated with developing and promoting the museum to meet the identified needs of the market (see Unit 10).

Marketing mix   A balance of factors – product, price, place and promotion – which museums can control in order to influence people's attitudes towards a museum (see Unit 10).

Market intelligence   Information about the market, including composition and trends (see Unit 9).

Marketplace   The specific social and economic context within which a museum operates (see Unit 9).

Market research   The study of the different habits, attitudes and interests of the users making up the market for a museum (see Unit 9).

Market segment   An identifiable range of users or non-users within the market with shared characteristics (see Unit 9).

Market share   The extent to which the museum attracts users in the overall market (see Unit 9).

Market survey   A programme of investigation into the structure and nature of the market (see Unit 9).

Market penetration   The degree to which a museum is successful in attracting users from the market as a whole and from particular market segments and encouraging take-up of services (see Unit 9).

Micro-environment   A small space that can be controlled in terms of relative humidity and other environmental factors for special categories of material (see Unit 57).

Museum manager   Any member of staff with responsibility for managing resources – people, collections, finance, buildings or equipment. It is used in this book to show that many people in a museum contribute to its effective working.

Museum product   An amalgam of the quantifiable and non-quantifiable factors that go to make up the personality and identity of a museum in the mind of the user (see Unit 10).

Outreach   The methods by which a museum can take services out into the community that it serves through, for example, touring exhibitions or School Loan Services (see Unit 17).

People-mover   A vehicle in which users ride through display or presentation areas in museums (see Unit 24).

Pepper's Ghost   A presentation technique based on mirrors that allows one image to replace another (see Unit 25).

Performance measurement   Measuring a museum's or a person's performance against agreed objectives and standards (see Unit 82).

Preventive conservation   The processes by which a museum's collections are stored, displayed, handled and maintained in ways which do not lead to deterioration (see Unit 55).

Public relations   The management of the relationship between the public and the museum (see Unit 38).

Recording thermohygrographs or electronic hygrometers   An item of equipment used for the continuous recording of temperature and relative humidity levels on a weekly or monthly chart (see Unit 57).

Relative humidity (RH) Relative humidity is a ratio of water vapour in the air to the amount that it can hold if fully saturated, and is expressed as a percentage, for example 55 per cent RH (see Unit 57).

Remedial conservation The processes involved in repairing damage to collections, using specialist conservation techniques that are reversible. The need for remedial conservation is often due to poor collections management and inadequate preventive conservation measures (see Units 63–4).

Service Level Agreement A contract between a funding agency and a museum, setting out what the museum will deliver in return for how much financial support.

Stakeholders Those groups of people with a real interest in the museum. Stakeholders will include funding bodies, sponsors, Friends, universities, government, collectors' groups etc. Some are more important than others!

Tableau A presentation technique consisting of a reconstructed setting with life-size models of people or animals (see Unit 24).

Thesaurus A list of agreed names, to ensure consistency in cataloguing objects. A thesaurus usually provides synonyms, broader and narrower terms, and 'preferred' terms. Also known as 'vocabulary'.

UV-monitor An item of equipment electrically operated that measures the proportion of ultra-violet light falling on an object or display/storage area (see Unit 56).

Visitor profile The nature and demographic make-up of the museum's visitors (see Unit 11).

Volunteers' organisation An organised group of people who provide practical support to museum staff on a voluntary basis (see Unit 91).

Select bibliography

The titles listed here have been selected as the basis of a good working library for a small to medium-sized museum. They are all English language titles and have been listed with their ISBN numbers for ease of reference. They have been arranged to reflect the structure of *Museum Basics*.

▍SECTION 1 INTRODUCTORY

American Association of Museums *Codes of Ethics and Practice of Interest to Museums* AAM 2000 ISBN 0931201691

Baghli, S., Boylan, P. and Herreman, Y. *History of ICOM (1946–1996)* ICOM 1998 ISBN 9290122439

Boswell, D. and Evans, J. *Representing the Nation: Histories, Heritage and Museums* Routledge 1999 ISBN 041520870X

Carbonell, B. M. (ed.) *Museum Studies in Context* Blackwell Publishers 2003 ISBN 0631228306

Cuno, J. (ed.) *Whose Muse? Art Museums and the Public Trust* Princeton University Press 2004 ISBN 0691032157

Davis, P. *Ecomuseums: A Sense of Place* Leicester University Press 1999 ISBN 0718502086

Dicks, B. *Culture on Display: The Production of Contemporary Visitability* Open University Press 2003 ISBN 0335206573

Edson, G. *Museum Ethics* Routledge 1997 ISBN 0415152909

Fforde, C., Hubert, J. and Turnbull, P. (eds) *The Dead and Their Possessions: Repatriation in Principle, Policy and Practice* Routledge 2004 ISBN 0415344492

Giebelhausen, M. (ed.) *The Architecture of the Museum* Manchester University Press 2003 ISBN 0719056101

Hein, H. S. *The Museum in Transition: A Philosophical Perspective* Smithsonian Institution 2000 ISBN 1560983965

Kavanagh, G. and Frostick, E. (eds) *Making City Histories in Museums* Leicester University Press 2001 ISBN 0718502728

Kreps, C. F. *Liberating Culture: Cross-cultural Perspectives on Museums, Curation and Heritage Preservation* Routledge 2003 ISBN 0415250269

Mauries, P. *Cabinets of Curiosities* Thames & Hudson 2002 ISBN 0500510911

Merriman, N. (ed.) *Public Archaeology* Routledge 2004 ISBN 0415258898

Pearce S. M. (ed.) *Museums and Their Development : The European Tradition 1700–1900* Routledge 1998 ISBN 0415193079

Spalding, J. *The Poetic Museum: Reviving Historic Collections* Prestel 2002 ISBN 3791326783

Thompson, P. *Voice of the Past: Oral History* Oxford University Press 2000 ISBN 0192893173

Weil, S. E. *A Cabinet of Curiosities: Inquiries into Museums and Their Prospects* Smithsonian Institution Press 1995 ISBN 1560985119

Weil, S. E. *Making Museums Matter* Smithsonian Institution Press 2002 ISBN 1588340007

Witcomb, A. *Re-imaging the Museum: Beyond the Mausoleum* Routledge 2002 ISBN 0415220998

▍SECTION 2 THE MUSEUM AND ITS USERS

American Association of Museums/Committee on Audience Research and Evaluation *Introduction to Museum Evaluation* AAM/CARE 1998 ISBN 0931201470

Black, G. *The Engaging Museum: Developing Museums for Visitor Involvement* Routledge 2005 ISBN 041534557X

Caulton, T. *Hands-on Exhibitions: Managing Interactive Museums and Science* Routledge 1998 ISBN 0415165229

Chadwick, A. and Stannett, A. *Museums and Adults Learning: Perspectives from Europe* National Institute for Adult Continuing Education 2001 ISBN 1862010218

Claxton, G. *Wise Up: The Challenge of Life-long Learning* Bloomsbury 2000 ISBN 1582340927

Cunningham, M. K. *Interpreters' Training Manual for Museums* AAM 2004 ISBN 093120190X

Diamond, J. *Practical Evaluation Guide: Tools for Museums and Other Informal Education Settings* AltaMira Press 1999 ISBN 0761989404

Dodd, J. and Sandell, R. (eds) *Including Museums: Perspectives on Museums, Galleries and Social Inclusion* Department of Museum Studies, University of Leicester 2001 ISBN 189848919X

Donnelly, J. F. (ed.) *Interpreting Historic House Museums* AltaMira Press 2002 ISBN 0759102511

Durbin, G., Morris, S. and Wilkinson, S. *A Teacher's Guide to Learning from Objects* English Heritage 1990 ISBN 1850742596

Errington, S. (ed.) *Using Museums and Centres to Popularise Science and Technology* Commonwealth Secretariat 2001 ISBN 0850926688

Falk, J. and Dierking, L. *Learning from Museums: Visitor Experiences and the Making of Meaning* AltaMira Press 2000 ISBN 0742502953

Falk, J. and Dierking, L. (eds) *Lessons Without Limit: How Free-choice Learning is Transforming Education* AltaMira Press 2002 ISBN 0795101604

Falk, J. and Dierking, L. *The Museum Experience* Whalesback Books 1992 ISBN 0929590074

French, Y. and Runyard, S. *The Marketing and PR Handbook For Museums, Galleries and Heritage Attractions* The Stationery Office 1999 ISBN 0117026492

Goodacre, B. and Baldwin, G. *Living the Past: Reconstruction, Recreation, Re-enactment and Education at Museums and Heritage Sites* Middlesex University Press 2002 ISBN 1898253439

Hein, G. E. *Learning in the Museum* Routledge 1998 ISBN 0415097762

Hooper-Greenhill, E. *Writing a Museum Education Policy* Department of Museum Studies, University of Leicester 1991

Hooper-Greenhill, E. *Museums and their Visitors* Routledge 1994 ISBN 0415068576

Hooper-Greenhill, E. *Museums and the Interpretation of Visual Culture* Routledge 2000 ISBN 0415086337

Kalfatovic, M. R. *Creating a Winning Online Exhibition: A Guide for Libraries, Archives, and Museums* ALA Editions 2002 ISBN 0838908179

Kentley, F. and Negus, D. *Writing on the Wall: a Guide for presenting Exhibition Text* National Maritime Museum 1989 ISBN 0948065087

Lord, B. and Dextor-Lord, G. (eds) *The Manual of Museum Exhibitions* AltaMira Press 2001 ISBN 0759102341

MacDonald, S. *The Politics of Display:Museums, Science and Culture* Routledge 1997 ISBN 0415153263

McLean, F. *Marketing the Museum* Routledge 1996 ISBN 0415152933

McManus, P. M. *Archaeological Displays and the Public: Museology and Interpretation* Archetype Publications 2000 ISBN 1873132670

Merriman, N. *Beyond the Glass Case: The Past, the Heritage and the Public* University of London, Institute of Archaeology 2000 ISBN 0905853377

Miles, R. S. *The Design of Educational Exhibits* Routledge 2001 ISBN 0415239648

Moffat, H. and Wollard, V. *Museum and Gallery Education: A Manual of Good Practice* The Stationery Office 1999 ISBN 0117026956

Noble, W. and Lord, G. *Access for Disabled People to Arts Premises: The Journey Sequence* Butterworth-Heinmann 2003 ISBN 0750657790

Pearce, S. *Objects of Knowledge* Athlone Press 1990 ISBN 0485900017

Royal Ontario Museum *Communicating with the Museum Visitor: Guidelines for Planning* Toronto 1976

Sachatello-Sawyer, B. *et al. Adult Museum Programs: Designing Meaningful Experiences* AltaMira Press 2002 ISBN 0759100977

Sandell, R. (ed.) *Museums, Society, Inequality* Routledge 2002 ISBN 0415260604

Serrell, B. *Exhibit Labels: An Interpretive Approach* AltaMira Press 1996 ISBN 0761991069

Sixsmith, M. *Designing Galleries: The Complete Guide to Developing and Designing Spaces and Services for Temporary Exhibitions* Arts Council of England 1999 ISBN 0728707802

Talboys, G. K. *Museum Educator's Handbook* Gower 2000 ISBN 0566081733

Velarde, G. *Designing Exhibitions: Museums, Heritage, Trade and World Fairs* Ashgate 2001 ISBN 0566083175

Xanthoudaki, M., Tickle, L. and Sekules, V. (eds) *Researching Visual Arts Education in Museums and Galleries: An International Reader* Kluwer Academic Publishers 2003 ISBN 1402016379

▌SECTION 3 THE DEVELOPMENT AND CARE OF THE MUSEUM'S COLLECTIONS

Ashley-Smith, J. *Risk Assessment for Object Conservation* Butterworth-Heinemann 1999 ISBN 0750628537

Bachmann, K. (ed.) *Conservation Concerns: A Guide for Collectors and Curators* Smithsonian Institute 1992 ISBN 1560981741

Belk, R. W. *Collecting in a Consumer Society* Routledge 2001 ISBN 0415258480

Buck, R. A. and Gilmore, J. A. (eds) *The New Museum Registration Methods* AAM 1998 ISBN 0931201314

Clark, K. (ed.) *Conservation Plans in Action: Proceedings of the Oxford Conference* English Heritage 1999 ISBN 1850747520

Clavir, M. *Preserving What is Valued: Museums and First Nations* University of British Columbia Press 2002 ISBN 0774808616

Corr, S. *Caring for Collections: A Manual of Preventive Conservation* The Heritage Council 2000ISBN 1901137244

Dewe, M. (ed.) *Local Studies Collection Management* Ashgate 2002 ISBN 0566083655

Fahy, A. *Collections Management* Routledge 1995 ISBN 0415112834

Gardner, J. B. and Merritt, E. E. *The AAM Guide to Collections Planning* AAM 2004 ISBN 0931201888

Hatchfield, P. B. *Pollutants in the Museum Environment: Practical Strategies for Problem Solving in Design, Exhibition and Storage* Archetype Publications 2002 ISBN 1873132964

Holm, S. A. *Facts and Artefacts – How to Document a Museum Collection* Museum Documentation Association 2000 ISBN 1900642050

Keene, S. *Digital Collections: Museums and the Information Age* Butterworth-Heinemann 1998 ISBN 0750634561

Keene, S. *Managing Conservation in Museums* Butterworth-Heinemann 2002 ISBN 0750656034

Knell, S. *Care of Collections* Routledge 1994 ISBN 0415112850

Knell, S. J. *Museums and the Future of Collecting* Ashgate 2004 ISBN 0754630056

Lavendrine, B. *A Guide to the Preventive Conservation of Photograph Collections* Getty Conservation Institute 2003 ISBN 0892367016

Legget, J. *Restitution and Repatriation: Guidelines for Good Practice* Resource: The Council for Museums 2000 ISBN 0948630914

Lord, B. *et al. The Cost of Collecting: Collection Management in UK Museums* The Stationery Office 1989 ISBN 0112904769

Mack, J. *Museum of the Mind: Art and Memory in World Cultures* British Museum Press 2003 ISBN 0714126373

Paine, C. (ed.) *Standards in the Museum Care of Archaeological Collections* Museums & Galleries Commission 1992 ISBN 0948630159

Paine, C. (ed.) *Standards in the Museum Care of Biological Collections* Museums & Galleries Commission 1992 ISBN 0948630183

Paine, C. (ed.) *Standards in the Museum Care of Geological Collections* Museums & Galleries Commission 1994 ISBN 0948630205

Paine, C. (ed.) *Standards in the Museum Care of Larger & Working Objects* Museums & Galleries Commission 1994 ISBN 0948630264

Paine, C. (ed.) *Standards in the Museum Care of Musical Instruments* Museums & Galleries Commission 1995 ISBN 0948630337

Paine, C. (ed.) *Standards in the Museum Care of Photographic Collections* Museums & Galleries Commission 1996 ISBN 0948630426

Paine, C. (ed.) *Standards in the Museum Care of Costume and Textile Collections* Museums & Galleries Commission 1998 ISBN 0948630590

Paine, C. *Godly Things: Museums, Objects and Religion* Leicester University Press 1999 ISBN 0718501535

Pearce, S. (ed.) *Interpreting Objects and Collections* Routledge 1994 ISBN 0415112893

Pearce, S. *On Collecting: An Investigation into Collecting in the European Tradition* Routledge 1995 ISBN 0415075610

Pearce, S. *Collecting in Contemporary Practice* Sage 1997 ISBN 0761950818

Pye, E. *Caring for the Past: Issues in Conservation for Archaeology and Museums* James & James 2000 ISBN 1902916107

Thickett, D. and Lee, L. R. *Selection of Materials for the Storage or Display of Museum Objects* British Museum Press 2004 ISBN 0861591178

Tressel, G. *Museum is to Touch* Association of Science Technology Centres Reprint edition 1984 ISBN 9991749195

SECTION 4 THE MUSEUM AND ITS BUILDINGS

Dorge, V. and Jones, S. *Building an Emergency Plan: A Guide for Museums and Other Cultural Institutions* Getty Trust 1999 ISBN 089236551X

Lord, B. and Lord, G. D. *Manual of Museum Planning* The Stationery Office 1999 ISBN 011702659X

Thomson, G. *The Museum Environment* Butterworth-Heinemann 1986 ISBN 0750620412

SECTION 5 THE MUSEUM AND ITS MANAGEMENT

American Association of Museums *Museum Job Descriptions and Organizational Charts* AAM 1999 ISBN 0931201616

American Association of Museums *Museum Visitor Services Manual: Resource Report* AAM 2001 ISBN 0931201772

Anderson, G. (ed.) *Museum Mission Statements: Building a Distinct Identity* AAM 1997 ISBN 0931201411

Bierbaum, E. G. *Museum Librarianship* McFarland Inc. Publishers 2000 ISBN 0786408677

Burcaw, G. E. *Introduction to Museum Work* AltaMira Press 1997 ISBN 0761989269

Chitty, G. and Baker, D. *Managing Historic Sites and Buildings* Routledge 1999 ISBN 0415208157

Corsane, G. (ed.) *Heritage, Museums and Galleries: An Introductory Reader* Routledge 2004 ISBN 0415289467

Edson, G. and Dean, D. *Handbook for Museums* Routledge 1996 ISBN 0415099536

Fitzherbert, L. *Effective Fundraising: An Informal Guide to Getting Donations and Grants* Directory of Social Change 2004 ISBN 1903991404

Fopp, M. A. *Managing Museums and Galleries* Routledge 1997 ISBN 0415094976

Genoways, H. H. and Ireland, L. M. *Museum Administration: An Introduction* AltaMira Press 2003 ISBN 0759102945

George, G. *Starting Right: A Basic Guide to Museum Planning* AltaMira Press 2004 ISBN 075910557X

Hill, L. and Whitehead, B. *Complete Membership Handbook: A Guide to Managing Friends', Members' and Supporters' Schemes* Directory of Social Change 2004 ISBN 1903991501

International Council of Museums (ICOM) *Code of Ethics* ICOM 2005

Kilgour, E. J. and Martin, B. *Managing Training and Development in Museums* The Stationery Office 1997 ISBN 011495853X

Kotler, P. and Kotler, N. *Museum Strategy and Marketing: Designing Missions, Building Audiences, Generating Revenue and Resources* Jossey-Bass 1998 ISBN 0787909122

Lawrie, A. *The Complete Guide to Business and Strategic Planning for Voluntary Organisations* Directory of Social Change 2001 ISBN 190036087X

Lord, B. and Lord, G. D. *The Manual of Museum Management* The Stationery Office 1997 ISBN 0112905188

Skramstad, H. and Skramstad, S. *A Handbook for Museum Trustees* AAM 2003 ISBN 0931201837

Stiff, M. *Managing New Technology Projects in Museums and Galleries* Museum Documentation Association 2002 ISBN 1900642107

Suchy, S. *Leading with Passion: Change Management in the 21st Century Museum* AltaMira Press 2003 ISBN 0759103666

Index

Boxed text, study examples and figures are indicated by *italic* type. Key word definitions are indicated by **bold** type.